Fighting Poverty in Africa:
Are PRSPs making a difference?

Fighting Poverty in Africa:
Are PRSPs making a difference?

Edited by David Booth

Overseas Development Institute

Cover background photo: Machinga district, Malawi by Tom Slaymaker,
ODI Water Policy Programme

A CIP Publication data record may be obtained from the British Library

ISBN 0 85003 688 7

© Overseas Development Institute 2003

Published by the Overseas Development Institute,
111, Westminster Bridge Road,
London SE1 7JD

Typeset at the Overseas Development Institute
Printed by the Russell Press Ltd, Nottingham

Contents

Acknowledgements and disclaimer

This book is based on a study commissioned by the Technical Group of the Strategic Partnership with Africa (SPA), the forum of bilateral and multilateral development agencies on assistance to low-income Africa. Financial support for the study and for the production of the book was provided by German Technical Cooperation (GTZ), Japan Bank for International Cooperation (JBIC), Netherlands Ministry of Foreign Affairs, Norwegian Ministry of Foreign Affairs, Swedish International Development Cooperation Agency (Sida), Swiss Agency for Development and Cooperation (SDC) and UK Department for International Development (DFID).

The study team and the Overseas Development Institute are grateful for this support as well as for the time and effort contributed to the research by donor-agency personnel, government officials and ordinary citizens in all the African countries included in the study. On the other hand, none of the organisations or individuals mentioned, including ODI, is responsible for the analysis or opinions contained in the book. The work was commissioned as an independent study, and responsibility for it rests with the authors of the individual chapters and with the editor of the volume.

The production of the book has benefited from the excellent editorial assistance of Margaret Cornell, Pippa Leask and Tammie O'Neil.

David Booth
29 Sept 2003

Acronyms

AfDB	African Development Bank
CAS	Country Assistance Stategy (World Bank)
CCA	Common Country Assessment (UN)
CDF	Comprehensive Development Framework (World Bank)
CG	Consultative Group (donor-government forum)
CWIQ	Core Welfare Indicators Questionnaire
DAC	Development Assistance Committee (OECD)
DANIDA	Danish International Development Agency
DFID	Department for International Development (UK)
ESAF	Enhanced Structural Adjustment Facility
EURODAD	European Network on Debt and Development
GTZ	Gesellschaft für Technische Zusammenarbeit (German)
HDI	Human Development Indicator
HIPC	Highly Indebted Poor Countries (initiative)
HIPC2	Enhanced HIPC
IDA	International Development Association (World Bank)
IFI	international financial institution
iPRSP	Interim Poverty Reduction Strategy Paper
JSA	Joint Staff Assessment
MTEF	Medium-Term Expenditure Framework
NORAD	Norwegian Agency for Development Co-operation
ODA	Official Development Assistance
OECD	Organisation for Economic Co-operation and Development
PD/GG	Participatory Development and Good Governance Group (DAC)
PER	Public Expenditure Review
PERC	Public Expenditure Reform and Credit (World Bank)
PFP	Policy Framework Paper
PMS	poverty monitoring system
PPA	participatory poverty assessment
PRGF	Poverty Reduction and Growth Facility (IMF)
PRS	poverty reduction strategy
PRSC	Poverty Reduction Support Credit (IDA)
PRSP	Poverty Reduction Strategy Paper
Sida	Swedish International Development Co-operation Agency
SIP	Sector Investment Programme
SPA	Strategic Partnership with Africa
SWAP	Sector-Wide Approach Programme
UNCTAD	United Nations Conference on Trade and Development
UNDAF	United Nations Development Assistance Framework
UNDP	United Nations Development Programme
USAID	US Agency for International Development
UEMOA	Union Economique Monétaire Ouest-Africaine

Chapter 1: Introduction and overview

by David Booth*

PRSPs have helped to mainstream anti-poverty efforts in national policy processes in Africa. However, the seven country experiences synthesised in this chapter reveal differences as well as commonalities. Can vicious circles of patrimonial politics, state weakness and ineffectual aid be replaced with virtuous ones, based on greater national ownership of anti-poverty effort? This is still uncertain. PRSPs add value to technocratic reforms in public management, by opening new spaces for policy dialogue, but those reforms remain vital, especially in regard to the budget. For their part, donors need to be prepared to take risks and impose some disciplines on themselves. The hypothesis that PRSP processes can promote changes leading to more effective poverty reduction needs refinement, but remains plausible.

1.1 Introduction

Are Poverty Reduction Strategy Papers (PRSPs) making a difference? This book explores that question, drawing on the early evidence from seven countries of sub-Saharan Africa. The contributions derive from a multi-country study of PRSP processes in Africa commissioned by the Strategic Partnership with Africa (SPA), the joint forum of multilateral and bilateral development agencies on assistance to low-income Africa. Eight country studies and a synthesis report were presented to the SPA Plenary session in January 2002 and fed into the first review of the PRSP approach by the World Bank and IMF in the first quarter of 2002 (IMF and IDA, 2002a, b). Further work was done to update the findings during 2002–3.[1]

---

* Poverty and Public Policy Group, Overseas Development Institute, London. I am grateful to Alison Evans and Laure-Hélène Piron for helpful comments and substantive textual suggestions on earlier versions of this overview. Howard White, Charles Harvey and Jan Kees van Donge peer-reviewed the whole report on which the book is based, making numerous helpful comments. Andrew Lawson, David Hoole, Mick Foster, Andy Norton and John Mackinnon contributed as members of an internal review panel. Inputs from a number of SPA member organisations, especially the IMF, also proved valuable. However, the study was commissioned to give an independent view of the PRSP process, and it is more than usually necessary to make the disclaimer that the authors formed their own final judgements and bear sole responsibility for these.
1. Shortened versions of the chapters were previously published in David Booth

Background

PRSPs were introduced in late 1999 as a device to help ensure the proper use of debt relief under the Enhanced Highly Indebted Poor Countries facility (HIPC2). Preparation by the national government of an Interim PRSP (iPRSP) was set as one of the conditions for reaching Decision Point, and substantial effective relief, under the HIPC2 scheme. A full PRSP, prepared in consultation with other national stakeholders, became, along with other 'triggers', a condition for HIPC2 Completion. However, PRSP processes have since assumed wider significance, both for poor countries and for international development co-operation.

First, PRSP documents have taken the place of the former Policy Framework Papers as the required statement of recipient government objectives for the purposes of adjustment lending by the IMF and concessional credits from the World Bank. Increasingly, bilateral development agencies have taken their lead from this and, in one sense or another, reorganised their own country programmes with reference to national policies set out in PRSPs. Second, both the large international financial institutions (IFIs) have introduced new lending instruments avowedly designed to support the implementation of PRSPs – a Poverty Reduction and Growth Facility (IMF) and a Poverty Reduction Support Credit (World Bank/IDA). These are not merely formal changes, or new labels for established activities. They reflect long-term shifts in the policy thinking of the IFIs, and the senior management of both the Fund and the Bank mean them to signal fundamental changes in the way those organisations do business.

The PRSP initiative has already stimulated much debate, some controversy and a considerable informal literature in the form of website material, reports and working papers. This book represents the most substantial formal publication on the subject to date. It attempts to provide an interim report on PRSP experience in Africa that is both hopeful and realistic.

The contributors do not adopt a single view, partly because the countries they have studied are different and partly, no doubt, for reasons of temperament, discipline or affiliation. But, compared with the radical sceptics who lie at one end of the continuum of opinion about the PRSP initiative, this collection could be regarded as constructively critical. Compared with the other end of the spectrum, its authors take very seriously the structural obstacles to genuine, non-cosmetic improvements in the domestic policies of African countries and the way these interact with aid.

We start from the belief that the PRSP initiative represents, at least potentially, a non-trivial change in the way international support to poverty reduction in developing countries is framed and delivered. We believe that it provides an opportunity to address some critical problems in both the

(ed.) 'Are PRSPs Making a Difference? The African Experience', *Development Policy Review*, 21(2), March 2003.

governance of poor countries and the institutional framework of development assistance. In particular, it could be the solution to the chronic tendency of much aid for poverty reduction to undermine the conditions of its own success, by weakening the capacities of governments and other national institutions to act for themselves.

It is by no means a foregone conclusion that it will work in this way. On the contrary, the aid business will surely require more than greater understanding and better intentions at the top to really transform itself in the required ways. And rather more important, examples of successful engineering of national social and political change on the scale anticipated by the more radical versions of the PRSP vision are rather rare in history. For this reason, we have made an effort, in approaching the African PRSP experience to date, to temper hope with realism, avoiding both cynicism and naivety.

Scope of the work

The SPA study was focused on PRSP *processes*. It set out to investigate the extent to which poverty reduction policies, programmes, practices and monitoring systems were being institutionalised in selected African countries. It was intended to provide some early feedback on the degree to which the new elements introduced into IFI conditionality by the Enhanced HIPC framework were leading to poverty reduction plans that benefit from greater country ownership and, therefore, promise to be more effective.

Attention was focused on three main topics:

- the attitudes, commitments and plans of governmental and non-governmental stakeholders, including multilateral and bilateral donor agencies;
- the institutional changes that were being introduced, especially in respect of: (a) public financial management and (b) participation in policy-making and other aspects of the governance framework; and
- the development of PRSP monitoring and information systems.

It is worth underlining that the research undertaken did not involve a systematic assessment of PRSP documentation or any other aspect of the content of the strategies being developed by countries. The principal focus was on processes and institutions. This seemed justified on the grounds that a substantial improvement in how governments define and manage poverty reduction policies is the main precondition for improving what they actually deliver in terms of actions and results.

The research was initially based on case studies of the experience of seven countries: Benin, Ghana, Kenya, Malawi, Mali, Rwanda and Tanzania. Mozambique was added at an early stage, taking advantage of a study commissioned separately by the Swedish International Development

Cooperation Agency and the Norwegian Ministry of Foreign Affairs. Ghana was the subject of a case study, but the PRSP process in Ghana changed gear so radically after the main research was done (because of the election victory of President Kufuor's New Patriotic Party) that a mere updating of the findings for the purposes of this publication was considered impractical.[2] Results from just seven case studies are therefore being published.

The topics outlined above were investigated in three phases, over a two-year period. Phase 1 (September 2000-January 2001) was an initial scoping exercise, designed to identify key issues for further investigation and provide a baseline against which to gauge later developments. This was based on in-country interviews and documentary work of about two weeks' duration. Phase 2 (February-October 2001) involved more extended research in the study countries, with somewhat widened terms of reference and a larger effort of analysis and synthesis. Phase 3 consisted of report dissemination in several countries, and a systematic updating of information across the whole set.

All of the study countries were in principle eligible for Enhanced HIPC relief, apart from Kenya, where concessional loans were not available for much of the past decade, and a major accumulation of domestic debt took place instead.[3] Most countries in our sample submitted their Interim PRSPs, satisfying the main conditions for the HIPC2 Decision Point, during the middle months of 2000. Tanzania was permitted to proceed quickly to complete and submit a full PRSP in 2000, although HIPC2 Completion awaited the PRSP's first annual review. The other countries moved at different speeds towards presentation of their PRSPs during 2001 and 2002.

In most cases, our research began during the culmination of the iPRSP phase, while the main research in-country coincided with a fairly advanced stage in the consultations and other work on the full PRSP. The country study teams each conducted between 25 and 50 interviews in each stage of the research. Interviewees were treated both as 'key informants' and as stakeholders whose opinions on different subjects were of substantive interest to the study. Some care was taken with the conduct of the interviews and their interpretation. In all cases, the picture that emerged came from the combined and cross-checked testimony of the different actors, not from the views of individuals on their own.

Phase 1 interviewees included senior government officials with responsibility for the PRSP process or poverty monitoring; officials of other echelons of government (for example, line Ministries); parliamentarians,

---

2. Instead, we draw on the interim results for Ghana of the more recent evaluation of the Comprehensive Development Framework. That study has the same lead author – Tony Killick.

3. In 2000, Ghana had opted not to seek HIPC2 relief but then, under the NPP government, changed its position, with significant implications for the place of the PRSP in national policy.

including members of opposition parties; private business representatives; heads of civil society membership organisations; leaders of national or international NGOs; independent consultants and academics; technical assistance personnel; and embassy, donor-agency and IFI staff. In all cases, interviews were conducted with individuals in several different categories.

In Phase 2 of the study, informants were re-interviewed and attempts were also made to widen the range of stakeholders consulted, with greater efforts to include those living outside the national capital and formal 'development' spheres. Coverage of donor perceptions and intentions was also increased.

Arriving at an overview

An obvious difficulty facing the synthesis of findings in an exercise such as this is that the different countries are indeed different, and much of the interest is embedded in the detail. In our reports for the SPA, we attempted to handle this by entering key information and 'pointers' from the country studies in analytical matrices. The main text then provided an overview of the analysis in the country reports, discussing the issues that emerged for at least significant sub-groups of countries. This chapter retains the substance of that approach.

The remainder of the chapter is organised into six sections. The next section clarifies further what we think is the challenge of PRSPs, and includes a review of how the initiative originated, plus an overview of the main features of the context at the country level. The following five sections explain what emerge as the major findings and practical implications, particularly but not exclusively for donor agencies, of the country studies. The concluding section sums up and returns to what we take as the principal 'hypothesis' underlying the PRSP initiative – the major factor that will affect whether, in the long term, it makes a difference to poverty reduction efforts in Africa or not.

1.2 Politics and aid: asking the right questions

The PRSP initiative may prove ephemeral, a passing fashion in the ever-changing world of international development. There is also a distinct possibility that PRSPs will make a real difference – that they will have a greater impact on development practice and outcomes than the debt relief with which they were initially associated. HIPC2 may very well pass into history mainly as the occasion when PRSPs were born.

These are strong claims. Understanding how they can be made calls for clarity about the situation out of which the PRSP initiative arose, and the kind of challenge it represents. Contrary to some superficial appreciations of the initiative, it does not arise from a naïve assessment of the past and present obstacles to effective poverty reduction in aid-dependent countries. Nor does it imply a renewal of faith in the simple efficacy of 'strategic' thinking, as reflected in official policy documents.

The nature of the issue

The phrase Poverty Reduction *Strategy* Paper has a literal meaning and an aura of solemnity that are potentially deceptive. Some of the language in which PRSPs are discussed is strongly reminiscent of the early days of 'development planning', in the 1950s and 1960s, when the world seemed a simpler place than it does now. The concept of a PRSP might seem to imply that the reduction of poverty is more straightforwardly amenable to rational thinking and action than we know to be the case. Is there not an element of naïvety in the concept, one that could sow the seeds of later disillusionment?

There certainly is some basis for this concern. But the possibility raised by PRSPs is not whether the world has changed in some fundamental way, so that the obstacles to a simple-minded 'rational planning' approach have suddenly disappeared.

On the contrary, the PRSP challenge arises from the observation that the world remains very much as it was. It stems from the almost unreserved failure of all previous instruments and processes to achieve significant breakthroughs in the field of poverty reduction in the poorest countries, especially in Africa. It raises the possibility that, against this background of failure, small adjustments in ways of doing certain things might make a significant difference.

The adjustments in question are not so much about 'planning' as about appreciating processes of structural change, particularly within the domestic societies and governance institutions of poor countries, and their decisive influence on the outcomes of development efforts. It is by no means suggested that the need to make concessional funding and debt relief conditional upon changes in policies and institutions within recipient countries has disappeared. What *is* claimed is that a shift in the emphasis of conditionality, focusing more on policy processes oriented to particular sorts of outcomes, and less on specific preconditions, just might make a crucial difference.

The origins of the PRSP proposals reflect some combination of:[4]

- disappointing poverty reduction performance in most highly indebted and aid-dependent countries throughout the last 20 years, despite substantial changes in policies and institutions;
- growing recognition of the importance of the national policy context for aid effectiveness;[5]

---

4. A vast literature might be cited under each topic; some representative landmarks would be World Bank (2001); White and Killick (2001); World Bank (1998); Devarajan et al. (2001); Killick (1998) and Foster et al. (1999).
5. The particular form of this argument advanced in *Assessing Aid* (World Bank, 1998), using econometric results to suggest extremely low aid effectiveness in

- increased awareness of the limitations of conventional conditionalities for levering some of the critical changes;
- a search for new instruments with which to justify a major new debt-reduction initiative.

The PRSP principles extend and largely incorporate the ideas previously developed around the World Bank's proposals for a Comprehensive Development Framework (CDF) governing development co-operation in borrowing countries. The following are key elements in this thinking.[6]

- Policy-making for poverty reduction should take the form of a *country-led* strategy process, in which government engages in *dialogue* with other constituents of the national society, resulting in greater national ownership of the decisions taken.

- It should be *results- or outcome-oriented*, starting from an analysis of poverty and its causes and working backwards to the design of appropriate policies.

- The thinking should be *comprehensive* in its coverage of different macro, sectoral and cross-sectoral issues that affect poverty reduction processes and prospects.

- The basis for international support should be a form of *partnership*, in which all funding sources are drawn together in a co-ordinated way around a strategy developed under the leadership of the recipient government.

- This is visualised as a *medium- to long-term process*, implying a need for medium-term commitments as well as careful consideration of appropriate timing, performance criteria and monitoring arrangements.

Process conditionality?
Behind the PRSP initiative, there is a belief that 'process conditionality' (Foster et al., 1999) may succeed where previous forms of conditionality, focused on specific policy measures, have failed. A central hypothesis is that refocusing IFI approaches, in the context of HIPC2 and the new lending instruments, will enable the adoption of poverty reduction policies and programmes that benefit from greater national ownership and commitment than has been the case in the past. This in turn will lead to greater effectiveness and sustainability of anti-poverty action.

Any study of PRSP experience needs to concern itself with whether this

---

unfavourable policy environments, is contested (e.g., Tarp, 2000). However, in a more generic form the proposition is increasingly accepted.
6. This draws on World Bank (2000) and IMF and IDA (1999, 2000).

hypothesis seems likely to prove true. This does not mean that we are reaching the stage where a rigorous test is possible – far from it. However, we do think it is reasonable to start asking several related questions: whether there has yet been a sufficiently clear shift towards a new form of conditionality; in what respects national ownership of poverty reduction efforts has been enhanced so far; what else could usefully be done to strengthen any benign, and weaken any corrupting, effects; and whether, on current evidence, the hypothesis remains plausible and/or needs to be refined.

Politics matters

Underlying the research reported in this collection is a common belief that poverty reduction policy is, for better or worse, embedded in living political systems. This implies that the PRSP experiment will work through the political systems and policy processes of the countries concerned, or it will not work at all. PRSPs will either engender new relationships and dynamic processes within countries that result in poverty policies being handled in a new and more effective way, or they will not. What happens in this respect will be a highly political issue, in two senses. First, for all their limitations, formal political systems are a powerful influence on what happens in every country. Second and probably more important, the informal arrangements and understandings that determine policy and its implementation are also 'political', not merely technical.

It follows from this that an important part of the study has been to establish a realistic framework of understanding of the political background, its constraints and possibilities, in each of the country cases. All the other chapters in the book include a brief consideration of these issues. Here, we attempt an overview.

From a social and political perspective, the country contexts we are concerned with contain some significant contrasts. From the point of view of a study of the institutionalisation of poverty reduction strategies, the commonalities are also important.

The country contexts

An initial generalisation is that in all cases we are dealing with semi-democratised states in which domestic politics tends to be patronage-based, with fragmented party systems and weak civil societies. We may also say that all have quite fragmented policy processes. That is, they are characterised by poor co-ordination both between different centres of decision-making, and between the formulation and implementation of policies. In addition, these countries share high levels of financial and institutional aid dependency. This produces low accountability to domestic actors, and contributes also to the persistence of clientelism and policy fragmentation. At a more technical level, public expenditure and revenue management systems have, at least until recently, been only weakly driven by public policy objectives.

Administrative systems have similarly been characterised by low morale and weak performance incentives.

These features are among the problems that the PRSP initiative is intended to address. At the same time, they affect the range of outcomes that can reasonably be expected from PRSP processes. In a sense, the central issue we are addressing is whether PRSP-related changes can get enough of a foothold before being overcome by the very structures and processes they aim to transform. As will become apparent, different country experiences to date suggest different answers to this fundamental question.

To what extent does the thumb-nail sketch just given apply uniformly to the eight countries in the study, and why? We deal immediately with the domestic institutional issues and then turn to the propositions about the aid relationship.

Semi-democratised states

The majority of our countries participated in the tide of re-democratisation that began in the late 1980s, and several were pioneers of this process in their sub-regions. The outliers in this respect are Mozambique and Rwanda, where in different ways the legacies of regional conflict and civil war still bear heavily on what is politically possible. In the general case, there is a multi-party system, governed by elections, at least at the national level. There is press freedom, and competitive mass media – led in most cases by FM radio – have developed strongly, leading to better public information and debate.

While in these respects the conditions for national dialogue on fundamental issues such as poverty have improved, the quality of the democracy that has been institutionalised is heavily conditioned in almost all cases. In the language of political science, it is a 'neo-patrimonial' democracy.

Pure patrimonialism – or 'prebendalism', to use another common term – occurs where the resources of the state are treated as the patrimony of the ruler, not as public wealth in the modern sense. Official servants and their retainers are rewarded by access to the spoils of office – by prebends, rather than salaries. Neo-patrimonialism prevails where similar principles operate to a greater or lesser degree within the context of a bureaucratic state structure, with authoritarian or liberal-democratic constitutional trappings. Characteristics of neo-patrimonialism include presidentialism or the 'big man syndrome', systematic clientelism and the use of state resources for political legitimation (Bratton and van de Walle, 1997: Ch 2; van de Walle, 2001: 49-60).

It is generally considered that African democratisation processes have been heavily influenced by persisting, and even increasing, patrimonial tendencies. This in turn is reckoned to account for several other features of the actually existing democracies in the region, which are highlighted in several of the country chapters.

One is the tendency for opposition parties to be numerous, unstructured (one-man bands in many cases), non-ideological and beset by regular defections to the governing group. Another is the related infrequency of substantial political change, in which the historically-dominant party or leader is replaced through an election on a programmatic basis. Finally, civil society – in its classic European sense – barely exists, both because the economy is insufficiently differentiated, and because systematic clientelism involves the constant cooptation of independent institutions by politicians and the state.

The possible exception, in this respect, is Ghana. Until recently firmly among the countries covered by the description above, Ghana is today an ambiguous or borderline case. On the basis of a hard-fought electoral campaign at the end of 2000, one party was replaced in power by another on a fairly clear programmatic basis. For certain, neo-patrimonialism may not be dead in Ghana yet. Doubts arise from the possibility that, whatever the new government's initial intentions, there is a deeper level of political institutionality that will in due course reassert itself. But the case for seeing the neo-patrimonial tradition as clearly dominant over the more inclusive liberal-democratic tendencies no longer exists. In the medium and long term, this may mean that the prospects for pro-poor policy making of a new type are better in Ghana than in most of our other cases.

It is not part of the business of this study to contribute to the portrayal of Africa as a region where 'nothings works' and there is only conflict, backwardness and decay. We use such concepts as neo-patrimonialism and clientelism as standard social science terms that are not only applied to poor developing countries. We do not see them as wedded to a particular evolutionary scheme of progress. Their point is to help us to be *realistic* about what is specific to the countries we are dealing with. To borrow the title and the theme of the book by Chabal and Daloz (1999), 'Africa works': African polities and societies may not provide very well for their people, but understanding why that is the case entails understanding their own particular principles of operation, including their moral underpinnings;[7] it is not assisted by an approach that only emphasises the way such societies fall short of supposed international norms.

This may be illustrated by the case of Benin, whose political system is described as based on the association of local and regional elites with the government through dense clientelistic networks. While these relationships reduce the capacity of the state to function effectively in regulatory and administrative spheres, especially at the local level, it has also provided welcome political stability and social peace.

---

7. Ekeh (1975) made the classic case that the moral principles governing the 'public' and the private spheres in Africa are comprehensively different from, rather than inferior to, those that developed historically in Europe. Gould (1997) explains well how understanding African societies involves steering a course between sentimental traditionalism and performance standards imported mechanically from other realities.

Not only is the way Africa works not just a catalogue of failure, but the structures and processes responsible for undergirding the whole affair are by no means just African. As the country chapters argue, the clientelism and 'rent-seeking' that typify the real policy process in all of the study countries to a greater or lesser degree are both cause and consequence of an aid relationship that serves its nominal purposes very poorly. Apart from being heavily indebted, the countries are highly dependent on aid, both financially and, more important, in institutional terms. Institutional aid dependency is understood here as including a loss of capacity to make and implement planning decisions arising from the gross imbalance between domestically generated revenues and the actual or potential availability of external finance.

Fragmented policy processes

If the contributions to this study differ from the mainstream political science literature on Africa (e.g. the Chabal and Daloz source just cited) it is not primarily on issues of substance. It has more to do with a greater interest in operationally-relevant reform issues. We are interested not just in why things are the way they are, but whether the PRSP initiative might make a difference, and whether there are particular constraints that might be a focus for improved interventions. This implies going beyond the general features of the social and political context – though their pervasiveness makes them important – to focus on some of their specific manifestations, which are the sites of struggle (for struggles there also are).

Most of these issues have to do with what we have called generically the fragmentation of the policy process. This has various dimensions. Some, such as the rather general tendency for cabinets not to function as effective decision centres with joint responsibility, are quite direct reflections of the nature of the political system. Where patron-clientism is the dominant form of politics, ministries tend to be more like fiefdoms than centres of delegated authority. Cabinets therefore do not guarantee policy decisions. Permanent Secretaries and their equivalents do not necessarily participate actively in policy discussions within ministries, and so on. Decisions get taken, but there are no guarantees that they are even in principle consistent with each other.

Other features are equally widespread but harder to pin down to specific structural causes. There is typically a large gulf between policy formulation and implementation, with implementation constraints and past failures not generally feeding back into an appreciation of what might constitute good policy. This characteristic is not exclusive to poor African states, and to some extent is a feature of policy processes everywhere. However, it is particularly marked in the countries covered by this study. One source is surely the underlying reality – more acute in Africa than elsewhere – that there may well be rewards of various kinds from having the 'right' kind of policies (those currently in favour internationally), but few from having policies that work in the sense of achieving intended results.

Underlying political incentives and constraints powerfully determine all of the above but not necessarily in a completely deterministic fashion. The disconnection between policies and results has been reinforced in the countries in our sample, as well as in most wealthy countries until quite recently, by the traditional approach to public finance management, and equivalent weaknesses in the management of public services. Given the way the budgets and staffing arrangements of ministries and other official agencies have typically been managed, it is hard to see how incentives to improved performance could ever have prospered, whatever the overarching politics. It is for good reason that budget and civil service reforms designed to increase orientation to results are on the public agenda of most African countries, including those in our sample.[8]

The progress and setbacks that such efforts at deliberate change have encountered are very much a part of the country context for PRSPs. The relationship between PRSP processes and public finance reforms in particular is central to this study. As will become clear, the country experiences support the notion that this is a key interface for the purposes of a wider assault on public-policy incoherence. However, it is also clear that to be successful the reform effort needs to be multi-pronged, and to have a strong element of political as well as technical-bureaucratic change.

The aid relationship and the critique of projects

The countries included in the study are all very poor in terms of average living conditions. They are also highly indebted and, with one exception, eligible for debt relief under HIPC2. Most of the countries face a much more healthy situation, in terms of their basic macro-economic balances, than a decade ago, but several still experience basic stabilisation problems and periodic difficulties in their external financial relations, including Kenya (and, from our original set of countries, Ghana). Most have experienced growth but not enough to reduce poverty substantially or quickly.

It seems likely that high aid volumes, whatever the form of aid delivery, foster institutional aid dependency. Some research – focused on the ability of states to translate a given level of GNP per capita into improvements in human development – suggests that states which rely heavily on aid are less effective than those that draw substantially on other income sources, such as general tax revenues (Moore, 1998; Moore et al., 1999).

All aid may have the effect of weakening accountability to domestic actors, which in turn may reduce effectiveness in poverty reduction. However, there are also grounds for concern about specific modalities of aid delivery. The loss of public planning and implementation capacity that we have identified as the core of institutional aid dependency is believed by many to arise particularly from the dominance in the aid relationship of the *project* modality.

---

8. A rich source on these processes is a series of papers produced at ODI and synthesised in Foster et al. (2002), Roberts (2003) and Holmes (2003).

The case for sector support and other forms of programme aid or direct budget support has been built up on the basis of concerns about the project modality of development assistance in particular.

The dominance acquired by the project modality in recent decades is a response to a deep-seated imperative. Donors have resorted to building parallel management structures and separate accounting arrangements for their aid as a means of avoiding the inefficiency and unreliability of mainstream government procedures. The reasons for the continued popularity of projects are not entirely unsound. However, there is increasingly wide recognition that they contribute in a vicious circle to the persistence of the difficulties to which they are a response. Projectised donor funds divert skills and attention away from mainstream processes of development management in a country, and undermine incentives for officials to spend time on reform and strategic thinking at the centre.

The damage is recognised to be worse if project design is supply-driven; that is, motivated by donor incentives to disburse grant or loan funds for particular purposes, and/or if the aid is tied. However, these may be more usefully regarded as exacerbating factors rather than the principal problem. In a project framework, under conditions where projects are the dominant form of aid, real 'national ownership' of poverty reduction efforts is most unlikely to be achieved. Effectiveness in meeting goals is likely to be reduced as a result.

Project aid has indirect effects on state capacity, as well as direct ones, and the indirect effects may be the more important. We have said that domestic political patterns cannot be considered separately from the nature of the aid relationship. The modal type of patronage-based political system referred to earlier might well exist in the absence of aid. Policy processes might still be fragmented (as indeed they are in many parts of the world). On the other hand, it is clear that the social and economic relationships of project aid fit very easily into a system of patron-client relationships and can help to fuel it and strengthen its institutional foundations.

Benin and other countries in our sample are described as *rentier* states, on the basis that public revenues have been dominated historically by rents (e.g. from the international port of Cotonou) rather than taxes on capital or labour. Aid has reinforced this characteristic and generalised it. It may also be argued that aid, particularly in the project form, encourages a culture of rent-seeking across both the public and the private sector, and that this has continued to be the case despite the move to more market-based economies. In turn, this fertilises the ground for the continued growth of social and political relationships based on patrimonial principles.

A vicious circle
It is worth saying again that there are important effects going in both directions. Once firmly established, the patron-client type of social and political order generates a type of policy process and pattern of behaviour

among the generality of public servants that provide justification for persisting with projects. In Benin, Tanzania, Mali, Rwanda and elsewhere, there is an almost closed circle of mutual reinforcement, in which lack of trust in government systems leads to the building of parallel systems, which undermines incentives at the centre while doing nothing to build up systems that might inspire greater trust.

Many of these linkages, and the dilemmas they pose, have been widely recognised by both donor and government representatives. This is particularly the case in two of the study countries, Mali and Tanzania. The OECD DAC Aid Review of Mali, which highlighted the very low level of donor accountability to government in that country, has been well received and influential. The 1997 agreement between Tanzania and its main development partners following the Helleiner Report recognised many of the same issues. Moving towards a new form of aid partnership that successfully avoids the troubles outlined above has not proven easy in those two countries or anywhere else. It is in part for that reason that the PRSP initiative poses such an important and difficult challenge.

Previous poverty policies

A final element of general context needs to be noted. In none of the eight countries except Rwanda is the PRSP process the first experience in developing a national poverty reduction strategy. Some initial efforts, particularly in the form of improvements in the availability of basic data on poverty conditions, were already undertaken in response to the Social Dimensions of Adjustment initiative in the early 1990s. A more substantial and sustained effort followed the Copenhagen Social Summit (1995) and was reinforced by the sequence of international agreements on poverty reduction goals that culminated in the UN's Millennium Summit.

Among the international agencies, UNDP in particular committed itself strongly to facilitating and providing technical support for national poverty strategies, and encouraging international learning from these experiences (UNDP, 2000; Grinspun, 2001). From our country studies and other sources, it is clear that these efforts did help in various ways to place poverty more squarely on public agendas and promote attempts to tackle it in a more deliberate way.

This forms an important part of the context for PRSPs. However, it would be a serious mistake to see PRSPs as just more of the same. In several important respects, previous poverty reduction programmes and strategies in the study countries took a form that differs systematically from the PRSP approach as we understand it.[9]

First, poverty reduction was typically handled as a special activity, added on to existing programmes and thus requiring special structures and activities.

---

9. Unfortunately, while the UNDP evaluation study on this previous phase (Grinspun, 2001) provides much relevant information, it does not highlight these differences.

Second, the emphasis was on providing a new focus for project funding, not on influencing the processes of public resource allocation through the national exchequer. Thus, Mali created a new Social Development Ministry to host its SNLP. This was not oriented to transforming existing government activities, but to securing funding for new ones. Kenya created a Poverty Eradication Commission in the Office of the President, and Tanzania a National Poverty Eradication Division in the Vice-President's Office, with purposes that were not dissimilar. Ghana's National Poverty Reduction Programme was an UNDP-funded unit, physically located in the planning commission (NDPC), managing a range of 'pilot' schemes. In none of the study countries, including Mozambique, Kenya and Malawi, were previous poverty policies integrated with the macro-economic framework or linked institutionally with the budget and the overall management of public expenditure.

Third, where the national poverty-reduction efforts did include strategic policy declarations, these showed a tendency to be vague statements of aspirations. They were not based on a thorough assessment of previous policies and approaches. Given the fragmented type of policy process described earlier, it is not surprising that they were typically not implemented to any significant degree (donor-funded projects excluded). Malawi's Poverty Alleviation Programme (1994), Ghana's 'Policy Focus for Poverty Reduction' (1996) and Tanzania's National Poverty Eradication Strategy (1997/98) would be cases in point. Most such documents did not even reach the next step of being translated into a time-bounded action plan. Thinking was results-oriented, but only at the level of final goals.

Those things having been said, previous poverty plans have in a number of cases absorbed considerable national effort. Sometimes, this has included broad participation by non-governmental interest groups and experts. In some cases, previous plan processes are considered to have acquired extensive national ownership, according to the criterion that large numbers of stakeholders are aware of them and have some degree of identification with them. Mali's SNLP is a leading example of this.

Broad stakeholder involvement is not the only possible, or perhaps the most important, criterion of national ownership that needs to be applied, as discussed later. However, the fact that some previous exercises in national poverty planning benefited from some level of public recognition was an important feature of the context into which PRSPs were introduced. In asking the question 'Have PRSPs made a difference?', we are in part placing the spotlight on these specific weaknesses of previous international efforts to kick-start vigorous anti-poverty action in the study countries.

The argument in outline

These, then, are the elements of the PRSP question, as we see it. Can policy-process conditionality succeed where other forms of conditionality have failed? Will PRSP processes begin to effect changes before being overcome by the patterns of behaviour they are intended to transform? And have international aid policies changed enough in response to the challenge of PRSPs?

The following five sections outline what seem to be the answers, based on the three years or so of experience in the study countries. The section titles convey five major conclusions, whose thrust is to suggest that in some quite important ways PRSPs have made a difference for the better. In each section, however, some vital provisos are added, and recommendations are made about the need for greater or different efforts on the part of the main actors. The major arguments are:

- PRSPs have mainstreamed and broadened national poverty reduction efforts.
- Complementary reforms are essential, especially in the area of public sector governance.
- New spaces for domestic policy dialogue have been created.
- Monitoring processes may improve the quality of poverty reduction strategies.
- PRSPs invite a more substantial transformation of the aid relationship.

1.3   PRSPs have mainstreamed and broadened national poverty reduction efforts

Initial responses

According to the case studies, acceptance of the PRSP approach by African governments was swift. This was partly, perhaps overwhelmingly, because of the powerful incentive created by the prospect of HIPC2 debt relief.

In several countries, stakeholders perceived the PRSP exercise as being overwhelmingly motivated by getting access to debt relief and having little further significance. There are exceptions. For example, Rwanda's PRSP unit went out of its way to downplay or not mention the connection with HIPC relief, in order to encourage national stakeholders to treat the exercise as a real planning endeavour (not an exercise in nominal compliance, or merely a discussion on how to spend additional resources at the margin). Kenya also moved vigorously to institute a PRSP formulation process without the incentives associated with being eligible for HIPC2 relief. Elsewhere there were strong impressions of nominal compliance. For example, in Mali a very strong emphasis was placed on getting and considering how to spend the HIPC windfall.

The fact that the debt relief was 'front-loaded', meaning that the bulk of it was effectively available from Decision Point (i.e. coinciding with endorsement of the iPRSP) does not seem to have weakened this perceived linkage. This is partly because substantial new funding was also expected after completion. In Tanzania, the most advanced of our countries in PRSP terms, those in the know were concerned that the 'HIPC factor' had been a strong force driving the PRSP process, and that the energy devoted to it would certainly wane as soon as completion was achieved.

These kinds of concerns notwithstanding, governments in all seven of the countries covered by this study have invested substantial effort in doing what they think to be required to produce a good PRSP. The degree to which such effort signals commitment at all levels of the political and administrative hierarchy in our countries is more difficult to assess. In Kenya, Malawi and Benin, for example, an energetic process was driven primarily at the technical level, and political commitment was unclear or non-existent. Elsewhere (Mali, Mozambique, Rwanda and Tanzania) commitment to poverty-reduction goals at the political level seems less of a problem than the commitment to implement significant change in the ministries and the civil service at large.

We postpone further consideration of the ownership question to later. What is clear is that in all cases, a range of national stakeholders responded positively to the initiative. Although PRSPs were understood to be the result of additional conditionality, the new approach was not strongly opposed anywhere. Initial frictions arising from the particular policy backgrounds in some countries (for example, Mali) were mostly overcome between 2000 and 2001.

This may be considered unsurprising, and banal as a finding. It has seldom been the case that highly aid-dependent African countries have not acceded to the formalities of a new way of working that has been strongly advocated by the IFIs, with the backing of major bilateral donors. However, our study suggests that PRSPs have already made a difference in some ways that go beyond formalities and are not banal.

Institutional impacts

Three important shifts are documented in the country studies:

- At an early stage, responsibility for coordinating countries' principal policy instruments for dealing with poverty shifted to Ministries of Finance.

- As a result of the PRSP initiative, there has been, across all of the countries to a greater or lesser degree, a move away from the traditional approach of focusing poverty reduction efforts largely on the social sectors.

- A more favourable institutional context has also been created for linking poverty reduction to discussions about budget priorities and the medium-term allocation of national and donor resources.

Shifts in institutional leadership on poverty
One of the most palpable and important effects of the PRSP process to date has been a shift in the institutional location of the principal responsibility

for poverty reduction within government systems. In most of the eight countries,[10] as well as others we know of, responsibility for guiding and/or implementing anti-poverty measures was formerly located in a weak social-welfare ministry (Mali), in a planning authority without resource-allocation powers (Benin, Ghana, Malawi) or in an appendage of a president's or vice-president's office lacking real authority to convene line ministries and other actors (Kenya, Tanzania). In these cases, the interest of the department or unit in developing a national poverty-reduction *policy* was compromised by the interest in managing poverty-focused donor-funded programmes, as discussed in the last section.

This has largely changed. PRSP preparation resulted, in one country after another, in the responsibility for poverty-reduction policy being taken over by the Ministry of Finance. One of the two countries in the sample where the institutional division of labour for leading the PRSP process remained unsettled in 2000 (Benin) has since resolved it in the expected way, with Finance taking the lead role and Planning providing support. On the other hand, Ghana confirmed its National Development Planning Commission in the leading role, becoming the only case in our original sample to buck the trend. In Kenya, the shift to Finance took place, but the change of government at the end of 2002 has placed a question mark over the outcome of the continuing rivalry between Finance and the Office of the President, home of the NPEP.

The background to these changes was the simple fact that PRSPs were being requested by the IFIs, whose natural interlocutors were Ministries of Finance. However, the implications are quite far-reaching. Where it has occurred, the shift to Finance has meant a significant upgrading of poverty policy in several respects.

Mainstreaming poverty: out of the social-sector ghetto

While not universally popular – partly because vested interests are involved – the assumption of a leading role by finance ministries has meant that poverty is more effectively 'mainstreamed' within government policy, seen as a policy concern for all sectors and cross-sectoral areas. Poverty reduction is increasingly seen as a goal of *all* sectors and cross-cutting policy areas, including those governing 'productive' activities such as agriculture. This change is important and was long overdue.

It is worth noting that this effect of the PRSP initiative may have been dampened by what appears to have been the impact of the HIPC2 conditionalities, namely to further increase the focus of public spending on health and education services (Killick, forthcoming, citing World Bank OED, 2003). As a result, PRSP implementation may reflect only to a limited degree the conceptual mainstreaming of poverty reduction that we are suggesting has taken place.

---

10. Including Ghana.

Linking poverty reduction to the budget

Making the linkage effective from poverty planning to public-expenditure management is, of course, not just a question of shifting around responsibilities (as discussed in Section 4 below). But thanks to the PRSP initiative, the institutional division of labour is now more favourable to that. Because Finance holds the purse strings, it means that poverty is more closely linked to central resource-allocation decisions and thus to the incentives that cascade down from budget decisions. This is important since, as pointed out above, previous national poverty reduction strategies tended to be both institutionally marginalised and unrelated to the national budget, and heavily oriented towards attracting new donor projects.

Together with removing poverty reduction from the limited field of action of the so-called social sectors, and reviving strategic thinking about the role of sectors such as agriculture, this is one simple but definite gain from the PRSP initiative that is unlikely to be taken away whatever the subsequent developments.

Missing links

The above shifts are significant and probably irreversible gains, affecting some aspects of the way governments work. On the other hand, the country experiences caution us against expecting too much too quickly from this relative 'mainstreaming' of anti-poverty efforts. Many of the corresponding gains in terms of performance and results remain potential rather than actual. Decisive further steps will be necessary to realise the potential.

The principal missing link is the difficult and to some degree technical one of improving public-sector governance discussed in Section 4. Others are obvious and non-controversial, and we deal with them first.

Information and understanding

Even today, after countries' full PRSPs have in most cases been agreed by cabinets and endorsed by the Joint Boards of the Bank and the Fund, the impact on public consciousness – even at the level of opinion leaders – remains shallow. Awareness of the existence of a PRSP (as distinct from the myriad of donor-supported projects and programmes) still tends to be limited to a few layers of officialdom in central government and to a limited range of non-governmental actors. Clear understanding of the distinctive features of the approach, and the degree to which it does and does not constitute a break with the past, is especially scarce. Full PRSPs have had a much larger impact on public consciousness than the Interim documents did. But there are big variations between countries in the degree to which even the full PRSP has made an impression, as recorded in the country chapters of this book.

A first policy message emerging from our research was, therefore, that further efforts are needed to spread understanding of PRSP principles within countries as well as between them. For the PRSP approach to work on the scale that is expected, it needs to be widely disseminated and understood across central and local government as well as within the research/advocacy community working outside of government. This was the case in 2000, and it remains the case in 2003. There has been useful learning in many countries on how to involve different actors in the drafting and consultation processes connected with PRSPs. However, this needs to be generalised to other dimensions of the PRSP process, and shared with countries where the tendency to create 'enclaves of understanding' has been more marked.

Disseminating information is a first step; translating the PRSP document into local languages is another; and both of these things have been done in a few countries. But sharing information is not the same as creating understanding. The latter will require a more systematic approach that engages relevant stakeholders in a continuous process of learning about the PRSP and its relationship to other policy and aid processes. The range of relevant stakeholders should not be narrowly defined, and certainly not limited to the technical levels of government.

In regard to inter-country sharing, the work of the World Bank Institute and the UN Economic Commission for Africa in hosting learning events has been very valuable. This could be usefully emulated at country level, providing a more consistent, joined-up approach to deepening understanding about the PRSP (i.e. linking it to other reform initiatives such as local government reform, sector strategy processes, anti-corruption measures and the media). Resident IFI staff should be encouraged to play an active role in such events, and not regard them as falling outside their sphere of responsibility.

How to promote the PRSP concept in-country

A further point is about the *content* of the dissemination of PRSPs in-country. According to our research, there is too little appreciation in most countries that the PRSP exercise has the potential to be much more than a new means of accessing external funds. The idea that a good PRSP could be the instrument for liberating countries from burdensome conditionalities and unwelcome external tutelage (donors agreeing to support country policies, instead of imposing policies as the price of aid) is not, as yet, widely appreciated. This could and should be a *central* message of in-country dissemination efforts.

1.4 Complementary reforms are essential

PRSPs are making a difference in limited but important ways, we suggest, and these effects will be magnified as more familiarisation occurs. But, to have the substantial positive results expected, PRSPs need to be credible – that is, to be capable of being implemented. The case studies suggest that this is going to be dependent on countries' making progress with longer-term, complementary reforms, especially in key fields of public sector governance, such as public expenditure accounting, budget reform and public service management.

The backlog of institutional reform

In most of the countries included in the study, institutional reforms covering these areas have been under way in principle for a number of years. But almost everywhere progress has been slow. In several countries, key initiatives are described as chronically stalled. This poses quite serious challenges to PRSP implementation, especially where basic conditions for predictability, transparency and accountability in public expenditure management are not yet (or no longer) in place.

To be sure, not all countries are in exactly the same situation. In countries where the basic conditions are favourable, Medium-Term Expenditure Frameworks (MTEFs) and other steps to make budgets more realistic and oriented towards outcome goals appear to be particularly important to the credibility of PRSPs. Where outcome-oriented, or programme-based, budgeting with a medium-term perspective has made headway, it is a short step to costing and prioritising PRSP goals. Otherwise, this can appear quite a daunting task.

The degree to which results-oriented reforms of public finance or civil service management were already in place and making headway was found, in the scoping stage of the study, to be a principal determinant of stakeholders' understanding of the purpose of the PRSP exercise. What might be involved in a *national* poverty reduction *strategy* was clear enough to officials who had already been involved in MTEF discussions, concerned with defining medium-term priorities on the basis of resource ceilings and outcome objectives. In such cases, the notion that resource ceilings should include the totality of public resources, including donor and government funds, and both capital and recurrent expenditures, was already accepted. This provided a fertile soil for acceptance of PRSP principles.

This was confirmed and reinforced by the larger body of evidence produced in the second phase of the study. Countries were found to be without exception investing substantial effort in their PRSPs; but understanding of what this was for was quite uneven, between as well as within countries. The degree to which it was being treated as a new departure, involving a substantial break with the more deplorable features of the aid relationship and its negative interaction with the national political economy, varied across countries. Moreover, attitudes seemed to vary systematically with the progress that had been made with previous initiatives in public management and especially public finance management.

Without exception, the countries where PRSPs seemed to involve little more than a repackaging of existing poverty-focused projects and programmes were countries where public management reforms were stalled or otherwise in trouble. The importance of the broader reform record was, moreover, not limited to its effects on the perceptions and understanding of stakeholders. It also affected the degree to which the PRSP could be considered realistic, grounded in a clear sense of priorities and capable of being implemented.

Why budget reform matters

Unless some mechanism is in place for assessing overall resource constraints (including, crucially, the national resources that set limits on the successful absorption of foreign funds), unrealistic wish-lists are likely to take the place of priorities. Unless Ministries and local government authorities have started budgeting by objectives, they lack any mechanism or incentive to contribute to strategic policy-making. Unless the Ministry of Finance is capable of enforcing expenditure ceilings and limiting Ministries' ability to do their own deals with donors and lenders, PRSP priorities will not begin to be respected. So long as civil servants can get better and more interesting work by selling their skills to projects than by improving and implementing government policies, PRSPs will have no more value than previous unimplemented poverty policies.

The country studies are unanimous on this point. Very little will be achieved by PRSPs if they are not complemented by increased impetus to a range of reforms in public-sector management. PRSPs might in fact be best presented as one part of a jigsaw puzzle, of which the centrepiece is the sort of exercise in medium-term financial planning associated with MTEFs. There are both negative and positive cases that support this view of the matter.

Negatively, the doubts expressed in the chapter on Benin about PRSP implementation prospects are strongly connected to worries about the slow implementation of programme budgeting and the failure of Bank-supported accountability reforms to touch the core problems of corruption and arbitrary power. In view of the nature of socio-political relations at the local level, decentralisation too emerges as a precondition for anything that would count as implementation of an anti-poverty strategy. In Mali, also, the inability of the Ministry of Economy and Finance to impose budget discipline on the rest of government is a fundamental stumbling block. In theory, programme budgeting has been being implemented since 1998, but little progress has been made.

MTEFs and PRSPs

In both Ghana and Malawi the stalled implementation of MTEFs, after several years of effort, has been a substantial obstacle to making PRSPs effective in those countries. Not only does it hinder a link being established between the strategy and the budget and its execution, but the enforceability of a range of other governance reforms is also affected – because this is conditional upon the linkage of funding to institutional performance that the MTEF promises.

In the Ghana case, the MTEF was thrown into disarray by fiscal mismanagement and bad luck in 2000. But institutional difficulties also stood in the way of a close relationship between the PRSP and the MTEF, some of which remained even after the National Patriotic Party (NPP) government made a fresh start with the PRSP process in 2001. In Malawi, the PRSP and the MTEF are not institutionally disconnected, but fiscal discipline has been seriously undermined by political decisions, and the old line-item approach to budgeting is said to have been reasserting itself, reversing the gains made in previous years.

Even in Tanzania, where the MTEF is not described as stalled, not enough has yet been done to give confidence that a virtuous circle of interactions between the PRSP and the central resource-allocation processes is being created. The fact that cash-limited budgets still have to be resorted to (so that the Treasury only disburses monies that it has in hand) means that sectoral MTEF ceilings do not lead to predictable disbursements. This reduces considerably the incentive effect on line Ministries (and now districts), and this is unquestionably a drag on the implementation of Tanzania's PRSP.

Many of the other countries in our sample are at an earlier stage in the implementation of public finance reforms. But, with that qualification in mind, they provide some positive lessons, underlining the usefulness of a close and synergistic relation between PRSPs and MTEFs and associated budget reforms. Kenya, until the sacking of key members of the Economic Recovery Team in April 2001, was a good example of MTEF-PRSP synergy, even though the wider field of accountability in government remained highly problematic. The potential for a joint evolution of MTEF reforms and efforts towards PRSP implementation also exists in Mozambique and Rwanda. But it is clear in both cases that much work remains to be done, and that capacity to do it is very limited.

Value-added from PRSPs

We have argued that PRSPs need MTEFs and other reforms of the same type. We have even suggested that MTEFs might be regarded as the centrepiece of a cluster of reforms on which both the likely character and the implementability of a PRSP depend. This naturally raises the question of how much the PRSP initiative contributes as such. If MTEFs and related governance reforms are what really matter, what is the value of having a PRSP as well? The question has particular point where, as found in several countries, the two exercises are led by the same over-stretched officials.

We are relatively sanguine about this. In the countries investigated, the PRSP does seem to have added value in at least two ways.

First, it has boosted the reform effort in general. In both Kenya (to April 2001) and Benin, it was thought that the joint impact of the MTEF and the PRSP was stronger than either would have been on its own, including the degree of encouragement provided to donors and IFIs to shift their aid instruments towards budget support. In both those cases and many others, such a change in aid modalities seems essential if poverty reduction is to be 'de-politicised', in the sense of becoming less tied up with particularistic patronage politics.

For Malawi, there seem to be doubts about whether the PRSP, or anything short of a political change at the top, will do much to revive the MTEF. There is also a suggestion of some backsliding on aid modalities, with HIPC2 funds going into special accounts after a period in which concessional funding was becoming more mainstreamed through the budget. Nevertheless, from both Malawi and Mali, there are indications that, even if the PRSP cannot do much for the national budget progress, it may have given impetus to some sector plans, thereby encouraging the development of common-basket funding of the sector-wide approach (SWAP) type.

In contrast with previous poverty-policy exercises in most countries, this stimulus may not be restricted to the social sectors, previously the main preserve of SWAPs. For Tanzania and Mozambique, it may extend to agriculture and cross-sectoral policy areas such as HIV/AIDS and environmental sustainability. At least the potential exists for imaginative new approaches in these areas, with governments leading fundamental rethinking rather than being content to allow policy to be driven by offers of project funding.

The second way in which the PRSP initiative adds value to the MTEF and related reforms is by opening new spaces for domestic policy dialogue on poverty. Given what we said in the previous section about the way policy is made in case-study countries, an essential innovation of the PRSP is to open up public debate, thereby potentially creating new sources of public accountability, on poverty issues. A PRSP process may create policy spaces in which more voices can be heard and chronically neglected policy bottlenecks can be exposed to a wider national constituency. In other words, PRSP processes may add a missing political dimension to what, in many countries, has tended to be a rather technocratic reform environment. The extent to which this has actually happened is the subject of the next section.

These observations suggest that a priority is to increase the linkage and synchronisation between PRSPs and complementary reform measures, with PRSPs placed in the lead. The PRSP initiative provides a suitable opportunity to breathe new life into dormant reform programmes, and increase the pace of implementation where some successes are being achieved. Without suggesting that the changes that are needed are easy or capable of being completed quickly, there is no doubt that the PRSP initiative has raised the stakes. Our country evidence suggests that, without fresh impetus to key complementary reforms, the effort that has gone into the PRSPs may be largely dissipated. That would be a heavy price to pay.

Incentives for countries and donors

On this issue too, the argument among in-country stakeholders should not revolve around the need to please donors and access funds. On the contrary, it should be about how a substantial *reduction* in donor influence might be achieved in the medium term if countries play their cards right.

Achieving PRSPs that satisfy the basic conditions for credibility and implementability is the key to the transformations in aid relationships that most actors say they desire. The DAC donors have committed themselves to the principle of building, first and foremost, on partner-country development frameworks (OECD, 2001, 2003). Action to reflect this commitment is to be expected and demanded. However, it is important to be realistic. The incentive for donors and IFIs to shift towards programmatic forms of support, and take more of a back seat, will be strong when countries reform their budgets and link their poverty reduction strategies to MTEFs. They will remain weak until this happens. Country leaders should surely regard this as a strong reason for quickening the pace of institutional reform.

1.5 New spaces for domestic policy dialogue have been created

Opening new spaces for domestic policy dialogue is one of the most important potential contributions of a PRSP process. Broadening commitment to poverty reduction efforts among national stakeholders is important as a source of both better policy ideas and stronger pressure to perform.

The needed transformations in Africa's fragmented, patronage-oriented policy processes depend crucially on this element in the PRSP initiative. Rather than a technically more powerful approach to planning, the PRSP is a way of ratcheting up the political costs and benefits associated with ignoring or doing something serious about poverty. It could lay the foundations of a new 'poverty contract', under which politicians and other leaders acquire new obligations and poor people gain new rights. However, many factors affect whether this is actually likely, beginning with the particular political moment or conjuncture into which the PRSP initiative was inserted in a given country.

The importance of the political conjuncture

The extremes among our cases are well represented by Tanzania and Benin. In Tanzania, the timing of the initiative favoured a strong governmental commitment to the PRSP. 2000 was an election year, and the governing party took the opportunity of HIPC2 to present itself as a trustworthy custodian of the country's international financial relations. HIPC2 and the PRSP probably helped to ensure an electoral victory for Tanzania's CCM. The resulting high-level political backing (added to the fact that several other building-blocks for a credible process were in place) led to a relatively fast-track transition from iPRSP to full-PRSP preparation, and then to a bullish Joint Staff Assessment of the final document as early as November 2000.

In contrast, in Benin the PRSP initiative became mixed up with electoral timetables with the opposite type of result. The presidential election process effectively delayed everything, and the initial steps towards PRSP drafting did not take place until April 2001. As a consequence, Benin was one of the last countries of our set to complete the process.

The study's findings on four other countries underline the point that national political conjunctures have proven critical to the reception and significance of the PRSP initiative. In Ghana, the treatment of the PRSP by the Rawlings government in 2000 suffered from the distracting effects of the elections expected at the end of the year, as well as from the policy of not seeking relief under HIPC2. The transfer of power then brought new distractions. Although the new government reversed the position on 'joining HIPC', thereby increasing the stakes in the PRSP process, it found itself preoccupied with re-stabilising the economy and implementing its election pledge to emphasise 'wealth creation'.

In Kenya, the PRSP process that was developing during late 2000 benefited from the boost to transparent public sector management given by the placing of the Economic Recovery Team of independent Kenyans led by Richard Leakey in key government positions. However, during the second phase of the study, the underlying system of presidential rule reasserted itself with some vigour. The majority of the ERT departed. The PRGF agreement with the IMF was again suspended for non-compliance, signalling the re-emergence of the stop-go cycle of Kenya's external financial relations. This did not necessarily mean that the Kenyan PRSP would have no benefits. It did, however, alter the range of outcomes that could be expected.

In Mozambique and Rwanda, deep political divisions and a violent past history affect in obvious ways the gains that might be made from an enhanced national poverty-reduction effort. They also place constraints on any immediately feasible national consensus. Both governments seem to have embraced the PRSP as an opportunity to move national reconstruction into a new phase. However, in Mozambique the disputed results of the 1999 elections left a legacy of inter-party relations that has limited the kinds of national agreement on the PRSP that can be achieved. Rwanda's political and strategic situation has been similarly constraining, for obvious reasons.

Gaining policy spaces

There were signs during the research in most of the study countries that the PRSP process was beginning to open up policy spaces in the hoped-for ways, creating a potential for greater changes in the future. New arenas were being created in which governments could be tackled by other national actors on what they are doing, or not doing, about poverty. The consultative processes organised by governments have been the subject of quite a lot of written comment, especially by NGOs, and several reports have focused closely on this aspect.[11] Together with the details reported in the country chapters in this collection, these support a number of generalisations about experience

---

11. e.g. Whaites (2002); Christian Aid (2002); McGee (2002) and Eberlei (2001).

in sub-Saharan Africa:

- Despite a rushed and unsatisfactory consultation process in most cases, the political profile of poverty issues in-country has been raised, and in some cases this may be a permanent effect.

- Where they are a significant force, NGOs and civil society organisations have mobilised to engage with national policy processes in a more strategic manner than before. In some cases, working relations between the government and development NGOs have improved.

- More substantial changes are to be expected as 'second-round' effects of the PRSP initiative, as more organisations appreciate the value of engaging with government at a policy level and set out to gain the capacities and resources to do so on an ongoing basis.

Quality of consultation processes

We will not attempt to summarise all the details of the consultation process undertaken in the eight study countries, but only give an overall flavour of what has been involved. In all cases, the full PRSP will have been influenced to some degree by a national consultative process. In most cases, this was in the form of national and regional workshops (the scale and number of the latter varying considerably from case to case). While in several instances, the process was unprecedented as an exercise in policy consultation ('the most participatory policy process in Malawi to date', and so on), it has often been less than completely inclusive of interested groups and parties.

In several cases, non-governmental or private-sector organisations have organised parallel consultations, sometimes with separate donor support (Mali, USAID; Benin, DANIDA, Netherlands). This was out of a sense that either the timetable or the procedures proposed by government were unsuitable, although in the case of Mali it is reported that the NGO exercise was completed in less time than originally scheduled by government. Elsewhere, protests at the narrowness of government proposals in the iPRSP phase led not only to a broader consultative process, but also to the inclusion of NGO-network representatives in thematic or sectoral working groups (e.g. the Malawi Economic Justice Network).

In many cases, there were concerns that the ideas and preferences expressed during the consultations would not figure as centrally as they should in the final drafting of the PRSP, which in all cases was a rather more closed process. We leave on one side for the time being the question of the quality of the inputs that were being offered.

The general picture, then, is that the consultation processes were more substantial than many observers expected in late 2000, and certainly more so than anything that was done during the preparation of the iPRSP. On the other hand, for most countries the words of the Mozambique chapter apply:

although 'a promising start', the consultations offered 'substantially less than full civil society participation'.

This somewhat faint praise calls for some qualification. Even experienced national observers of the process in Kenya regarded it as having been, by all relevant standards, not only efficiently organised but wide, deep and strongly 'owned' by all of the participant groups, if not by the national political leadership. The Kenya chapter reports that the process generated considerable national attention, partly because the spending of a relatively large sum of money on 'just talking' was picked up aggressively by some MPs and mass media.

Despite this, and perhaps a little because of it, the process was credited with raising the political profile of poverty issues. The ambitious scope of the consultations outside Nairobi also led to important gains in terms of NGO networking (national NGOs became better connected with those operating in the districts); better working relationships between local governments and church and development organisations in some districts; and benefits in terms of self-organisation and raised expectations in some communities. Several of these gains were due to the way the funding served to involve a suitable range of Kenyan organisers and researchers with relevant experience.

Upgrading of NGO roles and second-round effects

The Kenyan case notwithstanding, we maintain our claim that the possible second-round effects are going to be generally more significant than those achieved so far. In some countries, second-round effects started relatively early, leading to some concerns that they may not be sustained. The iPRSP process in Malawi stimulated the creation of a new organisation, the Malawi Economic Justice Network, which became a vocal and effective (which is not to say necessarily decisive) actor in the process.

In Tanzania, the consultation on the full PRSP was much criticised by the NGOs at the time, but it did prompt a flurry of organisation, communication and coalition-building that significantly improved their capacity to engage in policy dialogue with government and other actors. The first annual review of the PRSP was the occasion for further debate, in which NGOs participated. However, some of the more articulate NGOs – such as the gender network, which benefits from involving both academics and grass-roots' activists – were becoming critical of the rather 'instrumental' approach of both government and donors to encouraging NGO involvement. This suggests that careful thought needs to be given to appropriate means of maintaining the momentum for dialogue and advocacy on policy issues.

In Kenya too, there was a commitment in principle to maintaining the involvement of NGOs and academics after the drafting process was finished. The set-up for PRSP monitoring (to which we turn in Section 6) was seen as one way of doing this. But the study team felt that needed to be actively promoted if a discouraging phase of de-mobilisation was to be avoided.

In sum, in most of our countries there seem to have been spin-off benefits for NGOs, including a greater orientation to poverty as a policy issue – not just as a focus for projects; more effective networking among those organisations that already have some limited capacity for engagement in policy discussions; and identification of capacity-building needs that may be addressed in the coming years if resources are available.

Room for improvement

To summarise, there are grounds for being positive about the prospects for improved domestic policy dialogue (from an admittedly low base). On the other hand, some important qualifications do need to be added:

- In some cases, a rather narrow view of 'civil society' was taken, effectively excluding significant membership organisations such as trade unions and producer associations. There was also a general tendency to by-pass parliamentary institutions and procedures, and even, in some cases, key political processes within the executive arm of government. This was clearly unwise. Attempts to circumvent core political processes are not only contrary to the PRSP goal of national ownership, but are very likely to backfire.

- New voices started being heard – not in most cases 'voices of the poor' in a direct sense, but at any rate organisations with a different perception from the government's on the needs and problems of poor people. A limitation was that these expressions of view tended to generate 'shopping lists' of desirable objectives. They did not contribute much to the more difficult tasks of defining priorities, and finding new ways of attaining goals that have defeated previous efforts. This limited the ability of the consultation mechanisms to influence policy.

- There are perceptions within countries, particularly among the more combative NGOs, that PRSPs have not fundamentally changed relations between recipient countries and the IFIs. Some changes for the better are noted (for example, IFIs making substantial efforts to stand back from PRSP preparation and make space for national consultations). However, PRSP design in most countries did not start with a blank sheet of paper. Some of the most important decisions had been 'pre-empted' by prior government-IFI agreements, for example on PRGF conditionalities and HIPC triggers. This is an inevitable limitation at this stage in the process. However, ways need to be found of mitigating its more negative consequences.

A narrow vision of civil and political society
Overall, more efforts seem to have been made to include NGOs than membership organisations that might seem in principle to have greater claims

to represent civil society. For example, in Mali neither the trade unions, nor the important Cotton Producers' Association, participated. Private sector input was also notably lacking. The meaning of 'CSOs' seems to have been largely restricted to NGOs, despite the fact that, in the assessment of the study team, these are lacking in both legitimacy and technical capacity.

Parliamentary institutions have generally not been centrally involved in PRSP consultations. At the extreme, Rwanda had no elected national assembly. The participatory poverty assessment and other exercises undertaken in connection with the PRSP were ambitious and innovative in the context. However, they and ongoing efforts to rebuild national unity (with which they are apparently not well-connected) are deliberately working strictly from the bottom-up, starting with base communities rather than institutions of any sort, since even the churches are still felt to be compromised by their role in the genocide.

For Mozambique, too, it is reported that none of the planning instruments used by government are subjected to parliamentary debate. Opposition political views are not solicited by any other means either. While this has to be seen in the context of the delicate and particular post-conflict political situation in that country, the tendency for PRSPs to be seen as technical planning processes that are properly the affair of the executive branch of government, and not a subject for party-political debate, is rather general.

In view of these limitations, it has to be asked whether PRSP design processes have led to any significant transformations in the way countries make policy. They could easily be portrayed just as a new means by which donors ventriloquise their ideas about development. No doubt, the big battalions of civil and political society – the trade and professional organisations, political parties, parliaments and parliamentary committees – are typically under-resourced for their roles. They are often compromised, as vehicles for new policy agendas and independent pressure on government, by their involvement in networks of patronage. On the other hand, NGOs are not necessarily any less a part of the 'system'. The Benin chapter is eloquent in portraying them as integral to it, while reminding us that in its classic sense, civil society is a sphere that is both non-governmental and non-profit (whereas most local NGOs are for all practical purposes private businesses). In Mali, the president of the National Assembly is famously quoted as not recognising any significant civil society in the country other than that represented in parliament: '*La société civile, c'est moi!*'

However, it may be necessary to recognise national diversity in addressing these questions, and it is best not to go to extremes in either direction. It would not be sensible to discount the potential of a largely extra-parliamentary process in countries like Kenya that have substantial civil societies and private sectors, independent mass media and a large intelligentsia. On the other hand, as the Kenya chapter says this does not mean that it was wise for the consultations to have by-passed parliament to the extent that they did. This provoked some opposition to the PRSP that could and should have been avoided.

In any case, it would not be wise for PRSP consultations to be *restricted* to parliamentary parameters. Even in countries where parliamentary institutions function a great deal better, and party politics is more concerned with principles and less with personal loyalties, major changes in policy occur typically through an *interaction* of parliamentary and extra-parliamentary, social movements.[12] If PRSPs are to be a significant innovation, this will have to be true of them too.

What do PRSP consultations contribute to better policy?

A general observation in the country studies is that PRSP consultations, as they were conducted in the first round, generated 'shopping lists' or 'wish lists', not careful prioritisations or fresh thinking. This was probably inevitable. It is arguable that all that can be expected is that such expressions should be taken into account, and intelligently assessed, while the actual design of policies and actions takes place in the technical working groups.

It may not be particularly important, in that sense, if in mass consultations, the demands that are heard tend to be of a 'trade unionist' sort – that is, unrestricted and driven by sectional concerns and interests. What matters is that in such processes some voices are heard that are not usually heard, not heard so loudly or not heard by such senior officials. It would be welcome however if, among the welter of known concerns, there were also to be found some good ideas about how to deal with entrenched problems and what the real obstacles to better performance are.

The more encouraging signs in this respect are modest and anecdotal, but not for that insignificant. From Kenya, it is reported that concerns of pastoralists were articulated more effectively than usual. In Benin, senior planning officials who for the first time travelled outside the capital for the purpose of explaining government policies were surprised to learn that the principal problem in rural primary schools is that teachers do not turn up to work. In Tanzania, primary-school fees were abolished partly in response to the frequency with which school fees were cited as a constraint on poor people during the PRSP consultations. In other words, the consultations did to some degree function in the way that PPAs have sometimes done, drawing the attention of senior planners to issues of policy or implementation about which they ought to have been aware but perhaps were not.

This sort of thing is not unimportant but it is no substitute for the sort of thorough scrutiny of the problems in a given sector that makes for real policy improvement. It also presents the danger that politicians will be jumped into making policy 'on the hoof' in response to well-expressed public pressure,

---

12. A promising development in several countries is the establishment of regular links between parliamentarians and research-and-advocacy NGOs, with the latter providing briefings to support parliamentary questions or committee work. The Malawi chapter has an example.

and will make mistakes as a result.[13]

A further issue is the tendency noted in a number of our country chapters for the discussion of poverty-reduction policies to be limited to public-expenditure options and other 'technical' issues, and to skirt around structural-reform questions and anything that might be deemed political. Thus, issues of family-law reform and land distribution were effectively ignored in Benin, despite the evidence suggesting these as critical to the causation of poverty in the country. Women's inheritance rights were not to the fore in the Tanzanian PRSP debate. Nor were corruption and its causes.

The country chapters contain a number of efforts to explain the limitations of the current round of PRSP consultations, drawing on the stakeholder interviews. Cultural factors loom large in this. In Rwanda, there is what is termed a 'culture of obedience' that discourages people from expressing their real concerns. In Tanzania, the rural masses are said to have become both demobilised and disengaged during the era of economic and political liberalisation, so that reviving real interest in politics and policy may take a long time. Similar things could be said about the other countries. However, against this it should be pointed out that many of the limitations pointed out above are fairly general to public consultation exercises everywhere, including in very rich and quite democratic countries. They could almost be said to be inherent in the more unstructured types of participatory policy making. Recalling that, in addition, we are dealing with societies where taxation, and particularly income taxes, are an insignificant revenue source compared with foreign aid, the level of citizen engagement shown within PRSP consultations is actually quite remarkable.

What this suggests is that reviews of the experience of PRSP consultation should be paying attention to ways of structuring consultation that improve the quality of policy inputs. This is not necessarily a case for making it more formal, and certainly not for limiting it exclusively to the institutionalised political processes of countries. It does, though, mean addressing seriously the role of parliamentary committees, and the possible synergies between them and advocacy groups. It means making them more broadly political, in the sense of embracing organised as well as unorganised opinion. Whichever institutional framework is used, it involves getting the balance right between political pressure and technical quality.

National stakeholders and the prospects for change

The study found that national stakeholders entertain a fairly developed scepticism about PRSP processes, on two counts. In the first place, there are few who believe that a substantial reduction in the number and complexity

---

13. An example from an actual country, but not in our sample, is the cancellation of user charges in major hospitals as well as primary health centres, on the understanding that this will favour the poor, which has generated chaos in the referral system and mis-targeted the element of subsidy.

of IFI conditionalities is on the immediate agenda.

It is recognised that, in some countries, bilateral donors and some multilaterals such as the EU are providing budget support on a new basis, in which ex-post performance assessment linked to the PRSP is taking the place of prior conditions. However, there is a belief that the overall impact of the new array of financial support instruments will be an even greater 'cascading' of conditionalities. Not only is total conditionality likely to increase, but some of the recent additions to it do not seem particularly friendly to building policy ownership on the basis of the PRSP.

The most important issue of this sort is the one that is raised most acutely in the Malawi country chapter – that some of the HIPC2 'triggers' were agreed in a way that *pre-empted* national discussion within the PRSP process. In some instances, it was not a question of insisting on steps that any reasonable poverty-reduction strategy would necessarily include (e.g. broad fiscal discipline), but rather an insistence upon the implementation of schemes that are both controversial and questionable in the opinion of informed and engaged observers.

These concerns are justified. *Ex-ante* conditions and performance benchmarks agreed in the framework of relatively narrow, apex-level negotiations around HIPC2 relief, PRGFs or PRSCs do conflict, or are at least in tension, with a country-led decision-making process covering the same issues. It should be remarked, however, that national stakeholders' views about the relationship between the PRSP process and traditional conditionality are typically somewhat one-sided. There is little appreciation that changes in the scale and form of conditionality are dependent on the seriousness and quality of what is done in-country in and around the PRSP process. So far, there is little understanding that a reduction or streamlining of external conditions will be possible only as and when PRSPs yield up tough policy thinking and monitorable implementation proposals of their own.

The second subject of scepticism is the ability of governments to change their behaviour. More in some countries than in others, stakeholders doubt whether this well-intentioned attempt to change the basis of the aid relationship will do enough to alter the incentives facing government departments and their officials. This stems from the sorts of issues reviewed in the last section on country context. As we shall see, some of it seems justified by what has actually happened in the PRSP process so far. For the moment, we merely note it as a strong element in stakeholder expectations. It appears strongest where, as in both Ghana and Benin, though for somewhat different reasons, there is very little sign of the PRS process engaging with, or becoming linked to, reforms that attempt to transform the budgetary incentives of ministries and the work incentives of civil servants.

The way forward

The three types of concern just reviewed suggest two major priorities for action. First, donors should assist by providing broad-based, consistent, long-term support to participatory policy-making. Second, all PRSP partners need to be encouraged to work with greater transparency and openness, to increase trust and maximise synergies. Let us develop these proposals in turn.

Sustaining support and changing gear

On the first point, the country studies suggest that donors in general have been supportive of PRSP participation processes. Modes of delivery of this support include some exemplary experiences (involving pooled funding and arms-length delivery) and some that might have been better. Lack of co-ordination and excessive 'clientelism' are cited in some cases. Elsewhere, it is suggested that donors were rather short-term and instrumentalist in their support to the participatory processes of PRSP preparation.

How far these charges are accurate is of merely historical interest. The main point is to ensure that support is sustained, and does not go the way of other passing fashions among donors. In any case, now that PRSP formulation processes are all but completed, a change of gear is needed. This should involve a longer-term, more comprehensive and deliberately non-instrumental approach to strengthening participation in policy-making.

The following elements are likely to be helpful:

- Common-basket funding for policy work, under independent management of the trust-fund type, would help avoid situations in which NGOs and other 'donor-friendly' groups are strengthened at the expense of other parts of civil and political society (trade unions, professional associations and parliamentary groups).

- Formal political institutions matter for PRSPs, but they are not invariably well equipped to participate in policy debates on poverty. New forms of partnership for public policy debate are needed and should be supported; for example, parliamentary committees working with advocacy groups, and national research institutions developing policy ideas for political parties.

- The importance of politics to PRSPs should be reflected, furthermore, in the general attitudes of donor agencies and IFIs towards the PRSP experiment. Political developments are bound to imply uneven results between countries, and big setbacks from time to time. Politics brings risks and will test commitments. All development partners need to set realistic expectations and timescales taking into account possible political scenarios, if only to avoid disillusionment.

- Governments and donors should encourage wider, deeper and more multi-layered participation in PRSP processes, recognising 'civil society' as highly differentiated. The quality of the PRSP process and the quality of the policy thinking it generates depend on this. There is still a need to develop modalities of participation that yield a higher quality of debate on the more difficult issues, both technical and political. A more differentiated approach to participation in PRSPs is needed that would allow open forums, participatory appraisals, pressure groups, think tanks, research institutions and independent experts to contribute severally and in combination in the ways that suit them.[14]

- *All* phases of the PRSP need broad stakeholder engagement. Participation needs to start with design, but becomes more important as policy commitments begin to be implemented, annual reviews are scheduled and opportunities arise for disseminating and using monitoring information. Support to stakeholder involvement should not be allowed to lapse after the PRSP design stage. As argued in the next section, the monitoring phase is key, especially when strategy content is weak.

What openness implies

For some time to come, national ownership of PRSPs will be compromised, at least to some degree, by the fact that governments have already entered into HIPC, PRGF and concessional credit agreements with the IFIs, which are characterised by conditionalities of a traditional sort. This is largely inevitable, and not just for reasons of timing. Until PRSPs and PRSP performance-monitoring arrangements become substantial and credible, it is going to be difficult for the IFIs to abandon their conditionalities – although streamlining them and merging review processes around the PRSP are certainly on the agenda, as discussed at the end of this chapter.

The study suggests, however, that some of the current problems are not inevitable, and could be avoided. These are not caused by the fact that there are agreements reached separately between governments and the IFIs. They stem from the lack of openness and attention to public dissemination that sometimes still characterise their handling in-country.

Because the contents of agreements between governments and IFIs tend not to be made public, suspicions arise that they are actually 'secret'. In fact, all or large parts of most of the relevant agreements are published. But this does not do much to mitigate the problem, as little *active* dissemination is undertaken by either governments or IFIs. The latter tend to insist that this is government's responsibility and prerogative. This is formally correct but an insufficient response in the PRSP context.

This state of affairs undermines trust and the centrality of the PRSP in the policy-making process. There is also another cost, which is possibly as important. There are signs in some countries that national stakeholders mobilised in the PRSP process wish to hold governments to account on exactly

---

14. This was a main recommendation of the PRSP country studies commissioned by the UN Economic Commission for Africa for its PRSP Learning Group in 2001.

the same issues as are covered in PRGF and other formal agreements. In other words, there is a potential for useful synergies between international pressures for reform and a strengthened domestic accountability. However, the hand of domestic pressure groups is weakened if the government's commitments to the IFIs are unknown, or in any way obscure.

The damage on both counts needs to be reduced, and synergies between external and domestic policy thinking and accountability maximised. This could happen if *all* participants were more active in explaining and disseminating the content of agreements. We suggest that this could be done without compromising the IMF's obligations and the legitimate place of confidentiality in the case of market-sensitive information, etc. *All actors*, including bilateral donors and advocacy organisations as well as government units and IFI resident missions, should be invited to play a part in an information policy aimed at building trust and strengthening the positive linkages between PRSPs and related agreements.

1.6   Monitoring processes may improve the quality of poverty reduction strategies

Monitoring arrangements are an important focus of this study, but they have generally been the last things to be considered within PRSP formulation processes. In most PRSP documents, the proposals under the heading of Monitoring and Evaluation are rather thin and problematic. However, as country authorities have turned their attention to implementation and the required annual progress reviews, discussion of options and instruments for monitoring has attracted more interest.

We consider the experience on monitoring and information under three headings:

- the general approach to PRSP monitoring;
- the anticipated relationship between the supply of and demand for PRSP-related information; and
- the roles donors are assuming in relation to PRSP information requirements.

Approach to monitoring

What is PRSP monitoring *for*? What is its purpose? Most African PRSP documents have been rather unclear on this issue, as reported elsewhere (Booth and Lucas, 2002). One result is that the required selection of indicators to be the basis of monitoring continues to be rather indiscriminate. Although they purport to be strategic, the documents are typically weak in the 'middle'. They do not explore very well how the prioritised actions can be expected to be better at achieving the outcome objectives than similar actions have been in the past. The critical intervening variables have not been identified, so it is not clear what are the critical things that need to be monitored.

The case-study countries do not provide any exceptions to these generalisations. In several countries, further work is being done to refine an initial, over-long indicator list. However, there is a rather heavy focus on measuring final outcomes or impacts for poor people – that is on the goal level in logical-framework terms. Intermediate results get relatively little attention. Consequently, attention is being given to types of information that will be relatively slow to arrive and hard to interpret from a policy-assessment point of view. Sources of quick feedback, which could suggest timely policy correctives, are being neglected.

There is some danger that the emphasis that has been placed on results- or outcome-orientation in propagating the PRSP idea (and the CDF idea before it) has created the impression that it is only the final level of outcomes that is now worthy of serious attention, so that monitoring inputs (e.g. tracking public expenditure) and intermediate outputs and outcomes can safely be downgraded. Alternatively, it may just be that deciding on what needs to happen 'in the middle' to achieve agreed goals is always the hardest part. It may be, too, that there is sound and relevant thinking in the framework of certain sector programmes that is not being sufficiently used, as suggested for Mali.

This insufficiency recalls what we said about stakeholder perceptions of the PRSP initiative. There is, as yet, too little general appreciation of the potential role of appropriate and credible progress benchmarks in liberating countries from external conditionality. The difference between this and second-guessing what it is that the IFIs want to see (or, worse, deciding what targets might most easily be achieved) is not at the moment very apparent.

The design of a monitoring and information system cannot, with the best will in the world, entirely solve this problem. It is a planning problem rather than a monitoring problem. Nevertheless, if PRSP stakeholders can remain involved in arrangements for PRSP monitoring, the latter could provide points of entry back into the strategic debate. If neglected and difficult issues are constantly being raised in a relatively high-profile way by the monitoring authorities, incentives to the better conceptualisation and more effective implementation of poverty-reduction efforts could strengthen.

Poverty information: supply and demand

What sorts of monitoring systems are currently being proposed for PRSPs? We can separate this question into two parts. There is the matter of how the necessary information is to be supplied – that is, what instruments are being developed to meet different levels of monitoring. And there is how the demand for, and use of, information is likely to evolve. We consider these in turn.

Improving the supply of information
In principle, a large range of survey- and non-survey data-collection

instruments are appropriate to PRSP monitoring. The different instruments have different strengths and weaknesses as applied to the different levels of monitoring (final impacts, intermediate outcomes, outputs, inputs, etc.). Apart from the household expenditure surveys that have led the way on final impact monitoring, there are a range of lighter survey instruments that serve particular purposes, including picking up evidence on intermediate processes. Routine data collected through administrative reporting structures and management information systems have some advantages and some well-known weaknesses. Notably, they are facility-based and hence are bad at measuring the reach of existing services. A range of participatory and more qualitative techniques are also available, including some that have traditionally focused on multidimensional aspects of final outcomes, and others that assess implementation.

It seems clear from our country cases that a large number of new household surveys have been commissioned. The information on poverty profiles and trends is about to improve significantly almost everywhere thanks to PRSP-related initiatives. This is good and particularly important for enabling better diagnostic work that can feed into improved policy designs.

'Light' surveys of different kinds are proposed in several countries (for example, Mali, Mozambique, Tanzania). Uncertainties remain, however, as to whether the CWIQ type of survey that uses a short, machine-readable questionnaire, focusing on service-use rather than expenditure, is going to have a major role to play. Doubts about relative costs, and questions about the usefulness of the service-use results, are still being considered.

Matching the upsurge of household-survey work, participatory poverty assessments have been completed in Rwanda and Tanzania. So far, PPAs have focused mainly on assessing impacts and other final-outcome issues such as the meaning of poverty in the eyes of poor people. It is hoped and expected that future generations of PPAs will become progressively more concerned with intermediate processes and policy-implementation issues. The same is true of the units for Qualitative Impact Monitoring (QUIM) that have been set up in several countries (Benin, Kenya, Malawi). In principle there is no reason for such arrangements not to be oriented primarily to providing quick feedback on policies that are being implemented, those that are not, and what immediate difficulties need to be drawn to public attention.

The demand side

There have been previous periods of upsurge in data supply comparable to the one we are observing in connection with PRSPs. The Social Dimensions of Adjustment initiative in the early 1990s led to a significant improvement for a period in the availability of poverty data. It was, however, donor-driven and not sustained. Much of the data was under-utilised. The lack of effective demand from potential users within the country has been a chronic problem.

Demand for information is of course a function of the incentive to use information that is generated by a given kind of public-sector management system. Once again, the principal constraint on the design of an appropriate monitoring system lies outside the sphere of monitoring. Weak demand for poverty-related information until now is a reflection of the fact that although governments are committed in principle to poverty-reduction objectives, neither ministry budgets nor the employment conditions of civil servants have been closely linked to meeting public-policy objectives.

This is beginning to change, and may have been given an additional fillip by the PRSP initiative, as we suggested in Section 4. The growth of new pressures and demands for accountability from parliamentary and non-governmental sources may also help in the long term. However, the particular challenge that arises, at this point, is how to stimulate new sources of demand for information on an interim basis until the more fundamental changes have a chance to kick in. What is needed is imaginative stop-gaps that build on whatever strengths the PRSP design process has had to provide a pole of attraction for the information that will become available.

A very important point is well articulated in the Rwanda chapter. What is needed is not simply the analysis and recycling of raw information, but above all better understanding of certain issues. There is, in most countries, a considerable body of dispersed and under-utilised information (Rwanda). There are also data that are in principle available but in practice almost impossible to obtain, particularly by national researchers and interest groups (Benin). Systematising information and making it available in accessible forms is an important first step. However, what is *most* needed is the building up of a stock of understanding and knowledge about processes that lead to poverty-reducing outcomes. This is a much more challenging analytical task. It is one in which international cooperation has a role to play.

Alternative institutional models
In several countries, poverty *Observatoires* exist or are being set up, with terms of reference that, in some cases, include the full range of tasks just identified. The key question, however, is whether they are set up in such a way as to stimulate data use in a framework of enduring weakness in demand. One approach that has proven its worth in Uganda is to locate a small technical unit very close to the budget office in the Ministry of Finance, so that when the new incentives created by budget-reform process begin to generate demand for poverty information, this is immediately noticed and responded to.[15] Mozambique, Rwanda and perhaps Benin seem to be following that model.

In many other countries, the institutional framework has yet to be defined, but poverty monitoring has been historically located away from the Ministry of Finance, in a national statistical bureau, a planning agency or a president's or vice-president's office. The logic that has so far brought PRSPs under the wing of Finance in most countries does not yet seem to have been applied to

---

15. In Uganda, poverty-focused public expenditure gets special protection from budget

monitoring.

It is not a question of centralising all information-generation and utilisation in a single institution. That would be out of the question, and is not a feature of the Uganda model. The monitoring system will always need to involve a network of institutions. That would be expected to include in most cases a statistics department or agency, sectoral planning units, and any non-governmental organisations that have a commitment to participatory monitoring. The question is not whether to have a unit or a network, but whether it is strategic to have a well-resourced and well-placed unit that assumes the principal responsibility for making things happen (as opposed to a mere secretariat to a committee, with ultimate responsibilities remaining dispersed).

Tanzania provides an interesting contrast, and a model that seems deliberately to avoid the approach of Uganda. Although the PRSP itself said little on the subject, the arrangements for monitoring have since been laid out in detail in a Poverty Monitoring Master Plan. Four working groups were convened to cover all aspects of PRSP monitoring, including analysis and research. The agreed arrangements take a broad 'stakeholder approach', in which all interested parties are included and responsibilities are shared out. Ambitious in conception, this may be complex and time-consuming to maintain, and could result in a vacuum of responsibility. Particular doubts arise about whether effective tracking of policies and detection of implementation snags can be delivered by such a system.

Whichever of these basic models is adopted, it will be important – at least until public-sector management reforms become effective – to build in the active participation of non-governmental stakeholders. This does not automatically mean NGOs, although in some countries they will be the most appropriate participants. Academics, parliamentary committees and trade union leaders, could also be considered. The point is to ensure that PRSP monitoring does not come to be treated as a largely technical business, and that any issues that have arisen in the PRSP design process, whether or not they have figured in the final document, are constantly brought up, and publicised.

Donor roles in information systems

The options just reviewed will, if they are successful, avoid the need for donor-driven poverty monitoring. For the foreseeable future, they will not make it unnecessary for donors to provide funding for data collection and to support research. However, they do underline the importance of revisiting the modalities of donor support for monitoring and information. The case

---

cuts; in preparing their medium-term Budget Framework Papers, sectors of government are invited to make the case that particular programmes should qualify for such protection (see Williamson and Canagarajah, 2003, for a full explanation).

for basket funding, on a grant basis, seems particularly strong, and now that the initial surge of new survey work is over, there is time for this to be organised and to be channelled through the national budget.

To the extent this happens, it should help to prevent the type of unseemly occurrence that has been reported for one country where the sample size of the household survey was determined more by donor disbursement pressure and rivalry than by technical arguments and considerations of sustainability.

There may be a good case for special units, and even projects, to pioneer new methods such as participatory assessment and qualitative monitoring, particularly where the intention is to bring NGOs into a sphere traditionally dominated by government. However, donors should not allow their own delivery mechanisms and convenience to determine this. Nor should they overlook the importance of placing such units where they are likely to have the most influence.

Donors may be able to influence the shape of monitoring and information systems by their contributions to PRSP-related dialogue, as well as by where and how they spend their money. If that is so, they should be offering resistance to the recent tendency for final-outcome measurement to get all the attention. It has to be recognised that this is related to absorptive capacity (surveys use money quickly and with predictable results; investments in improving MISs typically do not). This applies to PPAs and QUIM as well as to quantitative data: partly because it has been done before, it may be simpler to ask general questions about poverty than to get seriously to grips with why poor people don't use government health services or what to do about crop disease. Renewed efforts are needed to ensure that these more challenging tasks are also tackled.

1.7 PRSPs invite a more substantial transformation of the aid relationship

The PRSP approach supports recipient countries in determining their own policies and assuming leadership of their own policy-making processes. This means confronting the tendency of much aid to undermine the conditions of its own effectiveness by weakening the capacities of government and other national institutions to work for themselves. It implies taking PRSPs as an opportunity to move the aid-reform agenda decisively forward.

Donor conduct matters

Country examples in our study support the idea that the way donors behave in-country can either support or frustrate national poverty reduction efforts. PRSPs are giving new significance to widely recognised difficulties with project-oriented approaches. Projects stand accused of cultivating patron-client relationships, encouraging a rent-seeking orientation in government and influencing domestic politics towards patron-client models that work against state effectiveness and accountability. Also, because they by-pass government systems to a greater or lesser extent, projects contribute to skill shortages and weak incentives in government. This sets up 'vicious' circles in which the form of aid delivery undermines national policy-making capacity and, in turn, helps to justify further by-passing of national institutions.

In contrast, PRSPs provide an opportunity to initiate a new type of 'virtuous' circle. In this scenario, the adoption of stronger national policies on poverty coincides with a shift by donors towards sector programmes or general budget support, and the wider adoption of common approaches and procedures by donors and concessional lenders. This means more aid that uses, and thus helps to improve and increase confidence in, government systems, leading to a gradual phasing out of by-pass solutions.

It is clear that the potential of the PRSP to contribute to this kind of advance in the aid relationship depends on the quality of the national policy process. But realising the potential also depends on donors' being proactive in promoting the chain of events that most of them wish to see. Our study suggests three policy messages for donors, one about aid modalities, one about common procedures and one about the desirability of donors' 'benchmarking' their own performance as well as that of recipients.

New aid modalities: risks versus costs

The first contention is that, to realise this potential, donors must build more actively on the common ground that exists among them in regard to new aid modalities. Changes in aid modalities have a crucial role to play in enabling national policy-making to be driven by overarching poverty reduction/growth priorities rather than by offers of project funding. Without suggesting a uniform approach, we would argue that – in addition to pursuing the important but difficult aid harmonisation agenda – donors and IFIs need to make stronger moves to change their aid modalities towards those that use national systems. Not all national systems call for the same timetable of change, and not all donor organisations will be able to move at the same pace. However, quite a lot of shared commitment in principle exists. It is a question of finding effective ways of taking the agenda forward.

There are inevitably concerns within the donor/IFI community about when and how to make the shift to programme modalities, such as direct budget support. But currently different rules are being applied by different agencies in the same country settings, without any obvious basis for the difference. The World Bank's due-diligence tests are clearly set out, but they are somewhat more demanding than the rules applied by other agencies. Urgent work needs to be done between donors/IFIs and governments to spell out and agree the necessary conditions for moving away from project assistance and towards programme support.

It is not entirely clear at present whether on balance modalities such as budget support pose greater fiduciary and developmental risks. But if they do, this needs to be set against the large potential benefits from the virtuous circle scenario, and the heavy institutional and other costs of continuing with the old model of aid relations. The donor community as a whole needs to convince itself on this point.

The multiplication of review processes and frameworks

A similar sense of urgency needs to be adopted in respect of performance assessment and review processes. A more proactive approach is needed to accelerate the shift to common performance assessment and streamlined review processes. The core of the PRSP (and CDF) concept is to reduce the number of uncoordinated demands made on recipient governments, by focusing on country-led criteria and processes. But there is little evidence to date that this has happened.

In fact, review processes seem to have multiplied with the introduction of PRSPs. Except under some SWAP arrangements and the few cases of coordinated general budget support, donors and IFIs continue to work to different performance assessment frameworks, with different timelines and procedures. The study was unable to identify a single instance of review processes being merged, or performance assessment moving in behind the PRSP. This no doubt reflects the early stage reached in the PRSP processes, and the fact that most of the strategies have been slow to set up credible performance assessment arrangements. However, this too needs to be approached proactively, and without waiting for perfection to be achieved.

Review processes need to be streamlined, within agencies, between agencies, and between agencies and governments. Streamlining conditionality around the PRSP would be the basis for building stronger, longer-lasting partnerships in support of a nationally defined agenda. This certainly means reducing the number of separate review processes, by merging some and eliminating others (for example, absorbing Consultative Group meetings into PRSP annual reviews). Wherever reasonably possible, the form of merger should be to subordinate externally-led processes and criteria to those that enjoy the most country ownership, normally those of the PRSP.

Benchmarking donor performance

These changes will not happen without coordinated international effort, and a deliberate setting of targets for streamlining performance assessment based on current or attainable best practice across countries. Definite timetables should therefore be agreed for:

- taking the next step forward in countries where most has been achieved so far in bringing lending and budget support performance criteria into line with those indicated by the PRSP; and

- extending current best practice to a further group of countries.

In other words, donors and IFIs should be benchmarking their *own* performance on implementing PRSP/CDF principles, and monitoring themselves and each other in this regard.[16] Some immediate symbolic actions, such as cancelling a forthcoming Consultative Group in favour of a PRSP review, would have value in signalling a clear intention in this direction.

1.8 Conclusions

The body of this chapter has drawn together the more general findings and major conclusions from the study of PRSP experience, placing the accent on practical obstacles and possible ways of moving forward. In this final section, we sum up on the question 'are PRSPs making a difference?'. As a first step, however, we return to the 'hypothesis' outlined in the Introduction that visualises changes in IFI policy leading, through greater national ownership, to more effectiveness in poverty reduction efforts.

Revisiting the PRSP hypothesis

In the Introduction, we pointed to the belief held by exponents of the PRSP approach that a 'policy process conditionality' in which recipient governments are expected to follow certain procedural steps, rather than accept specific policies, might succeed in generating commitment to poverty reduction where previous forms of conditional lending and aid have failed. The underlying hypothesis, derived from the literature on adjustment lending, says that national ownership of policies has been the crucial missing link. If process conditionality were to result in anti-poverty strategies that enjoyed more national ownership (while also being results-oriented, comprehensive and medium-term), then there would be a greater likelihood of their implementation. Such programmes would also be more sustainable, because they would enable a new type of partnership between donors and recipients, based on the leadership of the latter.

This is not, in our view, a hypothesis that is ready for rigorous formulation and testing against systematic evidence. Quite a lot of preliminary work would be necessary to work up what is at most a preliminary working hypothesis into testable form, and assess what sort of evidence would be needed, over what time-scale, to give us firm conclusions. On the other hand, we can

---

16. Instituting a system for doing this has been adopted by the Budget Support Working Group of the SPA as the principal element of its work programme. Following action-learning missions to three African countries at the end of 2002, this group has designed an annual survey to be administered in two dozen countries to track progress and problems in aligning budget support with PRSPs and national systems.

certainly ask several questions, First, has the new conditionality already produced policies that are more nationally owned than they otherwise would be? Second, on the basis of evidence so far, is the hypothesis still plausible? And does it need to be refined in any important respect?

Some of the country chapters reach conclusions, on the basis of stakeholder interviews and the researchers' own observations, as to the degree to which different levels of ownership have been achieved. We summarise these and follow their implications presently. It should be said that almost all of this discussion refers to the level of national ownership of the PRSP *process*, which is at most the first step towards the national ownership of particular policies (privatising coffee marketing; providing universal primary health care, etc.).

The meaning of ownership is central here. If there are variables to do with the way policies are handled within countries that seem likely to affect effectiveness and sustainability, are they well captured by 'ownership'? Does the concept need to be broken down into constituent elements that have, or might turn out to have, different significance within the causal chains leading from international policies to effective poverty reduction processes? The latter does seem to be the case, as we now suggest.

Definitions of national ownership

This is not the place for a full review of the research literature on policy ownership. Instead we make use of an overview treatment of the subject, which has the virtue of having been applied in a major empirical study. Killick (1998: 86-8) contains a useful short discussion that draws together the well-known contribution of Johnson and Wasty (1993) with suggestions from Haggard and Kaufman (1992) and other sources. This concludes that five different issues are salient in assessing levels of national ownership:

- the locus of programme *initiation* (mainly external agency, or mainly recipient government?);
- the intellectual conviction of key policy-makers or ministries (the *technocratic dimension*);
- support of the top political leadership, as demonstrated by dramatic up-front actions (the *political dimension*);
- *broad support* across and beyond government, for example, derived from a broad-based campaign to elicit support; and
- *institutionalisation* of the measures within the policy system ('stabilising expectations around a new set of incentives and convincing economic agents that they cannot easily be reversed').

Morrissey (2001: 6-8) has argued that the focus on ownership is misplaced, as well as being problematic from other points of view (it does not translate well into French or Portuguese, etc.). Attention should be concentrated, instead, on levels of *commitment*, this being understood to encompass both preferences and the political capacity to articulate these.

Morrissey's substantive argument is not inconsistent with the findings of our study. He is primarily concerned to dismiss the notion that intellectual *origination* of policies – their selection and design by government – is a key issue. He maintains that this is both unrealistic and unnecessary: it does not fatally compromise the prospects of a policy's being effectively implemented that it has been taken 'off the shelf', for example, from a donor or international agency source.

We have no trouble going along with this. It implies, among other things, that the fact that the PRSP processes are an external initiative, from the point of view of all the study countries, is not a major problem for the assessment of ownership. However, this does not seem to provide a reason for jettisoning the concept of ownership, and replacing it with commitment. Instead, we can simply agree with Morrissey that the first of Killick's criteria may be less significant than has been thought, so that attention shifts to the next two levels, which are in fact about different sorts of commitment. Lastly, the substitution of the alternative concept of commitment would rule out the fourth criterion, institutionalisation. We have found that criterion to be rather important.

What the country experiences suggest

There are two initial questions that can be asked of the study findings: how do the countries' PRSPs shape up in terms of the different dimensions of ownership identified? And what may be said about the relative weights to be attached to the different dimensions?

Recalling that we are concerned with ownership of the PRSP process and not specific policies, ownership on the first dimension (initiation) is obviously low in all cases. Even though it may have drawn on wide international experience, the PRSP initiative came to each country from Washington. That, in itself, does not seem to have been seen as a problem. With the temporary exception of Mali in 2000, governments do not seem to have been reluctant or unable to acquire ownership *ex post*, taking the basic design 'off the shelf' in Morrissey's terms.

The findings suggest that ownership on the remaining dimensions is variable within and between countries. In other words, the PRSP initiative and the incentives put in place around it have not (yet) been sufficient to generate full national ownership, even in terms of the process. The country researchers also argue in several cases that having plenty of ownership in one or two of these dimensions and not in others is potentially damaging to the coherence and implementability of the plans. That is, effectiveness and sustainability are likely to be compromised.

In all cases, ownership is quite strong in the 'technocratic' dimension, but in most countries this has so far been rather narrowly shared. As we said at the beginning, even knowledge about the PRSP sometimes does not extend very far outside the central economic ministry. Nearly everywhere, local governments and regional authorities have been quite lightly involved and can scarcely be considered party to any 'intellectual conviction' that exists at the centre.

In one case (Mali), the study team concluded that lack of commitment further down the administrative hierarchy, reflecting the poor level of general motivation in the civil service, was a greater worry than commitment at the top. In Mali, national ownership of plans in any thoroughgoing sense is not seen as a realistic objective, given the dominance of donors in the country. Nevertheless, even small steps towards mainstreaming poverty reduction efforts into national systems would be welcome.

The more general case is that the political dimension of ownership does not match technocratic commitment, and this is a potential source of real difficulty, if only because PRSP implementation will call for accelerated progress with other reforms to which the major obstacles are political. This conclusion emerges loud and clear from the chapters on Benin, Kenya and Malawi. For Mozambique and Rwanda, it seems that there is quite strong political support, but this is narrowly based and certainly does not extend beyond the governing party. In Tanzania, high-level political support for the PRSP is not questioned, but willingness to actually implement it is.

As implied by our discussion in Section 5, the achievements in terms of building a broad base of support across civil society are modest to date, but it may be too early to assess all the effects. This dimension is important because of the possibility that broadened interest in government policies on poverty could result in the government being held to account more than in the past. At least in Malawi, new structures have emerged that may fulfil this purpose to some degree, although the authors of the Malawi chapter insist that this will be no substitute for external financial pressure. The same may turn out to be the case in Kenya, with the same proviso.

Finally, the country studies lend support to the idea that the final dimension – institutionalisation – is critical. The arguments in Section 4 about the value of embedding the PRSP in the MTEF and the budget process, or vice versa, are relevant to this issue. The reports on Kenya, Mali and Rwanda argue particularly strongly that mainstreaming of poverty reduction, in the sense of articulating the goals of the strategy with the budget, and then using budgetary incentives to force line Ministries and districts to pay attention to them, is the most critical dimension of national ownership.

Necessary refinements
It seems to follow from this that at least one refinement of the hypothesis about ownership should be adopted before any more formal testing is contemplated. As far as strategy processes are concerned, all five of Killick's dimensions of ownership seem important, with the possible exception of the first (initiation). Political ownership at the top is the real challenge, and ownership as institutional mainstreaming is hardly less critical. The hypothesis about the sources of effectiveness and sustainability remains plausible, so long as these qualifications are noted.

What might refute the hypothesis at the end of the day is suggested by the conclusions of the Tanzania study. These say that even a PRSP benefiting from a moderately high degree of national ownership may not prove a very effective instrument for achieving poverty reduction objectives, because it may be too weak analytically or (what amounts to the same thing) backed by too little real implementation capacity.

That remains a serious possibility, one that goes outside the scope of the present study. To the extent that it emerges as a pattern, further questions will need to be asked – about what the sources of these deficiencies are (revisiting our themes in the second section); whether they reflect insufficiencies of the policy consultations (not so much their exclusiveness as their tendency to generate shopping lists, rather than critical reflection on past failures); and whether these are deficiencies that may be corrected, in time, as PRSP review and revision processes acquire more substance and become better embedded in national political economies.

Are PRSPs making a difference?

We are now in a position to consider the more general and informal question with which we started. Are PRSPs making a difference, in that they are helping to shift policies and practices in the right direction? Despite the caution suggested by what we have just said, there seem to be grounds for answering this question positively – but only after reminding ourselves of the scale of the obstacles that have to be overcome.

All of the main messages from our country reports are about the need for realism. The international community must keep its feet firmly planted on the ground and avoid being carried away by its own rhetoric on PRSPs. Realism is needed, moreover, on both sides of the aid relationship. Donors should ensure that they do not set excessively high standards of PRSP performance as preconditions for their support. Governments and other national stakeholders should not overestimate the likely scale of additional resources that are going to be generated. They should be aware that promised improvements in aid modalities are unlikely to materialise without further efforts on the recipient side. These cautions are important because erroneous impressions on these issues are a potential source of future disillusionment.

It seems evident that the adoption of PRSPs has brought some limited but important gains in all cases. The mainstreaming of poverty reduction – the beginning of its integration with macro policy and with the budget – is a palpable step forward.

The gains in this regard are much stronger in some countries than in others, but for reasons that can be specified. Where mainstreaming in terms of the national budget is still in doubt, some new impetus may have been imparted either to stalled budget-reform processes or else to sector-development plans and SWAPs. In cases like Tanzania, where numerous reform initiatives and changes in donor behaviour preceded the PRSP, the additionality from the PRSP may seem slight. Where there has been little such change, the PRSP could be the instrument that begins to break the vicious circle of off-budget project aid diverting capacity from mainstream tasks.

In some countries, all of the gains may seem fragile as well as somewhat speculative. But the most important changes may turn out to be different across countries – more to do with central resource-allocation and public management in some countries, more to do with opening new spaces for fundamental policy debate in others.

At the time of the research, the gains in Kenya certainly seemed fragile in the first respect, but they looked substantial in the second. Poverty reduction was considered by the study team to be higher on the national agenda than ever before. Government had been opened up in some significant ways, and new actors brought into the aid relationship. The creation of new constituencies for the monitoring of government performance also seemed a positive factor in Malawi, with the qualification that even more might have been achieved if the IFIs had been more transparent.

How does politics matter?

We have set out as a general theme of this study that policies and practices with relevance to poverty are determined politically in poor, highly-indebted countries, just as they are in more affluent ones. We think that the coming of PRSPs reflects, among other things, growing international recognition of this elementary fact. It is not sensible, from the point of view of effective pro-poor reform, to try to by-pass national political processes. It is not possible to achieve significant results in that way.

The gamble on which the PRSP approach is based is that if governments are obliged to discuss poverty and what they are doing about it with their citizens, they are likely to regard these things more seriously, and to be held to account more effectively. If this happens, it will involve processes that are formally or informally political. Politics matters, and, while nothing is guaranteed, politics *can* work in ways that are favourable to reducing poverty.

What could be the implications for donor and IFI behaviour of recognising these general truths? This requires us to be a little more specific about the kinds of ways in which politics has seemed to matter for the PRSP processes we have investigated.

We indicated in Section 5 how the particular political conjuncture in various countries affected the PRSPs' initial impacts and subsequent timetable. We can now add some further observations drawn from the country chapters.

In Tanzania, the bottom line, politically speaking, seems to be that party-competition is not effective, because of the systemic factors that constantly erode and atomise opposition groupings (Zanzibar excluded). This not only means that there is no decisive internal pressure on government to implement its own anti-corruption commitments. It also implies that there is little scope for hard-hitting policy debate. National consultations of the PRSP type are never likely to provide a substitute for that. For comparable though not identical reasons, political arrangements in Malawi do not encourage real policy debate.

In Benin, institutionalising PRSP principles would call for a 'regime change' (that is, something more than a change of government or President). That will only come from a political coalition that does not presently exist, although its elements may. Civil society, in the sense of NGO networks as presently constituted, are not the solution to this problem in Benin, as they are in a real sense part of the 'regime' that needs to be changed.

The latter is not so true in Kenya. On the other hand, in Kenya there certainly is an institutionalised political system, centred on presidential patronage, that has been a key factor blocking reforms, particularly the local government changes, that are called for by the PRSP. The Moi succession issue substantially impeded progress with the PRSP up to the end of 2002. In Mali, a superficially similar conjuncture had a different effect. The fact that President Konaré was not seeking re-election in 2002 created the expectation that there would be greater attention to both poverty reduction and public probity during the interlude before a new President was sworn in.

These observations suggest some specific recommendations that we take up below. However, the general implication is that those interested in a successful outcome of the PRSP experiment may need to bide their time and look to the slightly longer term. Overall, there is a need for expectations about PRSPs to be well managed, as suggested in the Tanzania chapter. One aspect of sensible management will be the recognition of the possibility that otherwise promising national processes will be blown off course in quite a major way from time to time by political events. In principle, the reverse is also possible but it would be wise not to expect that to happen very often.

What could be done better? Messages for governments, IFIs and donors

Much of the advice that our findings suggest is country-specific, and is contained in the chapters that follow. We limit ourselves here to recommendations that seem generalisable to some degree, focusing on just two topics for each of the constituencies we are addressing.

What could governments do better?

What PRSPs promise to countries, in terms of their ability to determine their own approach and free themselves to some degree from the tutelage of the IFIs and donors, depends a great deal on what governments do. From the experience we have reviewed, two things stand out particularly:

- There is very little indeed to be gained from placing anti-poverty policy and PRSP drafting in an enclave position relative to the rest of government, especially one that has little connection with the management of public expenditure. While few countries are now following that path, those that are should clearly reconsider. The gains from involving parliaments and parliamentary committees at a much earlier stage should also be looked at more closely.

- Donors and IFIs are being encouraged quite rightly to take some risks in introducing aid modalities that give recipients better value. But in this respect much depends on whether PRSPs give a tough-minded and credible account of what needs to be done to reduce poverty and how this is to be done. Only if they do this can they begin to displace and make redundant externally-imposed preconditions and performance benchmarks.

What could the IFIs do better?

Two issues seem to be particularly worthy of attention from the side of the IFIs. As emphasised in our progress reports to the sponsors of this study, one is the threat or actuality of 'process overload'. The other is transparency about conditionality.

- It seems that IFI staffs are now being fairly widely credited with delicate handling of PRSP processes as such. On the other hand, the range of joint reviews involving national officials with the IFIs, other multilaterals and bilateral agencies is regarded as being seriously out of hand – particularly in some of the countries that have gone furthest with PRSPs. Further thought clearly needs to be given to merging review processes or otherwise easing the burden on officials.

- No one is expecting the rapid disappearance of IFI conditionality, and even among national stakeholders there are some who defend it vigorously. However, it seems much less clear that there is any virtue – in the era of PRSPs – in secret conditionalities, or in agreements that are only publicised at government initiative. Synergies between domestic accountability and external conditionality do seem to be possible. The IFIs should consider seriously adopting rules that allow greater openness vis-à-vis the publics of the countries they are negotiating with.

What could the donors do better?

Donors seem to be supporting PRSPs in appropriate ways, with degrees and kinds of involvement varying according to country needs and preferences, not just reflecting agency biases. The country studies suggest two particular areas of concern, one about direct support to PRSP processes and one about changing aid modalities in response to PRSPs.

- The charge of 'instrumentalism', levelled at unnamed bilaterals in connection with their support to NGOs involved in Tanzania's PRSP, bears further consideration. The point of PRSPs is to institutionalise more participatory policy making, which is not going to be the task of a single day. We have suggested that second-round effects of PRSP consultations are likely to be much more important than first-round ones. A question that this clearly raises for donors is whether their current efforts in support of deeper and richer policy dialogue in PRSP countries have a sufficiently long time horizon. Some consideration might also be given to whether the recipients of support are the right institutions within a medium- and long-term perspective.

- The topic of alternative aid modalities is sensitive, and not susceptible to simple treatment. Even enthusiasts of new aid instruments recognise that different approaches are suitable for different conditions at the national and sectoral levels. On the other hand, the case has been made in this report that some measure of risk-taking on the donor side is going to be necessary if PRSPs are going to work to break the vicious circles of institutional aid dependency that have hampered poverty reduction efforts in Africa for so long. In addressing this fundamental challenge, more of the same is not an option.

References

Booth, David and Lucas, Henry (2002) *Good Practice in the Development of PRSP Indicators and Monitoring Systems*. ODI Working Paper No. 172. London: Overseas Development Institute.

Bratton, Michael and van de Walle, Nicholas (1997) *Democratic Experiments in Africa: Regime Transitions in Comparative Perspective*. Cambridge: Cambridge University Press.

Chabal, Patrick and Daloz, Jean-Pascal (1999) *Africa Works: Disorder as a Political Instrument*. Oxford: James Currey.

Christian Aid (2002) *Quality Participation in Poverty Reduction Strategies: Experiences from Malawi, Bolivia and Rwanda*. London: Christian Aid.

Devarajan, Shantayanan; Dollar, David R.; and Holmgren, Torgny (eds) (2001) *Aid and Reform in Africa*. Washington, DC: World Bank.

Eberlei, Walter (2001) 'Institutionalised Participation in Processes Beyond PRSP'. Study Commissioned by the Deutsche Gesellschaft für Technische Zusammenareit (GTZ) GmbH. Duisburg: Gerhard Mercator University.

Ekeh, Peter (1998 [1975]) 'Colonialism and the Two Publics in Africa: A Theoretical Statement'. Reprinted in Peter Lewis (ed.), *Africa: Dilemmas of Development and Change*. Boulder, CO: Westview Press.

Foster, Mick; Fozzard, Adrian; Naschold, Felix; and Conway, Tim (2002) *How, When and Why does Poverty get Budget Priority? Poverty Reduction Strategy and Public Expenditure in Five African Countries*. ODI Working Paper No. 168. London: Overseas Development Institute.

Foster, Mick; Healey, John; Martin, Matthew; and White, Howard (1999) 'Linking HIPC II Debt Relief with Poverty Reduction and Wider Aid Issues: Some Reflections and Suggestions'. Paper for DFID, London.

Gould, Jeremy (1997) *Localizing Modernity: Action, Interests and Association in Rural Zambia*. Helsinki: Finnish Anthropological Society.

Grinspun, Alejandro (ed.) (2001) *Choices for the Poor: Lessons from National Poverty Strategies*. New York: UNDP.

Haggard, Stephan and Kaufman, Robert R. (eds) (1992) *The Politics of Economic Adjustment*. Princeton, NJ: Princeton University Press.

Holmes, Malcolm with Evans, Alison (2003) 'A Review of Experience in Implementing Medium Term Expenditure Frameworks in a PRSP Context: A Synthesis of Eight Country Studies'. Draft ODI Working Paper. London: Overseas Development Institute.

IMF and IDA (2002a) 'Review of the Poverty Reduction Strategy (PRSP) Approach: Main Findings'. Washington, DC: World Bank/International Monetary Fund, 15 March.

IMF and IDA (2002b) 'Poverty Reduction Strategy Papers (PRSP): Progress in Implementation'. Washington, DC: World Bank/International Monetary Fund, 13 September.

IMF and IDA (2000) 'Poverty Reduction Strategy Papers – Progress in Implementation'. Washington, DC: World Bank/International Monetary Fund, 7

September.

IMF and IDA (1999) 'Heavily Indebted Poor Countries (HIPC) Initiative – Strengthening the Link between Debt Relief and Poverty Reduction'. Washington, DC: World Bank/International Monetary Fund, 26 August.

Johnson, J. H. and Wasty, S. S. (1993) *Borrower Ownership of Adjustment Programs and the Political Economy of Reform*. Discussion Paper No. 199. Washington, DC: World Bank.

Killick, Tony (forthcoming, 2004) 'Politics, Evidence and the New Aid Agenda', *Development Policy Review*.

Killick, Tony with Gunatilaka, Ramani and Marr, Ana (1998) *Aid and the Political Economy of Policy Change*. London: Routledge for the Overseas Development Institute.

McGee, Rosemary et al. (2002) *Assessing Participation in Poverty Reduction Strategy Papers: A Desk-based Synthesis of Experience in sub-Saharan Africa*. Brighton: Institute of Development Studies at the University of Sussex.

Moore, Mick (1998) 'Death without Taxes: Democracy, State Capacity, and Aid Dependence in the Fourth World', in Mark Robinson and Gordon White (eds), *The Democratic Developmental State*. Oxford: Oxford University Press.

Moore, Mick; Leavy, Jennifer; Houtzanger, Peter; and White, Howard (1999) *Polity Qualities: How Governance Affects Poverty*. IDS Working Paper No. 99. Brighton: Institute of Development Studes at the University of Sussex, December.

Morrissey, Oliver (2001) 'Pro-Poor Conditionality and Debt Relief in East Africa'. Paper prepared for the WIDER Development Conference on Debt Relief, Helsinki, 17-18 August (available on the WIDER website).

OECD (2003) *Harmonising Donor Practices for Effective Aid Delivery*. Paris: Development Assistance Committee, OECD

OECD (2001) *DAC Guidelines on Poverty Reduction*. Paris: Development Assistance Committee, OECD.

Roberts, John (2003) *Managing Public Expenditure for Development Results and Poverty Reduction*. ODI Working Paper No. 203. London: Overseas Development Institute.

Tarp, Finn with Hjertholm, Peter (ed.) (2000) *Foreign Aid and Development: Lessons Learnt and Lessons for the Future*. London: Routledge.

UNDP (2000) *Overcoming Human Poverty: UNDP Poverty Report 2000*. New York: United Nations Development Programme.

van de Walle, Nicholas (2001) *African Economies and the Politics of Permanent Crisis, 1979-1999*. Cambridge: Cambridge University Press.

Whaites, Alan (ed.) (2002) *Masters of Their Own Development? PRSPs and the Prospects for the Poor*. Monrovia, CA: World Vision International.

White, Howard and Killick, Tony with Kayizzi-Mugerwa, Steve and Savane, Marie-Angelique (2001) *African Poverty at the Millennium: Causes, Complexities, and Challenges*. Washington, DC: World Bank/Strategic Partnership with Africa.

Williamson, Tim and Canagarajah, Sudharshan (2003) 'Is There a Place for Virtual Poverty Funds in Pro-Poor Public Spending Reform? Lessons from Uganda's PAF', *Development Policy Review*, Vol. 21, No. 4, July.

World Bank, Operations Evaluation Department (2003) *Debt Relief for the Poorest: An OED Review of the HIPC Initiative.* Washington, DC: World Bank.

World Bank (2001) *World Development Report 2000/2001: Attacking Poverty.* New York: Oxford University Press for the World Bank.

World Bank (2000) 'Poverty Reduction Strategy Papers: Internal Guidance Note'. Washington, DC: World Bank Group, Operations Policy and Strategy, 21 January.

World Bank (1998) *Assessing Aid: What Works, What Doesn't, and Why.* New York: Oxford University Press for World Bank.

Chapter 2: Benin

by Thomas Bierschenk, Elisabeth Thioléron and Nassirou Bako-Arifari*

Under Benin's neo-patrimonial multi-party democracy, political continuity and social peace have been achieved at the cost of political immobilism. Major reform projects have advanced very slowly at best, relying heavily on donor-financed expertise and external pressure. At the same time, poorly coordinated and rather clientelistic aid has been a major factor in limiting the coherence of government action. This chapter suggests that it would be unrealistic and even dangerous, under these conditions, to expect very much very fast from the PRSP approach in Benin. The 'regime change' that is called for will require at least a substantial shift in donor behaviour, co-ordinated progress with stalled public management reforms and a step-change in the politics of reform in the country.

2.1 Introduction

It has been said that 'Institutionalising the impetus of reform requires a deliberate effort to take the issue of poverty beyond narrow agendas to make it a truly national concern and a subject of national debate and decision-making. In other words, it means transforming poverty reduction into a non-partisan issue beyond the individual or group interests and of particular donors and their funding modalities' (UNDP, 2001: 7). This chapter assesses to what degree this is happening in Benin. It asks whether the new elements introduced into IFI conditionality since the beginning of the Enhanced HIPC process are leading to poverty reduction plans that benefit from country ownership and, therefore, promise to be more effective.

The chapter is based on two field missions, in November 2000 and June 2001, a report submitted to the SPA in September 2001, and an updating of this with information on events up to April 2002. It reflects the authors' state of knowledge up to July 2002.

The chapter contains five substantive sections. The next section sets the country context, the third explains the scope and limits of the PRSP process in Benin, while the fourth assesses the prospects for the institutionalisation of a new approach to poverty reduction policy in the country. The fifth and the sixth sections briefly review the prospects for PRSP monitoring and a new approach to the aid relationship.

* Respectively Johannes Gutenberg University, Mainz, Germany; ODI Associate, Paris; and National University of Benin, Cotonou.

2.2   Poverty reduction and the policy context

Macro-economic performance and poverty

Benin is one of the poorest countries in the world, ranking 151ˢᵗ on UNDP's
HDI list of 174. Taking the $1 per day per head threshold, over 80 percent of
Benin's population can be considered poor and roughly one third is below
the national poverty line. A further 18 percent are considered vulnerable.
Income distribution and living standards vary greatly between regions and
between rural and urban areas.

The Beninese economy is almost entirely 'informal'. There are virtually
no manufacturing industries. Agriculture accounts for approximately 40
percent of GDP and provides 70 percent of domestic exports and 75 percent
of all employment. Cotton is the only significant export. Benin has the largest
informal sector of 27 African and Latin American countries for which
comparable data exist (Joekes and Houedete, 2000: 5). Cross-border trade
and micro enterprises are at the heart of the informal economy and account
for approximately 50 percent of total GDP (World Bank, 1994). The economy
remains inherently fragile, because of its dependence on world market prices
for cotton and on the overall business environment in Nigeria, to which the
Autonomous Port of Cotonou largely caters.

Economic growth has been positive in recent years, averaging 5 percent
between 1995 and 1999, and attaining 5.3 percent in 2000. A number of
signs tend to indicate that growth could be sustained in the coming years,
provided there are no external shocks. Savings and investment rates rose
from respectively 12.7 percent and 17.9 percent of GNP in 1996 to 15 percent
and 19.8 percent in 2000. Credit to the economy increased from CFA F154
billion (US$ 206 million) in 1999 to CFA F194 billion (US$ 259 millions) in
2000. The net government position gained CFA F2.2 billion between 1999
and 2000.[1]

However, neither good macroeconomic performance nor the various
poverty reduction initiatives of the last fifteen years have succeeded in reducing
poverty. The impact of growth has been considerably reduced by high
population growth rates during the same period, with average real per capita
growth not exceeding 2.3 percent. It has been estimated that it will take 38
years for Benin to reach the IDA threshold of $895 per capita GNP at currently
forecasted real per capita GDP growth rates (US/GAO, 2001: 50).

The aid context and debt

The country is heavily dependent on aid, which financed over 30 percent of
public expenditure and 80 percent of public investment over the 1992-97

---

1. These figures were obtained from a senior official from the Finance and Economy
    Ministry.

period. Undoubtedly, the country's good democracy and human rights track record since the 1990s has impacted positively on development aid levels. This phenomenon is referred to in Benin as the 'democracy bonus' (*prime de la démocratie*). Several interviewees from the donor community privately expressed the opinion that the country was in fact 'over-assisted'.

Ten major donors provide the bulk of Benin's Official Development Assistance (ODA), with Germany, the World Bank/IDA, France, the EC and Japan in the lead. Two thirds of ODA are allocated to the social sectors. However, because of administrative and other shortcomings, relatively little of this aid is absorbed. According to the most recent *Rapport sur l'état de l'économie nationale* (République du Bénin, 1999), Benin consumes barely one third of all external aid committed (only 52 percent of loans and 28 percent of grants were disbursed in 1999).

The low absorptive capacity, combined with poor project design and delayed implementation of both projects and loan agreements, have impacted negatively on the economy. To increase the efficiency of service delivery the government is increasingly targeting vulnerable groups via decentralised cooperation. This orientation is contributing to a proliferation of national and international NGOs operating in Benin.

External debt stood at US$ 1.3 billion in 1999. After submitting an iPRSP in late 2000, Benin became eligible for the Enhanced HIPC initiative, under which total debt reduction would be US$ 460 million over a 20-year period.

An incomplete democracy

Benin is often cited as a model democracy in the African context. Since the peaceful regime change of 1989/90 that is referred to locally as the 'democratic renewal', presidential and parliamentary elections have been fair and free. The country enjoys free and lively media (over 57 private and government newspapers, 42 private and two government radio stations, and two national television channels, apart from the foreign ones accessible via satellite). The Constitutional Court has played admirably its role as guardian of the Constitution and there are no political prisoners in the country. The country has also been spared major outbursts of ethnic and social violence since 1991. In view of a regional context that is not very enabling in this respect, this must be acknowledged as a major political achievement of the country's political elite.

Despite these achievements, the pluralist democracy and rule of law triggered by the democratic renewal have remained in important respects incomplete. Both on the national and on the local level, the political system is characterised by a high degree of clientelism, institutional and legal pluralism, politicisation of administration, rampant corruption and weak state regulatory and implementation capacities. The country's heavy dependence on aid is the context for the prevalence of rent-seeking in the closely articulated economic and political spheres.

The distinctive features of Benin's political system are most noticeable at the local level. The reform of decentralisation, on the agenda since 1993 when the government organised a widespread consultation process on the issue, is only now being completed, with local elections held in December 2002 and January 2003. The type of political system until now in place at the local level could be described as a 'negotiated political order' that is neither democratic nor despotic. Rather, it is based on the principle of participation via clientelist networks dominated by local elites (Bierschenk, 2000; Bierschenk and Olivier de Sardan, 1998).

One of the major features of this system is its high degree of institutional and legal pluralism. Local political arenas are multi-centred, with representatives of the central government unable to impose decisions on powerful local players. Decisions are based on complicated negotiations between local representatives of the central government, different segments of local political elites and a multitude of local institutional actors (traditional chiefs, development associations, NGOs, religious groups, local sections of political parties, peasants' organisations, the security forces, etc.). In the absence of a clear system of rules, regulations and sanctions, and given the number of local vetoing powers, these decisions are notoriously difficult to implement.

Local civil societies are barely developed and hardly differentiated from political elite networks. So-called civil society leaders often double as civil servants or politicians. In addition, the formal local economy is highly politically embedded: the larger private sector operators all depend to a very large degree on contracts with the administration. Indeed, the main local actors typically 'straddle' the sectors of polity, economy and civil society and have, as a rule, multiple identities and functions.

In this context, development strategies – like the PRSP approach – that assume a clear distinction between the spheres of politics, the economy ('private sector') and civil society seem somewhat naïve, as they do not take account of this peculiar form of local governance. At the national level, democratisation has remained in important aspects incomplete, and administrative and economic governance pose serious problems. There is a corresponding prevalence of informal politics that reduces the state's capacity for arbitrage and regulation.

Politics and civil society

To begin with, the national political system is highly biased in favour of the executive, and in particular the President. President Kérékou first held power, following a military coup, between 1972 and 1989. As a result of democratic elections, he has been able to regain and maintain this function from 1996 to the present. Throughout these periods, he has been very skilful in consolidating his position by associating, via clientelist links, a maximum number of segments of local and regional elite networks with the government machinery.

Governance by reciprocal assimilation of elite segments (to use a term of the French political scientist Bayart) has also been the basis of the relative political stability that the country enjoyed under the Marxist-Leninist regime from 1974 to 1989 and the pluralist democracy thereafter.

A disadvantage of Benin's 'inclusive' political regime is that it systematically weakens public debate. Opposition is either bought off or isolated. Parliament and its 83 members can easily be bypassed in the legislative and budgetary processes. Furthermore, it does not possess the technical capacity to challenge the administration, given the shortage of professional staff and the generally low technical skills of the MPs. As a result, Parliament has taken relatively few legislative initiatives.

This is compounded by the inability of political parties to organise policy debates. Parties are very light structures built around the personal ambition of individual politicians (or coalitions of 'big men' in the case of the larger parties) who are as a rule also their main sponsors. Internal conflicts are typically resolved by splitting up: in case of political defeat, the losing faction leaves the party and creates a new one.[2] It is thus not surprising that most parties have no political programme and no technical capacities in terms of policy analysis. MPs and parties are not elected on the basis of a programme but function as a link between the electorate of a given area and the national centres of power.

Strictly speaking, civil society is defined as an autonomous space composed of civil associations that pursue public goals. The sphere of civil society is distinct from both the state and the market. In this strict definition of the concept, CSOs are not only non-government but also non-profit organisations. In the current debate concerning Africa, a more restricted definition is often used, one that identifies civil society simply with NGOs.

Benin has a flourishing associational sector. Some associations, such as religious communities, have a long history going back to colonial times; some have existed since the revolutionary period but might have benefited from liberalisation after 1990 (e.g., community organisations, trade unions, professional associations); others appeared only just before or after the democratic renewal in the early 1990s (for example, NGOs, local development associations, cultural associations, agricultural producers associations). In 1999, it was estimated that there were more than 5,000 NGOs in Benin, of which more than 3,000 were officially registered (UNDP, 2000: 66).

---

2. This 'political transhumance', it could be argued, is not inconsistent with the interests of their electorate. Politicians are not elected to defend policy issues but to assure that government resources are channelled to their region of origin. To lose an MP to another party is not, however, in the interest of party leaders who are also expected to be the main providers for their party. A law, voted by Parliament in July 2001, stipulates that an MP who leaves the party on whose list he was elected loses his mandate (*Le Cordon*, 26.7.01); but in its present form, this law has been declared unconstitutional by the Constitutional Court.

The majority of Benin's NGOs, however, exist only on paper. Indeed, a large number of them are small business ventures that have been established by university graduates as a response to the reduction in employment opportunities within the administration after 1986. Furthermore, Benin's NGOs are hardly autonomous from the state. Many of them include at least one politician and/or civil servant.

To conclude this point, leaders of many so-called CSOs have multiple identities and straddle the world of politics and the private sector. Hence, in the Benin context, the distinction between civil society, the state and the market underlying much of the present development discourse needs to be seriously qualified; in Benin, civil society is weakly developed and has hardly emancipated itself from either the state or the market.

The liveliness of Benin's media and the freedom of expression they enjoy are an essential component of the country's image as an African (model) democracy. In fact, Benin can boast today a small number of very well qualified journalists. However, some exceptions apart, the media's potential as the carriers of an informed public debate on PRSP and other complex policy choices is rather limited.

In other words, the large majority of media in Benin should not be expected to run an in-depth discussion of PRSP and other policy choices on their own initiative and resources. However, they could be much more intensely used as information devices to inform the public on the policy stakes involved. Because of its nation-wide accessibility, in particular the radio would lend itself to such an information campaign. The very few serious journals and radio and television programmes that do exist, on the other hand, would need much easier access to information on the PRSP and specialised training to be able to discuss it in depth.

Political immobilism

Under Benin's neo-patrimonial multi-party democracy, political continuity and social peace have been achieved at a cost: political immobilism. Since the successful completion of the 'democratic renewal', all major reform projects have advanced only very slowly or have stalled. In each case, the initiative for these reforms came from outside; the formulation of reform projects relied to a large extent on foreign, and foreign-financed, expertise; and the degree of implementation was directly correlated with the degree of pressure from Benin's foreign donors.

We have noted Benin's heavy dependence on ODA for public expenditure in general and public investment in particular. Yet, institutionalised aid dependence is not a purely 'economic' phenomenon. It is directly articulated with the political system. Based on the idea that development aid can have, in the recipient country, the function of a 'rent', Benin's political economy has been analysed as a 'rentier state' (Bierschenk, 1993).[3]

Poorly coordinated aid – with each donor pursuing its own agenda, creating its own local clientele within and outside the government administration, working according to different funding cycles, timeframes and procedures – has been a major factor in limiting the coherence of government action. It has reduced even further the government's weak arbitration and regulation capacity. Actions are undertaken not because they are seen as priorities for the development of the country, but because they bring external financing.[4] Furthermore, clientelist politics, which we have identified as a major feature of Benin's political system, is encouraged and stabilised by institutionalised aid dependency. The PRSP approach interacts with this context, being constrained by it while at the same time trying to fundamentally alter it.

Previous poverty plans

Benin has a long history of anti-poverty policies and programmes going back to the late 1980s, with a rhetoric that, from the mid-1990s onwards, increasingly resembles that of the current PRSP approach. In late 1996, the incoming government under President Kérékou decided to draft a Three-Year-Development Plan (1998-2000) based on the results of recent surveys and analyses and a National Economic Conference. Following a social dimensions of adjustment philosophy, the objective was to consolidate economic growth while defining poverty reduction as a central policy objective. A year later, in 1997, a complementary strategy was initiated. Very much the personal initiative of the then Minister of the Plan, Albert Tévéodjre, a former senior official of the International Labour Organisation, this was

---

3. The notion of rent is used here in the Ricardian-Marxian sense of surplus revenues, which are not derived from investment in factors of production (e.g., capital or labour). In this sense, rents are 'unearned' revenues; they arise in situations where competition is limited by either natural or socio-political factors. In neo-classical economic theory, rent is a receipt in excess of the opportunity cost of a resource. Access to rents can be politically organised ('lobbying'). In this perspective, rent seeking describes the activity of economic actors who, by political and social means, compete for monopoly positions and preferential access to rents. A rentier state then is a state that receives considerable revenues from sources other than taxes on (internal) productive processes, e.g. profits and salaries. The possibility of having access to rent renders the state indifferent to the problems of internal mobilisation of factors of production. The concept had originally been used to analyse the political economy of Near Eastern (and other) oil-producing countries but can also usefully be employed to highlight certain features of aid-dependent poor African (and other) countries where aid plays a similar economic and political role. For an introduction into the large literature on the subject, see Buchanan et al. (1980) and Beblawi and Luciani (1987).
4. This theme is particularly well documented for West Africa. See for example Naudet (2000).

called the 'minimum basic needs' programme.

Other, more targeted measures were also undertaken. From 1997 onwards, thanks to improvements in the position of public finances, funds allocated to the health and education sectors were increased considerably. School fees for girls had been abolished in 1993, and in the school year 2000/01 all school fees were temporarily abolished. This ad hoc measure was funded with the 'savings' coming from the first round of debt relief under the Enhanced HIPC initiative. In 1999, a special fund was created to provide assistance to the needy.

These programmes were initiated in close cooperation with, and sometimes by, foreign donors, and they were often formulated on the basis of national consultative exercises, a 'National Conference', 'Round Table' or the like. There are thus important continuities of approach between the PRSP and what came immediately before. The current approach differs from these previous programmes, in the eyes of local stakeholders, mainly in that the IMF and the World Bank have decided to address poverty issues within the macro-economic framework, and that within the country, the lead has changed from the Planning Ministry to the Finance and Economics Ministry.

2.3   The PRSP process in Benin

A *delayed process*

The process for elaborating a poverty reduction strategy in Benin in relation to HIPC Initiatives 1 and 2 has been slow compared with other countries in Africa and elsewhere. For most of 2000, there was a tug of war between the Finance and Economics Ministry and the Planning Ministry regarding who would lead the process. Then the March 2001 presidential elections paralysed all political activity for months, delaying in particular the setting up of the institutional framework and the consultations with civil society. Only when the results were known and the new government of President Kérékou was in place did the CNDLP (*Commission Nationale de Développement et de Lutte contre la Pauvreté*) become effective and consultations with civil society finally began.

Only two officials had been involved in drafting Benin's iPRSP, which was adopted by government in June 2000. The Joint Staff Committee and donors who were asked to comment made a rather severe review of the document. Criticisms concerned the complex institutional structure suggested to conduct the PRSP process and the fact that it did not really reflect the quality of the analytical work on poverty that had been undertaken in the country, mostly with UNDP assistance, since the early 1990s. The comments concluded that much remained to be done before arriving at a comprehensive and coherent poverty-reduction strategy.

The design and monitoring of the PRSP process were coordinated within a three-tier structure created in December 2000. At the top was the already mentioned CNDLP presided over by the State Minister for Coordination of Government Action, Planning and Development, with the F&E Minister as Vice-President. The CNDLP has two organs: A Technical Committee that comprises staff from 8 Ministries (Planning, Finance and Economy, Rural Development, Industry, Education, Public Health, Interior, Social Protection and the Family), the Chamber of Commerce and Industry and the NUB; and a Permanent Secretariat (now called 'Technical Secretariat') in charge of day-to-day activities.

The CNDLP in fact never met during the preparation of the PRSP. Its Technical Committee met once, in August 2001, to examine the results of the technical studies commissioned by the TS as well as those of the departmental consultation meetings (see below). It would seem that the TS was the real driving force behind the PRSP. Once the tug-of-war between the Planning and the F&E Ministry was – temporarily – resolved, the TS was finally housed in the latter, and the Permanent Secretary of the Structural Adjustment Programme (one of the two authors of the iPRSP) was appointed Technical Secretary of the PRSP. The staff consists exclusively of economists. It is not clear to what degree all of them were actively involved in PRSP preparation.

In early 2001, the PRSP Technical Secretariat (TS/PRSP) commissioned five preparatory desk studies from national consultants. These studies synthesised existing research on the causes of poverty; identified its structural causes; evaluated major social, economic and financial policy initiatives since 1990 and their impact on poverty (two studies); and proposed an institutional framework for the implementation of the Poverty Reduction Strategy. These studies were finalised during the summer of 2001.

Participation in the process

At the same time, a series of consultations were carried out at different levels: ministerial; national, with the participation of civil society organisations (CSOs, such as the so-called 'National Forum on the Acceleration of Economic Growth'), and provincial, one seminar for each pair of departments, also with CSO participation. These provincial seminars were financed by the German GTZ and organised by one of the major national NGO/consultancy firms with which GTZ has long-standing contacts. This company had to work under enormous pressure.

The provincial seminars were prepared within three weeks. Most of the participants received their invitations and relevant documents (exclusively in French) less than a week before the seminar, some the night before. Obviously, this meant that CSO representatives could neither consult their base, nor seriously prepare the meeting as the participative approach had foreseen.

Each meeting lasted three days. Some 65 participants were invited, selected by the organising consulting firm in agreement with local government representatives: 30 from civil society, 34 from the regional government administration and 1 member of parliament. The seminars were conducted entirely in French, with no interpretation into local languages. Bearing in mind that the majority of Benin's population do not speak French, this was a fairly serious limitation. On the other hand, the consultations marked the first time since 1989 that high-level technicians from central government had toured the country to explain government policy initiatives to the population.

Participants whom we interviewed (whether from CSOs, Parliament, government or the donor community) regarded the utility of the provincial and national seminars as somewhat limited for two reasons. The first was the tight time-table, which did not allow serious preparation, and the second was the impossibility of prioritising problems and needs in a meeting of this kind. In particular CSO representatives were said to have attended the seminars in a trade unionist spirit; that is, to defend their particular interests.

The results were labelled 'shopping lists' by some. In any event, the general feeling was that there were very few new themes; that is, ideas not already dealt with in the voluminous literature on poverty in the country. There were some exceptions. People raised a number of socio-cultural issues that would be difficult, however, to address with any policy (e.g., cultural reasons for people not using latrines, etc.). And the meetings may have achieved a certain sensitisation of senior officials to the day-to-day problems of implementing government decisions on the ground.

An example would be the widespread absenteeism of primary school teachers in rural areas. This problem is well known to villagers and to any observer who has ever spent some time in rural areas. However, for the technicians from the Technical Secretariat of the CNDLP who participated in these seminars, this was an aspect of the actual functioning of public services of which they had been unaware until then. We discuss the potential of this kind of realisation by top civil servants of the true nature of 'problems on the ground' in the next section.

The government's programme

Throughout the middle months of 2001, the incoming government of President Kérékou was preparing a programme covering its 2001-5 mandate (*Programme d'Action du Gouvernement*/PAG). It seems that this was carried out as a parallel process to the PRSP preparation, with no reciprocal inputs. (It is, however, possible that some high-level staff, especially from the F&E Ministry, were also involved in the government programme.) The programme was officially adopted by the government in October 2001, together with the results of the UNDP-sponsored Long-term Perspective Study to which the government programme explicitly refers.

The Five-Year-Programme is articulated around seven key themes. While the fight against poverty is mentioned as a 'cross-cutting theme', the actions listed make it appear mainly the object of sectoral policies (mainly in the health and education sectors). Eight priority actions are foreseen under the heading of poverty reduction: developing essential social services, promoting employment and food security, fighting AIDS and malaria, rational management of the environment, promoting the family and women, and good management of population dynamics. The task of translating this cluster of actions into concrete measures was given to the Ministry of Health (major drafter) and the three Ministries in the educational sector.

In the meantime, considerable slippage set in in the drafting of the full PRSP. In July 2001, a small PRSP drafting committee was set up. It included four high level staff from F&E and Planning Ministries (the TS/PRSP and the Director of Economic Affairs from the former, a leading civil servant from the DSA section appointed as Vice Secretary of the PRSP and the Director of the Planning Unit, who is also President of the Technical Committee, from the latter) as well one staff member from the Planning Ministry who doubles as a GTZ-financed consultant to the PRSP process. The committee's role was to coordinate results from the PRSP process into a draft document.[5]

It seems that the full drafting committee never met, some of the key actors systematically sending low-ranking deputies. A first draft was produced in November 2001 but intra-government discussions on it and the second round of departmental consultations were blocked by the Minister of the Plan (now renamed *Ministre d'Etat Chargé de la Coordination de l'Action Gouvernementale, de la Prospective et du Développement* – MECCAG/PD) with the argument that it was not articulated with the government's Five-Year Programme (PAG). Things were further complicated by a 10-week strike of government employees in late 2001 and the political crisis produced by a split in the main opposition party that largely dominated political debate in early 2002.

It should be noted that the drafting of the PAG was coordinated by the MECCAG/PG, while the drafting of the full PRSP was undertaken by the lead F&E Ministry. In other words, the tug-of-war that had blocked progress on the PRSP in late 2000 and early 2001, resurfaced in late 2001.

Consequently, nothing happened until a small TS/PRSP delegation, including the Technical Secretary and his deputy, visited Washington in

---

5. At the same time, a private pressure group (*Espace Libéral*), funded in part by DANIDA and made up mainly of entrepreneurs, drafted an 'alternative PRSP' (in their terminology). The document was forwarded to the CNDLP in October 2001. It proposed further liberalisation of the economy, a systematic and nationwide investment programme to improve infrastructure (*grands travaux*), fiscal and legal reform, in particular the reform of land legislation, and the creation of a development bank as well as a building and loan society (*banque d'habitat*). However, judging from a survey of the press and from interviews, this alternative programme does not seem to have left much of an impact and has remained largely unknown to the larger public.

February 2002 to consult with the World Bank and the IMF. The delegation was apparently hoping to short-cut donors' criticism of the document. However, reactions were unexpectedly severe, particularly from the World Bank and the message given to the Beninese delegation was that the '50 percent job' done so far risked being rejected by the Joint Boards.

In March 2002, the draft was sent to other donors. It received equally severe criticisms that were formulated in a joint document of the European Union and its member countries. They concerned in particular i) the restricted (purely monetary) definition of poverty; ii) the weak diagnosis of the regional incidence of poverty and its structural causes; iii) the absence of a coherent link between the diagnosis and the strategies proposed; and iv) the lack of prioritisation and budgeting of the proposed actions. It was also noted that in reality the government was giving the PRSP second priority behind its Five-Year Development Plan and the UNDP-sponsored Long-Term Perspective Study.

In late April and early May 2002, the draft was also discussed in a second round of departmental consultations that were meant to produce poverty reduction strategies and proposals for a decentralised monitoring and evaluation system (via *Comités départmentaux de suivi*/CDS, see below). This time, each *sous-préfecture* was represented in the meetings. As in the first round, these consultations were sponsored by GTZ. The national forum originally planned as the concluding event of the participatory process was cancelled. The PRSP draft was discussed within the Economic and Social Council (a body representing business and trade union interests) and sent to Parliament without any further debate.

Despite the severe criticism by all major donors (which the TS/PRSP accepts only in part), the government remained optimistic that it would produce a satisfactory draft PRSP by the end of May 2002 that would be endorsed by the joint Board of the IMF and the World Bank. It was difficult to see how the draft could be dramatically improved in such a short time.[6]

However, the government's optimism may have been politically realistic in view of Benin's past record of successfully playing the 'democracy bonus' card. Donors were under heavy disbursement pressure, as most aid programmes were blocked as a result of the delays in the PRSP process. In fact, a number of donors already launched new poverty-reduction activities on a large scale (e.g., UNDP, which began a 2.7 million programme in April 2002) without waiting for the completion of the full PRSP.

---

6. In our view, its quality is not a result of poor analytical capacity in the relevant administrative services as such. Rather, it is the result of an inherently low capacity for efficient teamwork among high-level civil servants that would need considerable time to correct.

Stakeholders' views on the PRSP process

During our first mission, our interlocutors were already well aware of the conditionality underlying the initiative of the international financial institutions. Staff from the Planning Ministry commented that the PRSP was not much different from the existing DCPE (*Document Cadre de Politique Economique*/Policy Framework Paper), the only difference being the link between participation and debt relief. This feeling was confirmed during the second mission. For many observers, the PRSP simply replaces adjustment programmes, with increased demands on the government.

The new approach was also raising concerns that it might induce bilateral donors in particular to reduce aid amounts once debt relief was available. Others believed that the poverty strategy would result in increases in social spending that would raise the country's dependence on external aid.

From the beginning, many donors shared the perception that the government was rushing the PRSP process in order to achieve HIPC2 Completion Point, without which debt relief and access to other concessionary aid would be delayed. In fact, the government is said to have set the timetable for the elaboration of the PRSP and the consultation process without any pressure from the IFIs. The IMF facility and subsequent IDA credits and bilateral funding were not dependent on the PRSP process. Benin obtained its first Poverty Reduction and Growth Facility in November 2001.

The majority of stakeholders interviewed believed that the haste with which it had been prepared had a negative impact on the quality of the participatory process. However, it is difficult to tell whether consultations would have been more meaningful if the organisers had been given more time to prepare.

Government capacities and motivation

There were also concerns that capacity to implement the poverty strategy would be inadequate. The capacity problem was seen as the result of a number of factors, including unproductive use of staff time; poorly managed flows of funds and other resources; and weak motivation linked to low staff salaries and high levels of administrative corruption. Capacity problems were also a reflection of overly ambitious planning resulting from donor pressures to have their own particular interests included in work plans and their varied procedures and funding cycles used. These problems will not be resolved unless two things combine: the public administration's willingness to address, among other things, staff motivation through appropriate incentives, remuneration and sanctions; and donors' willingness to seriously question and change their own working methods.

In addition, many interviewees in all categories were convinced that the PRSP would be used by the public administration as a further opportunity for rent-seeking. This sentiment illustrates a serious lack of faith in the government's political commitment to reducing poverty and its ability to manage development. In fact, parliamentarians interviewed, even when not in opposition, were adamant in warning against a programme or budget support approach that would give money to a government that they see as financially unaccountable. This may seem unfair to a number of civil servants who appear highly committed to this mission. Nevertheless, there is much cynicism in Benin vis-à-vis the political elite. Questions were repeatedly raised about the extent to which resources freed by HIPC will be targeted to the poor.

Donor involvement

When we first conducted interviews in late 2000, we noted that most donors were in a 'wait and see' mode. At the same time, they admitted that focusing on poverty was a positive initiative that had arrived at a propitious time: i) good analyses related to poverty were already available and the PRSP offered an opportunity to bring them into a coherent whole; ii) the country's economic performance was encouraging and internal resource mobilisation was on the rise; iii) public expenditure management, including monitoring, was being revamped under pressure from the IFIs; and iv) the PRSP offered an opportunity to release additional resources through debt relief.

Consensus has emerged among bilateral donors since then to let the IFIs take the lead in the political and macroeconomic spheres. However, with a few exceptions they have been actively lending support to the PRSP process, at least financially and by providing technical assistance.

The support has been concerned, essentially but not exclusively, with:

- The participatory process. This was financed by two separate groups of donors to a total of approximately CFA F200 million (about US$270,000). As mentioned above, GTZ has funded the two rounds of departmental seminars, while the Danes and the Dutch have financed *Espace Libéral*, the lobby group made up of businessmen drafting alternative proposals to the PRSP.

- Technical assistance to a number of Ministries, in particular the F&E Ministry (e.g., to help install and manage the new computerised budgetary system and train local staff in its management). The sector Ministries are also assisted with their programming and budgetary process, including with separate units set up some years ago (e.g., the *Cellule* of the European Development Fund within the Ministry of Health).

- Assistance to the Technical Secretariat of the CNDLP with a managing unit housed at the F&E Ministry. The Netherlands and Denmark have signed a CFA F150 million (US$ 200,000) flexible agreement for this purpose.

- A *Fonds de Solidarité Prioritaire* (formely *Fonds d'Aide au Développement*) set up by the French to assist in the implementation of PRSPs. This fund, managed from Paris, is flexible and can be activated at any time to assist in the areas of statistics and macroeconomics, for specific sector projects, monitoring and evaluation.

The donor community kept a low profile throughout the period of consultations and the drafting of the PRSP. A number of agencies attended at least one of the departmental seminars (in Cotonou) as observers. Reactions were mixed: while the seminars and the forum on economic growth were found to be useful in terms of providing an opportunity for civil society to express itself, some regretted that they did not really tackle poverty in all its dimensions, including the more political ones. For instance, female poverty, social inequities, access to land and wealth redistribution were not discussed at all.

So far, the donor response to the capacity problem linked to the PRSP process has been threefold: to offer short- and long-term technical assistance ('institutional TA' for some of them); to set up parallel implementation units staffed by consultants; and to train technical staff, particularly in computer skills. This could have a high cost for the government in the long run, not only in terms of lack of 'ownership' and high transaction costs, but also in terms of nurturing the 'dependency' syndrome. The impact of TA is uncertain and, in any case, it should be evaluated within the context of annual PRSP and sector programme reviews. The alternative would be to rely more on the capacities of better-trained local staff, which can only be a medium-term strategy.

For a given agreed policy measure, there is a general tendency for the government to reduce its own contributions to the process every time donors increase their financial commitments. For this reason, we consider that in Benin the PRSP process has been over-financed. The risk of duplication of activities arising from the poverty strategy is real if donors fail to take the strategy as an opportunity to rationalise their own approaches and instruments.

2.4   What difference has the PRSP made?

The PRSP approach is an attempt to consolidate a number of previously developed approaches and to integrate them into a coherent framework focused on the overall objective of poverty reduction. The four key characteristics of the approach are: comprehensiveness, results-orientation, donor coordination and country ownership. Comprehensiveness and results-orientation indicate the need to link poverty reduction strategies to a reform of the budgetary system, with a view to making the link between alternative uses of public expenditure and poverty reduction more visible.

At the same time, comprehensiveness of approach and prioritisation of actions on the part of national governments will not be achieved unless and until donors coordinate their policies better. In other words, a fundamental change in the nature of the aid relationship is required. Finally, the approach rests on the premise that, to be effective, a poverty reduction strategy should be country-driven, based on widespread consultations and participation and largely 'owned' by key actors on all levels of national societies.

In this section, we deal with the issues of budgetary reform and national ownership. Monitoring is treated in section 5 and donor coordination in section 6.

Budget reform

Benin's budget reform is intended to improve the visibility, transparency and efficiency of public expenditures, with a view to increasing the impact of public spending on poverty. Apart from giving sector Ministries increased responsibility for defining their priorities and elaborating their own budgets based on results, the reform emphasises monitoring. The Finance and Economics Ministry retains overall control of the budget, arbitrates between the different Ministries and conducts negotiations with external partners.

Under the old budget system, the Planning Ministry prepared the investment budget and the F&E Ministry dealt with the operating budget. This arrangement is to be replaced by a unified budget that will be implemented using a number of key instruments:

- a Medium-term Expenditure Framework (MTEF), taking into account both domestic and external (aid) resources, including public debt;
- Public Expenditure Reform and Credits (PERC) for sector Ministries (all PERCs will eventually be integrated into the MTEF);
- an integrated computerised system for tracking public expenditures, the SYGFIP; and
- a two-pronged system for financial control and monitoring: at the level of the F&E Ministry through the Directorate for Financial Control responsible for supervision of all budgetary expenditures, and at the level of the Directorates of Inspection and Internal Audit in each Ministry. A new public works code operational since January 2001 is also meant to improve financial control.

Various fiscal reforms that began in the early 1990s will be consolidated. So far, they have focused on strengthening the fiscal administration to combat fraud, limit tax exemptions and increase fiscal revenues. Since 1994, revenues have been on the rise: The ratio of fiscal revenues to GNP increased from 11.7 percent in 1994 to 12.8 percent in 1996 and 16.6 percent in 2000, with a view to reaching the UEMOA benchmark of 17 percent in 2002.[7]

The reform process began in 1999 – that is, prior to the PRSP initiative – when the World Bank introduced PERCs in five Ministries (Public Works, Environment, Rural Development, Health, Education, Social Protection and Water). Two more Ministries were to be included in 2002 and eventually the PERCs will cover all Ministries and economic and social sectors.

The PERCs require an agreed policy and expenditure plan for each sector using a programme-budgeting approach (*approche budget-programme*), which is supported by the government and the donors. Since there are no sector investment programmes or sector-wide approaches to speak of, the PERCs can be considered to perform a somewhat similar function.

Status of the budget reform

By September 2001, the five Ministries that were identified in 2000 to test the reform had completed individual PERCs for 2000 and 2001, with assistance from the World Bank and other donors (e.g. European Commission). The PERCs include objectives, activities, monitoring and performance indicators within a logical framework that will be revised every year (the revision in 2002 was expected to reflect PRSP objectives more closely). Every three months each line Ministry is supposed to produce a financial budget and a physical implementation report with performance indicators linked to poverty reduction. The 2002 budget was not voted in parliament but implemented via presidential decree.

The five PERCs were to be integrated into the 2002-04 MTEF that was to be finalised in September or October 2001 by the F&E Ministry. When the consultants were in Cotonou in June 2001, a World Bank team was conducting a Public Expenditure Review combined with a multi-sector review to assist line Ministries in developing their own medium-term frameworks.

According to our interviews, the reform has already had a number of positive effects. The Planning Units (*Directions de la Programmation et de la Prospective*) in the relevant Ministries interacted better than before with the F&E Ministry on objectives and priorities in particular. This was a welcome change compared with the old budget system. It was hoped that increased feedback from the F&E Ministry on the decisions taken would alleviate some of the frustrations felt in sector Ministries.

A number of accompanying measures have been taken, in particular to strengthen the capacity of the internal and external auditing functions. 17 internal auditors from the *Inspection Générale des Finances* (IGF) have been trained; the Auditor-General (*Chambre des Comptes*) completed the first performance audit of the PERCs in 2001; and other audits were planned in 2001 at the level of the line Ministries. A new integrated and computerised

---

7. Data provided by the Director of F&E Ministry. UEMOA is the acronym of the West African Economic and Monetary Union.

system for tracking public expenditures (SYGFIP), though not fully functional, has been in place since early 2001 with French TA, including training. However, in summer 2001, our interviewees concurred that the system had set the reform process back for a number of reasons that are explained below.

Guidelines on the new budgetary system have been distributed to staff and the new Code for Public Works has been in use since early 2001. We were told that the strategy to fight corruption would be 'activated' in 2002. Meanwhile, the government's fiscal framework and UEMOA framework have been harmonised, and a common external tariff has been in place since January 2000.

The reform has inspired initiatives in favour of Parliament. The UNDP is assisting the Finance Commission by setting up a special unit to scrutinise the budget (*Unité d'Analyse Budgétaire*). The unit is expected to house at least three 'resource persons' over a three-year period.

Limits of the financial control apparatus

A tremendous effort is being put into the budget reform in terms of financial and human resources to make it operational as soon as possible. The reform has the potential to bring about positive improvements in the way the budget system operates and the poverty reduction strategy is being implemented. Historically in Benin, however, there are limits to such initiatives, as illustrated by recent comparative research on the fight against corruption (Bako-Arifari, 2001, Matthieu, 2001). Financial control has been used less as a means of regulating the administration than as a political weapon of the Presidency. As a result, the apparatus is rather weak, even compared with neighbouring African countries.

The government strategy has been to shift back and forth between the establishment of regular state mechanisms (e.g. the IGF, the *Directions d'Inspections et de Verification Interne*/DIVI within Ministries) and ad hoc measures inspired by the IFIs (e.g. the *Cellule de Moralisation de la Vie Publique*).[8] The IGF was suppressed in 1976, then rehabilitated in 1993, but without any resources until quite recently. The *Inspection Générale de l'État* created in 1976 was abolished in 1990 and rehabilitated in 1998 with no resources. The different DIVI are regularly used to house civil servants who have fallen into disgrace (often for not belonging to the political network of an incoming minister). Sometimes, these civil servants do not even have an office.

In other words, ad hoc measures and institutional creations to improve transparency and accountability have become profuse to the point of duplicating each other. They undermine regular state mechanisms while at

---

8. There are others, such as the Technical Committee in charge of elaborating a national strategy against corruption; ad hoc measures at the level of the F&E Ministry, etc.

the same time chronically lacking the resources to perform efficiently. The weakness of audit mechanisms is also a problem (US/GAO, 2001:42.)

More dramatically, the impact of these control mechanisms has been limited for other reasons linked to the nature of the political system. According to the comparative study by Marilou Matthieu (2001):

> The effectiveness of the instruments of control is nipped in the bud by a pervasive clientelism (political, ethnic, religious and kinship-based) that feeds off the recruitment and career progression of public servants, legitimises misappropriation, fosters impunity and allows personal favours to override sanctions when they are imposed. It is compromised by the discretionary power exercised by senior public figures, who have plenty of latitude to interfere with these organs and discredit everything they attempt to do … But rather than tackling the problem of concentrated discretionary power, the World Bank's strategy encourages its reproduction outside the state. The concern for improved accountability has been developed, but not the means of actually achieving it, which is equivalent to doing nothing, or to masking reality *(our translation)*.

According to Matthieu's study, the instruments that the IMF and the World Bank have installed in Benin since the mid-1980s to improve public finance management and minimise the risks of embezzlement (such as SYDONIA for customs) have been systematically sidetracked from their original aims. Others may have increased corruption. They certainly did not stop one of the biggest corruption scandals of the last few years, the privatisation of SONACOP, the state petroleum company. However, the problem is pervasive. Some state internal control mechanisms are considered to have helped to legitimise corrupt practices within the administration in the three countries studied by Matthieu. The unofficial 'toll system' (i.e., racketeering) generated by the one-stop shop (*guichet unique*) for tax collection is the latest of a generation of such practices. These findings are in line with other evaluations (e.g., EU/USAID, 1999; US/GAO, 2001; Bako-Arifari, 2001).

Few people interviewed were convinced that the new budgetary procedures would substantially modify illegitimate behaviour and result in increased spending for the poor. The prevailing view was that the patronage system, combined with semi-institutionalised corruption, would stand in the way of channelling money to those who need it most.

Bringing coherence to the various instruments around a poverty strategy

Undoubtedly, the PRSP initiative has helped to push the budget reform forward. While the decree on the reform of budgetary procedures was promulgated in 1999, it was only put into operation in 2000 and gained momentum in 2001. However, how the PERCs, the MTEF and the PRSP will fit together remains to be seen. The PRSP and the MTEF were being drafted separately, but staff from the PRSP Technical Secretariat were also involved in drafting the MTEF. A number of interlocutors indicated that a more polyvalent team of PRSP drafters could have included social scientists to guarantee that the pro-poor aspects will be better integrated into the strategy.

Another issue relates to the implications of the PRSP/MTEF/PERCs for budget decentralisation, including learning and feedback from implementation and service-delivery levels to the decision-making level. How this is going to take place without effective decentralisation is not resolved.

Ownership, participation and the politics of poverty reduction

In Benin as everywhere, the concept of poverty generates a number of interpretations. As mentioned above there had been continuous debate on poverty since the mid-1990s and even before, when issues were discussed under different labels like 'basic needs'. Not surprisingly, views on the subject differ.

There seem to be three major positions that have been articulated in the country. The first two emphasise economic growth as a precondition for poverty reduction but differ as to how to attain this objective. For some, growth is most likely to result from developing a service and entrepôt economy catering to the needs of the region (for an elaboration of this argument, see Igué, 1999). The research underlying this position has benefited from continuous donor support, mainly from France.

For others, growth calls for heavy, public-financed investments in infrastructure (this is the position of *Éspace Libéral*, the DANIDA-financed pressure group already mentioned). In both perspectives, poverty reduction would result from employment opportunities generated by economic growth.

The third position is less explicitly formulated but is the one that underlies much past government action. According to this view, poverty reduction is concomitant with improving access of the poor to essential social services, in particular health care and primary education. This position seems to have received support from UNDP in particular.

The government has not taken a clear position in this debate. Unsurprisingly, we found the then Minister of Industry, the President of the Chamber of Commerce and businessmen (but also some representatives of civil society, speaking during the departmental seminars, and a number of donors) taking the first or second view. The Health and Education Ministries, which under HIPC2 will benefit most from increased external resources, tended to take the third view. The labelling of the PRSP coordinating structure as the 'National Commission for Development and the Fight against Poverty' simply adds up the different strands, leaving the door open to different interpretations.

Income distribution, land reform and other sensitive issues are largely absent from public debate on poverty. One illustration of this is the proposed, but stalled, reform of family law that would make a major impact on the economic position of divorced women. These topics are not avoided because of pressure from outside, for example from the IFIs. Rather, there seems to be a tacit understanding among most major national and foreign actors to treat poverty reduction as a technical rather than a political issue.

Ownership and participation

Taking the operationalisation of ownership by Johnson and Wasty (1993, cited in Killick et al., 1998) as a point of departure, there is, in Benin, high ownership of the PRSP approach in the technocratic dimension, but low ownership on the three other counts.

First, as already mentioned, the PRSP is driven by a small group of high-ranking, highly competent, highly motivated and hard-working civil servants who have internalised the new approach. They have been in constant contact with donors for a long time (some in the context of the various Structural Adjustment Programmes, some in the context of the Social Dimension of Adjustment Programme) and are determined to make the new approach work. Furthermore, they are convinced that the obstacles that they themselves perceive, such as resistance from lower-level staff within their own Ministries, can be overcome.

Secondly, however, it would seem that even within the key Ministries such as Finance and Economics and Planning, detailed knowledge about the PRSP has remained the almost exclusive property of this core group. It is likely that the situation is no better at the level of the line Ministries (beyond their Planning Units) and certainly much worse at local administrative levels. In other words, people who will eventually have to implement the new approach are much less sensitised and informed than they should be, if they are to feel they belong to a team driven by a common national goal.

Thirdly, the locus of programme initiation is clearly seen as lying within the donor community, with one very high political authority quoted as saying, in an informal conversation, 'we do have to do this, don' t we, if we want to get the money from them'. As a qualification of this statement, we might add that there is also, in some quarters, a sense that with PRSPs the Bretton Woods institutions are finally coming on board on the matter of poverty reduction. There is certainly strong political support for the PRSP within the two Ministries directly involved (Finance and Economics and Planning). Elsewhere in government, however, the level of information does not seem to go very deep, and the PRSP was certainly not seen as the big issue for the incoming government teams following the 2001 elections.

One of the achievements of the new approach is that, for the first time since Benin turned to multi-party democracy in 1989/90, a number of high-level technocrats have gone to some lengths to explain a new policy framework at seminars held at both national and provincial levels.[9] This could be seen as a step in the right direction, foreshadowing significant changes across a broader range of issues if consultations on the PRSP outside the capital were eventually to be taken a little further (for example, becoming a regular exercise and reaching the local level).

In any case, the recent participation exercise has been limited and could certainly not be qualified as a 'broad consultation campaign' as some would have it. The provincial seminars reached only a tiny fringe of the population (a total of around 600 people participated, only half of whom were from outside the administration, out of Benin's population of 6 million). A proposal to precede the provincial seminars with similar ones at the district (*sous-préfecture*) level was refused by the TS/PRSP, who claimed that there was no time for it. The seminars suffered from the usual shortcomings of this kind of 'participative' meeting ('Round Tables'). With insufficient time for prior consultations, and in the absence of a system of local democratic representation, participants had no clear mandate from their base organisations, and certainly not a democratic one. The selection of participants was quite tightly controlled from the top. Participation was biased towards organised interests (whereas it is well known that 'the poor' are notoriously difficult to organise). Finally, the seminars had very limited capacities for prioritisation.

On the other hand, there is a real danger that the seminars raised expectations that will not be fulfilled. If that turns out to be the case, it will tend to increase the general cynicism among the population as regards the willingness and capacities of the government to effect fundamental policy reforms.

Some of the deficiencies of the first round of departmental seminars came from the particular approach taken to selecting participants, which was heavily biased towards local interests to the detriment of participants who would be able to defend a national perspective. Specialists in economic policy and poverty reduction strategies, e.g. from the universities or independent research institutions, were not invited to the regional seminars. Consumer defence associations are only now being created on the national level; at the local level they do not exist. Specialists of this calibre did participate in the national forum on economic growth; however, even the output of this seminar received the criticism that it was a 'shopping list'.

Parliamentary discussion of the PRSP

Whereas Benin's civil society was only marginally involved in the discussion of the PRSP, the country's political society was even more notable by its absence. Only one Member of Parliament was invited to each of the original

---

9. During the revolutionary period 1972/4 to 1989, intense information campaigns on government policies at grass-roots level were very common.

six departmental seminars (thus altogether only 6 out of total of 83). At the time of our June 2001 mission, the PRSP had not been explained to Parliament. As we have said, this conforms to habitual practice in Benin. There is no tradition requiring the government to present its programme to Parliament and to organise a debate on it. Therefore, opposition parties within Parliament, including their finance specialists, work with a very uneven level of information.

Consequently, few MPs are informed about the PRSP. When they are, it is often through unofficial channels or as a result of their personal links to particular donors (e.g., through participation in a UNDP-sponsored seminar that was held in Quebec in 2000). At the request of the President of the Finance Commission who had been informed of the PRSP process during that seminar, a 'sensitisation' session was planned in July 2001 at which officials from the TS/CNLDP were to inform parliamentarians of the state of PRSP preparations. However, this session never took place. Normally, the vote on the 2002 budget, to which the full PRSP would have been annexed, would have provided an opportunity for parliamentarians to discuss the PRSP. This opportunity was missed as the budget was implemented by presidential decree, and as the draft of the full PRSP was anyhow not ready by then.

A parliamentary discussion of the PRSP would be a precedent insofar as the government has never discussed its strategic planning in Parliament. While many Beninese doubt that MPs will be sufficiently prepared to contribute meaningfully to the debate, in the long run this precedent could indicate a larger role for Parliament in the discussion of strategic public policy choices.

Public discussion of the PRSP

As already noted, poverty and development issues are far from dominating the public debate. Media coverage concerns predominantly what in French is called 'politicians' politics' (*la politique policienne*), and in particular political scandals. As far as the PRSP is concerned, few journalists seem to have really grasped the breadth and the complexity of the approach.

The PRSP has received limited coverage in the media, with no systematic effort being made to brief journalists. We found that journalists of at least one private radio station claimed to have never heard of the document. In view of the serious shortcoming of the participative process which was remarked upon by many, it might have been worthwhile for the government to consider an intensive media campaign (in particular including Rural Radio with its exhaustive coverage of the country and its many programmes in local languages) as a serious complement, if not an alternative, to the approach chosen. In any case, the quality of popular consultations and participation would have certainly benefited from a much more relaxed calendar.

It is undeniable that, starting in the summer of 2001, poverty as a theme was increasingly publicised, in public seminars and in the media in general. Increasingly, the government presented its activities under the heading of 'poverty reduction', relegating formerly fashionable themes like 'good governance' and the 'fight against corruption' to the background. However, this reference to 'poverty reduction' remained rather vague and the PRSP was hardly ever invoked. In other words, there has been a remarkable change in official rhetoric: development activities – most of which were planned to be conducted anyhow – are increasingly relabelled as part of a general poverty reduction strategy.[10]

To conclude on this point, we would recall that at present there is very little analytical capacity in Benin outside the central administration to address the major issues of national development that are raised in the PRSP. Neither Parliament nor political parties (and certainly not the opposition parties) – nor civil society organisations, nor the media – are in a position to provide serious analytical feedback to the government and to play a meaningful watchdog function (although the President of the Chamber of Commerce and Industry claimed that there was internal capacity within the Chamber). Government's traditional propensity to keep information restricted does not help in this respect. But, in any case, the weakness of organised analytical capacity outside the central administration must seriously limit expectations as to what may realistically be expected from 'popular participation'.

2.5   Monitoring the PRSP: a second chance?

Benin's database for poverty analysis and monitoring is considered relatively satisfactory. Abundant literature on the subject already exists: the most recent edition of a regularly updated inventory of bibliographical references lists no fewer than 874 entries (République du Bénin/GTZ, 1998). For the first twenty years after independence, government statistical services relied heavily on French technical assistance. After the withdrawal of the French management in the late 1970s, and a period of decline during the 1980s, the government undertook to rejuvenate its statistical services in the early 1990s, with a strong focus on poverty-related indicators.

A number of surveys and studies were completed in this period. They include an agricultural survey (Ministry of Rural Development); regular surveys of living conditions in rural and urban areas (by the Ministry of

---

10. There are precedents for this. In 1989/90, after the fall of the Berlin wall, the Beninese political class showed a pronounced capacity for quickly adopting official discourse to changing geopolitical circumstances. Terms stemming from Marxist terminology disappeared from public speeches almost overnight (for example, the widespread use of 'comrade' was replaced by 'monsieur'). See Kohnert and Preuss (1992).

Rural Development and the National Institute of Statistics and Economic Analysis/INSAE respectively); collection of employment data in the formal and informal sectors (by the Ministry of Employment and INSAE respectively); and monitoring of consumer prices until 1995 (by the Observatoire des Prix, with units from different Ministries).

In 1997, the UNDP sponsored the publication of a *Manual of Poverty Analysis*, applied to Benin (Aho et al., 1997, now out of print). In addition, the UNDP-sponsored Long-term Perspective Study (finalised in 2000) contains an important section on poverty. The UNDP has also published results from the 2000 survey of living conditions in the rural areas prepared for the Rural Development Ministry.

In order to give more coherence to the collection of social indicators, an *Observatoire de Changement Social* was put in place, with UNDP support, in 1990. It is located in the *Cellule Technique de la Dimension Sociale du Développement* (GTZ-supported) at the Planning Ministry. The OCS is a network of functional units involved in data collection and analysis. It has been partly successful in coordinating these activities. Its main output seems to have been the regular compilation of results from studies undertaken by the various 'functional units', in the form of a bi-annual Social Report and the already mentioned Inventory. Due to late or insufficient reporting from those units, the Social Report does not always present the most recent data. In addition, INSAE has since 1992 produced a compendium of social indicators, the *Tableau de Bord Social*.

The information produced by the central agency, the *Observatoire du Changement Social* (OCS) and its network of units is largely quantitative. One notable exception is the 1995 study on the perception of poverty by the poor carried out by the Ministry of Rural Development with UNDP assistance. Some of the information produced by other institutions also contains qualitative information, for example the 1994 World Bank poverty assessment. Regular reporting on selected poverty issues is also done through the media, including the press, for example on the trade in children from rural to urban areas inside and outside the country. Following a general trend in Benin's press, there is a strong urban (and even capital city) bias in these reports.

One major problem with Benin's poverty monitoring database is its low degree of local ownership. Ever since they were established in 1960, the statistical services have been supported by development partners. All the surveys and studies mentioned above were either aid-financed, with foreign technical assistance, or were conducted directly by donors such as the World Bank and UNDP. They were discontinued when donor support was withdrawn (as in the case of the *Observatoire des Prix*). An example is data collected under INSAE's *Enquête Legère Auprès des Ménages* (ELAM), which were produced only some years ago but are already unavailable because of insufficient stocks. We were told that people who tried to obtain data kept at the Ministry of Rural Development were turned away and told to go to

UNDP.

To put it differently, after more than ten years of donor support, the human resources and financial requirements for data analysis and monitoring still seem to overstretch the government's own capacities. There is no reason to expect that this situation will change in the near future. On the contrary, a recent DANIDA evaluation concludes that massive technical assistance in this field is still necessary.

Another problem concerns the dissemination of findings and access to information, in particular for non-government stakeholders. The major findings of the studies are reported in the media. They are also disseminated through, usually aid-financed, national or departmental seminars organised by the government. This approach to dissemination has a long tradition in Benin, going back to the pre-1990 regime and even earlier. However, continuous access to the studies is difficult, certainly for the average citizen, but also for journalists, government units not directly involved in the data production and even, some time after their production, for the producing units themselves. This is in line with the general administrative routine of restricting information, which we have already referred to several times.

Different 'databases' (usually collections of the printed versions of studies) or documentation centres (libraries usually containing published material only) are located within different government units. The 874 studies mentioned above are to be found in no less than 27 different institutions, each of them holding only some of the studies. Access to most of these institutions is not predictable, and there is no guarantee that a particular study listed in the inventory will in fact still be available, the rate of loss being high. Out-of-print studies are not reprinted.

Thus, a citizen interested in a particular study has to go to the administrative unit that produced it, without being certain that s/he will succeed. For example, during our first mission it was impossible for us to get hold of the inventory mentioned above, although this is a major tool for anybody who wants to get a first overview of the state of poverty information in the county. Outside government offices, no independent Beninese data collecting and analysing capacity exists, at least not on a national scale. The situation is obviously even worse outside Cotonou.

We have been unable to establish whether public policies have been directly or indirectly influenced by information produced by the data monitoring system, except maybe in the health sector. Key actors hold the Cellule Technique of the DSD programme to be rather marginalised within the Ministry of Planning. Evaluations have pointed out that the data produced are on too general a level, and anyway are produced too late to inform policy. It also seems that as a rule, data collected are only analysed once, and are then not used for later analyses.

The database is rapidly going out of date, with most studies dating from the mid-1990s. The two exceptions are the Long-Term Perspective Study and the second survey of living conditions in rural areas. According to recent evaluations by DANIDA and the World Bank, the methodology for future poverty studies would need to be adjusted.

Finally, the poverty monitoring system suffers from a multiplicity of institutional arrangements caused by intra-administration conflicts over direct access to aid and competition between donors for leadership, as is the case elsewhere in government. The studies and surveys undertaken under the umbrella of the OCS are located in four different Ministries. Major national research institutions like the *Centre Beninois de Recherche Scientifique et Technique* (CBRST), the *Institut National de Recherche Agricole du Benin* (INRAB) and the National University of Benin (UNB), are not involved.

This might be justified by the argument that the data should be produced as close to potential users as possible. However, in our view this argument is not convincing for two reasons. First, as noted above, even data produced close to the presumed main user do not seem to have had a discernible impact on the strategic orientation of government policy. Secondly, it reflects a very state-centred and sector-based approach to poverty reduction, implying that the main actor in the area of, say, rural poverty is the Ministry of Rural Development. This approach to data production and storage sets up barriers to the production of a global and nationally-owned poverty agenda to which different stakeholders might contribute over and above the particular Ministry involved.

The iPRSP of June 2000 had a two-page section on 'Participation, Monitoring and Evaluation, and Coordination of the Strategy'. However, in spite of its title, it did not, in fact, contain a single sentence on monitoring and evaluation. Neither was monitoring a theme of the five preparatory studies undertaken for the full PRSP, or of the various (national and regional) consultations. In June 2001, we were told that a specific seminar was planned for July 2001, but this was later cancelled and the seminar never took place.

The draft PRSP contained a two-page section on Monitoring and Evaluation that differentiates technical from participative monitoring. Under the first heading, in substance a revitalisation and extension of the near-defunct *Observatoire du Changement Social* (OCS) was envisaged. Four types of actions were foreseen: i) the extension of the existing micro-financial model (MOSARE) to include poverty-related indicators; ii) two large-scale poverty surveys in 2002 and 2004, based on the model of previous UNDP-supported surveys (*Enquête léger auprès des ménages*/ELAM and *Enquêtes sur les Conditions de Vie en Milieu Rural*/ECVR) and including an improved method of data preservation; iii) budgetary monitoring in the context of the on-going reform of budget procedures (PERAC); and iv) the installation of a system of programme impact evaluation. These measures were to be reinforced by the integration of Benin into the IMF-sponsored General System of Data Diffusion (*Système Générale de Diffusion de Données*/SGDD).

As for participatory monitoring, committees (*Comités départementaux de suvi*/CDS) are to be set up in each of the country's 12 departments. They will comprise the *préfet* who will chair them; the mayors and vice-mayors of all departmental municipalities; a representative from each of the departmental producers' union (representing cash-cropping farmers), the Chamber of Commerce and the Parents' Association; and all the departmental directors of deconcentrated state services as well as a representative of civil society from each municipality. The role of these committees will be to oversee data collection and the monitoring of the implementation of the PRSP at the departmental level. It should be noted that this structure can only become operational after the implementation of decentralisation, e.g., once municipalities have been set up and mayors have been elected.[11]

2.6   Towards a new aid relationship

Donor co-ordination

There is no specific donor forum for dealing with poverty reduction, although donors do seize opportunities at field level to talk to each other individually or in small 'like-minded' groups. The PRSP offers an opportunity for the government to bring donors together around a coherent strategy. It seems that donors would in principle be willing to follow in this initiative, provided they find the government's approach convincing.

In our November 2000 report, we suggested that the Participatory Development and Good Governance Group set up by the OECD/DAC and led by the Swiss might be the appropriate option for donor coordination around the PRSP. We later confirmed that the PD/GG group now meets regularly *'pour faire le point'* (*Le Monde*, 26.6.01). Another donor group, made up of senior economists and led by the UNDP, does not seem to have met often and is considered a less suitable forum for coordinating around the PRSP.

From the beginning, the World Bank and IMF maintained some distance from the PRSP preparations while keeping other donors informed of major developments. The last Public Expenditure Review was conducted in collaboration with other donors (the European Union). Briefings are organised following Bank and IMF missions and relevant documents and correspondence seem to be shared. We were told in Benin that seminars on the PRSP were being planned with UNDP in a number of African countries to 'smooth things out', given the initial differences in Mali and elsewhere. Other multilateral institutions such as the AfDB and the West African Development Bank are also in the picture.

---

11. Benin's decentralisation laws foresee the replacement of the current 90-odd *sous-préfectures* by municipalities, with elected councils and mayors. Elections were held in December 2002/January 2003, and the councils and the mayors have been elected.

Towards a programme approach?

It is still too early to form an opinion on how much direct budget or sector support donors will be prepared to provide once the PRSP becomes operational. So far, the budget reform, which the government has been presenting since 2000 as a mechanism for implementing the PRSP, has attracted only a few donors (the World Bank and European Union). They are using modalities that seem to be evolving towards a programme approach. Others (Denmark, the Netherlands, Switzerland) have indicated their interest and may join in once they feel confident that the advantages outweigh the risks.

A third group, among them two of Benin's most important bilateral donors (France, Germany), are much more hesitant, as the adoption of a programme approach would constitute for them a fundamental shift from established practices, implying a need to change their funding cycles, timeframes and procedures in quite a fundamental way. Their hesitation also seems to be based on doubts about whether a rapid switch to a programme approach would in fact be appropriate in the existing political and administrative context.

In general, bilateral donors find it difficult to adhere fully to programme and/or sector approaches using government planning and implementation procedures. There are nevertheless more and more examples of a number of donors providing substantial sums via pooled arrangements. The budget reform may in due course help bring coherence to the various types of aid used in Benin. However, it is likely that the three types (budget support, sector support and project aid) will coexist for some time, until a critical number of donors feel confident enough to begin using government procedures.

2.7   Conclusions

In our view, it would be unrealistic and even dangerous (in the sense of raising expectations that will not be fulfilled) to expect too much too fast from the PRSP approach in Benin. In the last 40 years, Benin has seen many approaches to solving the problems of underdevelopment and poverty come and go, most of them donor-driven. There is widespread scepticism, if not cynicism, at all levels of Beninese society whenever a new approach is proposed.

Many of our interview partners perceived PRSP simply as another fad or 'slogan' invented by the development community which politicians are quick to pick up in order to keep the money flowing into the country. In fact, it would announce a revolution in the aid relationship if some day the government were to refuse a substantial amount of aid on the grounds that it did not fit with its own priorities. On a seemingly more banal, but in fact symbolically highly relevant, level, national ownership of the Poverty

Reduction Strategy might be enhanced if the approach were locally renamed in a way that made it sound less like one of the innumerable labels, acronyms and jargon-words that the international development community is so quick to invent.[12]

The PRSP approach is, however, more ambitious than anything the country has experienced since the demise of Marxism-Leninism, since it aims at a profound change in the nature of Benin's political economy as an aid-dependent neo-patrimonial democracy. In political-science terms, nothing less than a regime change is aimed at. Its success will largely depend on the building of mutual trust, as much between donors and the government as between the government and the population.

For this extremely ambitious objective to be realised, at least three conditions have to be fulfilled. First, the success of the PRSP approach depends to a very large degree on changes in donor behaviour. In fact, a key focus of the PRSP approach should be what is needed for a change in donor practices rather than focusing primarily on the way the government operates.

Will the PRSP be the common framework for a real country-donor partnership? In time, the process could generate policies that reflect the priorities of the government, rather than the un-coordinated preferences that emerge from the large number of donor projects. It could encourage donors to shed their conventional practices such as creating local clienteles and applying inflexible financial cycles, ex-ante planning and centralised decision-making. However, it should be clearly recognised that a number of bilateral donor agencies may perceive the change in donor-recipient relations as a threat to their established way of doing things and, in some cases, to their very existence. The new approach may also be a threat to some UN agencies, which act as intermediaries between the government and other donors. On the other hand, the apparently increasing willingness of donors to coordinate their positions vis-à-vis the government, as reflected in the joint statement by the EU and its member states on the draft PRSP, is an encouraging sign in this respect.

Secondly, as regards the government, the poverty reduction strategy must be matched by other reforms, in particular decentralisation, civil service reform and the eradication of corruption. These four policy measures form a 'package' that cannot be disentangled. This is not to say that the implementation of these other reforms would be a guarantee for a success of the PRSP approach. But it is a necessary condition. The fact that the decentralisation programme is finally moving forward is an encouraging sign.

Thirdly, a fundamental change in policy objectives and in the way the political system works is needed, and this cannot be the result of outside pressure alone. (There is in fact a kind of double bind in an approach that

---

12. Many key terms of the international development jargon – which are all in English – are notoriously difficult to translate into other languages. A case in point is the term 'ownership'.

tries to impose ownership from the outside.) There must be groups and networks of local reformers with the necessary political weight to carry out an ambitious reform programme. In this context, local alliances of reformers would certainly benefit from outside support. However, while individuals and small groups of local reformers can be identified, they do not seem to be connected with each other.

A more general implication of this point is that the concept of ownership needs to be seen in political, and not purely technical, terms. A political strategy would consist of supporting identified local actors inside and outside the government. This is currently done in one way, as many donors each have their own local sympathisers among government officials and sections, as well as among CSOs. What needs to be developed is the capacity of local reformers to link up among themselves.

Furthermore, in our view, two major trade-offs will need to be addressed in the implementation of the poverty reduction strategy. Again, in both cases, time is a factor.

The first is the trade-off between the ownership and the technical complexity of the process. While the rhetoric emphasises local ownership, the substance of the new approach and the instruments to implement it are quite complex. They call for massive amounts of external technical assistance to fill the local gap in capacity. This is problematic from the ownership point of view. In fact, we are inclined to conclude that the process is too complex for immediate national ownership to be on the agenda.

The problem would be easier to address if the PRSP were the only new initiative that officials were being asked to contend with. The profusion of different instruments introduced by the IFIs in recent years (PERs, PERCs, CAS, MTEF, PRSP), together with the exceedingly slow pace of reforms during the last ten years, have now resulted in a serious reform overload in Benin. This would indicate the need for the government to establish some priorities among the necessary reforms and to elaborate a timeframe for their implementation.

Another major trade-off is between participation and the (perceived) need to hasten the process so as to access the financial benefits linked to the PRSP. Up to now, the participatory exercises have contained a strong element of window-dressing. The different approaches to participation were initiated neither by the government, nor by Parliament or civil society, and are perceived by local actors as conditionality for access to debt relief.

In any event, advocacy of popular participation and consultation should be freed from an ideological fixation on a 'civil society' that does not exist in Benin, at least not as it is described in the textbooks. As with ownership, participation must be seen as a political issue, not a technical exercise. It is difficult to see how the present neglect of Parliament can be justified, no matter how great its weaknesses. If the capacities of Parliament are weak, consideration should be given to ways of raising them. Likewise, free flows of information should be considered a prerequisite for meaningful participation. In this connection the media should play a much more important role and journalists should be trained to discuss issues of substance. This implies a much greater willingness on the part of GOB to share important information, starting with policy documents.

The setting up of departmental monitoring structures is a positive first step, on condition that they become effective and are complemented with effective local monitoring committees. Here again, no real progress can be expected without decentralisation. The strengthening of independent users' associations, for example in the education and health sectors, and their involvement in evaluations would also be useful.

We have argued that it is unrealistic to expect positive impacts of the poverty reduction strategy in the medium as opposed to the long term, and that the poverty reduction strategy must be seen in the context of other reforms, notably decentralisation, civil service reform and the fight against corruption. These reforms are necessary, if not sufficient, conditions for the success of the strategy. Another necessary, but again not sufficient, condition for success is a profound change in the nature of the aid relationship.

It might be felt that there is a contradiction between the obvious magnitude of the problems requiring a whole array of interlocking reforms and our plea for giving the process more time. To conclude, we should therefore underline that having more time will only help on the basis of clear priorities, including a calendar spelling out the sequence of reform implementation. The PRSP approach provides the government of Benin with an opportunity to move in this direction.

References

Adjovi, Emmanuel V. (2001) 'Liberté de Presse et corruption au Bénin: La dérive du journalisme de marché', Cotonou, ms.

Aho, Gilbert; Larivière, Sylvain; and Martin, Frédéric (1997) *Manuel d'analyse de la pauvreté: Applications au Bénin*. Cotonou: Université National du Bénin and UNDP/Québec: Université Laval.

Alber, Erdmute and Sommer, Jörn (1999) 'Grenzen der Implementierung staatlichen Rechts im dörflichen Kontext: Eine Analyse der Rechtswirklichkeit in einem Baatombu-Dorf in Bénin' (Limits of Implementation of State Law in Village Contexts: An Analysis of Legal Realities in a Baatombu Village), *Afrika-Spektrum* 34: 85-111.

Bako-Arifari, Nassirou (1995) 'Démocratie et logiques du terroir au Benin', *Politique Africaine* 59: 7-24

Bako-Arifari, Nassirou (2001) 'La corruption au Bénin'. Draft research report. Parakou, Bénin (mimeo). See also http://www.uni-mainz.de/~ifeas/workingpapers/corruption.pdf

Banégas, Richard (1998) 'Marchanisation du vote, citoyenneté et consolidation démocratique au Bénin', *Politique Africaine* 69: 75-87.

Beblawi, H. and Luciani, G. (1987) *The Rentier State: Nation, State and Integration in the Arab World*, London.

Bierschenk, Thomas (1993) *Außenabhängigkeit und Intermediarität: Merkmale des Staates in Bénin* (Extraversion and Intermediarity: Characteristics of the State in Benin). Sozialanthropologische Arbeitspapiere/Socio-Anthropological Working Papers, 52. Berlin, Free University/Das Arabische Buch.

Bierschenk, Thomas, and Mongbo, Roch (eds.) (1995) *Le Bénin: Dossier thématique de 'Politique Africaine' no. 59.* Paris: Karthala.

Bierschenk, Thomas (1999) 'Herrschaft, Verhandlung und Gewalt in einer afrikanischen Mittelstadt' (Domination, Negotiation and Violence in an African Medium-sized Town), *Afrika Spectrum* 34: 321-48.

Bierschenk, Thomas and Olivier de Sardan, Jean-Pierre (eds.) (1998) *La démocratie au village: Le Bénin rural entre démocratisation et décentralisation.* Paris: Karthala.

Buchanan, J.N., Tollison, R.D. and Tullock, G. (eds.) (1980) *Toward a Theory of the Rent-Seeking Society.* Texas

Caramel, Laurence (2001) 'Une nouvelle approche pour contenir la pauvreté au Bénin', *Le Monde*, 26 June (Supplément *Le Monde Economie*).

European Union/USAID (1999) 'Macro-évaluation de la gouvernance au Bénin'. Cotonou (unpublished report).

Fondation Friedrich Ebert (1995) 'Le programme des partis politiques au Bénin: colloque international'. Cotonou: Fondation Friedrich Ebert (mimeo).

Fondation Konrad Adenauer (1997) 'Le financement des partis politiques et le statut de l'opposition au Bénin (Actes du séminaire du 27 janvier – 8 février 1997)'. Cotonou: FKA (mimeo).

Gbessemehlan, Victor and Rijnierse, Elly (1995) 'Les élections en milieu rural'. *Politique Africaine* 59: 70-81.

Hounkpe, Matthias, and Lalaye, Francis (2000/01) 'Pluripartisme au Bénin: Un défaut fatale de notre démocratie?', *Façons de Voir* (monthly journal), nos. 1-3, 15 Nov, 15 Dec and 15 Jan, Cotonou.

Hounkpe, Mattias, and Lalaye, Francis (2001) 'Le parlement béninois, cet inconnu', *Façons de Voir* (monthly journal), nos. 4-5, 15 Feb, 15 Mar and 15 Apr, Cotonou.

Igué, John O. (1999) *Le Bénin et la mondialisation de l'économie: Les limites de l'intégrisme du marché.* Paris: Karthala

Joekes, Susan, and Houedete, Thomas (2000) 'Creating a Framework for Poverty Reduction: Institutional and Process Issues in National Poverty Policy in Selected African Countries. Benin Country Report', Brighton, UK: Institute of Development Studies.

Killick, Tony (1998) *Aid and the Political Economy of Policy Change.* London: Overseas Development Institute in association with Routledge.

Kohnert, D. and Preuss, H. J. (1992) 'Vom Camarade zum Monsieur: Strukturanpassung und Demokratisierung in Benin' (From Comrade to Monsieur: Structural Adjustment and Democratisation in Benin), *Peripherie* 46: 47-70.

Le Meur, Pierre-Yves (1999) 'Coping with Institutional Uncertainty: Contested Local Public Spaces and Power in Rural Benin', *Afrika-Spektrum* (Hamburg): 187-211.

Matthieu, Marilou (2001) 'Une approche comparée de la lutte contre la corruption en Afrique subsaharienne (Sénégal, Niger, Bénin)'. Draft research report. Marseille (mimeo). http://www.uni-mainz.de/~ifeas/workingpapers/corruption.pdf

Mayrargue, Cédric (1999) 'Le Bénin dépuis le retour au pouvoir de M. Kérékou: «démocratie apaisée» ou paralysie politique?', *L'Afrique politique*: 107–124

Naudet, Jean-David (2000) *Trouver des problèmes aux solutions: Vingt ans d'aide au Sahel.* Paris: OECD.

République du Bénin (1999) *Rapport sur l'état de l'économie nationale. Développements récents et perspectives à moyen terme.* Cotonou: Cellule macro-économique de la Présidence.

République du Bénin/GTZ (1998) *Inventaire des études et enquêtes sur la pauvreté au Bénin* (3rd edn). Cotonou: MPRPE.

UNDP (2000) *Rapport sur le développement humain au Bénin (La gouvernance).* Cotonou: UNDP.

UNDP (2001) *Choices for the Poor.* New York: UNDP.

US/GAO (2001) 'International Monetary Fund: Few Changes Evident in Design of New Lending Program for Poor Countries' (Report to the Chairman, Committee on Foreign Relations, U.S. Senate). Washington, DC.

Westebbe, R. (1994) 'Structural Adjustment, Rent Seeking and Liberalisation in Benin', in J.A. Widner (ed), *Economic Change and Political Liberalisation.* London: 80-100.

World Bank (1994) *Benin: Towards a Poverty Alleviation Strategy.* Washington, DC: World Bank.

Chapter 3: Kenya

by Lucia Hanmer, Gerrishon Ikiara, Walter Eberlei and Carolyn Abong[*]

The future of the PRSP in Kenya is currently uncertain. Until the recent elections, there were considerable and well-founded doubts about the extent of high-level political commitment to economic and political reform, including the PRSP. Nevertheless, this chapter argues that the PRSP process was a highly positive experience for Kenya in a number of respects. A relatively thorough consultation exercise around the drafting of the document widened and deepened constituencies for pro-poor policy change between and within some parts of government and civil society. Synergies between the PRSP, budget reforms and a 'mainstreaming' approach to aid delivery were also revealed, but too briefly to reconcile differences among donors about how to support poverty reduction when the political context is unpromising.

3.1 Introduction

Donor relations with the Government of Kenya have experienced a 'stop-go' cycle that can be traced back to the early 1980s. Concessional lending is agreed on the basis of conditionalities, which the government reneges on, or implements half-heartedly. Lending is suspended when donors find that conditionalities have not been adhered to. Then, after a cooling-off period on both sides, new negotiations begin, leading to new agreements and new lending commitments, accompanied by new conditionalities.

The most recent cycle of this sort was completed just as the research for this article was getting under way in late 2000. In 1997 the IMF had suspended its loan disbursements agreed under the 1996 ESAF facility because of insufficient progress on governance in Kenya. IMF/World Bank lending restarted under the Poverty Reduction and Growth Facility agreed in August 2000. However, by the end of 2000, differences were already emerging

[*] Lucia Hanmer began the research for this chapter as a Research Fellow at the Overseas Development Institute and completed it as an Economic Adviser in the UK Department for International Development, both based in London. Gerrishon Ikiara and Carolyn Abong were staff members at the University of Nairobi, and Walter Eberlei is on the staff of the University of Duisberg in Germany. The team is grateful to all the individuals and organisations who took time off to talk to them about the PRSP experience and related issues, but the writers retain the responsibility for the accuracy of the reporting and the soundness of the overall analysis and recommendations.

between the IMF/World Bank and the Kenya Government. These led to the suspension of IMF lending in December 2000, after the Kenya Anti-Corruption Authority (KACA) was declared illegal. During 2002, a resumption of lending was on the cards, but never seriously entertained in the closing months of the Moi Presidency. Following the election of the National Rainbow Coalition (NARC) in December 2002 the early signs were that the lights were about to return to go once more.

Like the others in the book, this chapter draws on research for the PRSP study commissioned by the Strategic Partnership with Africa (SPA) in 2000. The study as a whole was concerned with the extent to which poverty reduction policies, programmes, practices and monitoring systems are being institutionalised in those countries, both HIPC and non-HIPC, in the region that have committed themselves to preparing PRSPs. Kenya is the only country in the original set of eight (including Ghana) where PRSP preparation is not linked to the conditions for Enhanced HIPC debt relief, but is a condition for access to new concessional lending from the IMF and the World Bank.

The Kenya country study was completed in two parts. An initial 'scoping' mission took place in November 2000, at which point Kenya's Interim PRSP (iPRSP) had been endorsed and the process leading to the preparation of a full PRSP was just beginning. The work was completed with a second phase of teamwork by the consultants starting in the second quarter of 2001, and by further follow-up research in mid-2002. The second phase of field research coincided with the consultation processes and debates in the culminating stages of full-PRSP preparation.

At the time of completing the chapter, the future of the Kenyan PRSP was rather uncertain. The document existed but had not been taken to the IMF/World Bank Boards for endorsement. There were considerable and well-founded doubts about the extent of official ownership of the PRSP and indeed the whole national economic and political reform programme in the country from the top levels of government down. Nevertheless, the presidential elections of December 2002 have injected new elements into the political scene. The NARC came to power on an election manifesto that includes pledges to eliminate corruption, to revive Kenya's ailing economy and to execute programmes to restore World Bank/IMF support. In its first days in power NARC was taking serious steps to fulfil these pledges, including publishing two anti-corruption Bills to be presented to Parliament. The IMF has indicated that it is keen to disburse aid as soon as prior actions that led to the suspension of the previous programme are fulfilled, and other donors too are indicating their willingness to work with the new government.

As the IMF has made it clear that updating the PRSP is one of the prior actions that will indicate that the new government is on the right track (*East African Standard*, 2003), what has been learned from the PRSP process will once again become relevant. Therefore, the questions posed in the other country studies in this collection remain relevant to the case of Kenya.

The chapter has six more sections. The next section explains further the particular context of the PRSP episode in Kenya. We then describe the main features of the process in Kenya, and what difference it appears to have made to the prospects for more effective poverty reduction efforts in the country. The last two substantive sections deal with monitoring and the dilemmas facing aid donors. A concluding section follows.

3.2 Poverty reduction and the policy context

Macroeconomic context

Kenya's failure to adjust in the 1980s and early 1990s resulted in deteriorating macro aggregates, negligible growth, rising unemployment, increasing poverty and growing tensions with the donor community culminating in the suspension of aid in November 1991. Growth averages per annum were: 1960-70 6.6 percent; 1970-79 4.6 percent; 1980-89 2.2 percent; 1990-99 1 percent. By 1994, the poverty headcount was estimated at 46 percent, having grown from an estimated 29 percent in 1974.

Aid suspension is widely viewed as the trigger for the radical economic and political reforms that were implemented between 1991 and 1995. The country's fiscal management improved from 1997 as deficits were reduced. However, by 1998 levels of domestic debt (KSh 25.4 billion or 3.4 percent of GDP) held by the government were becoming a threat to the resumption of economic growth.

The debt had accrued in the wake of the 1992 election when excessive monetary expansion was used to finance a large fiscal deficit (more than 10 percent of GDP) in 1992, which was widely suspected to have been used to fund the election campaigns. The result was severe inflation for the 1993-5 period, peaking at 60 percent in 1994. The problem was brought under control mainly through the use of short-term Treasury Bills at high interest rates. This build-up of short-term debt, in combination with declining savings rates, led to lending rates of around 20 percent in real terms during most of the 1990s.

Investment as a share of GDP experienced a major decline during the 1990s, falling from around 25 percent in the early 1980s to 15 percent in 1999. Projections used in the government's own Medium-Term Expenditure Framework (MTEF) do not show real growth rates exceeding population growth in the near future. Investor confidence continues to be low, owing to high costs of doing business as well as political uncertainty in the country. The infrastructure continues to suffer from high levels of dilapidation, while poor governance stifles efficiency, distorts market transactions and obstructs small- and large-scale private sector investment, production and organisation. As a result of the latest stand-off with donors, levels of domestic debt have escalated even higher, increasing to Ksh 233 bn in July 2002, around 24 percent of GDP (Central Bank of Kenya, 2002).

The Economic Recovery Team

Government and IMF documents point to increased official effort after 1998 to address the causes of financial instability and low growth (although this has shown no results yet in terms of improved growth or investment rates). Part of the progress is attributed to the introduction of the 'Change Team' or Economic Recovery Team to the top echelons of government during 1999-2001.

In 1999 six Kenyans, previously working for either the private sector in Kenya or international organisations overseas, were appointed to senior civil service posts for an initial two-year term. Dr Richard Leakey, a conservationist with an international reputation and a leading figure in Kenyan opposition politics, was appointed Head of the Civil Service, while other members of the team were appointed as Permanent Secretaries in the Ministries of Finance and Economic Planning, Agriculture, Transport and Communications, and Energy.

The brief of the ERT was to resuscitate the economy and undertake the required reforms, including the strengthening of governance and other pre-conditions for the resumption of aid. It included introducing a Medium-Term Expenditure Framework. However, in March 2001, the programme experienced a major setback as the government dropped three members of the team, leading to renewed tensions between the government and some key donors.

The first Kenyan budget prepared under the MTEF was presented to Parliament in 2000 and covered fiscal years 2000/01-2002/03. An Interim PRSP (iPRSP) was completed in July 2000, securing a PRGF agreement with the IMF. Preparation of the full PRSP remained on schedule up to mid-2001, with the draft report being presented at a national stakeholders' forum in June 2001. However, with the stand-off with the IMF and the changes in the civil service, commitment to continuing the PRSP and the MTEF was adversely affected.

Political and civil society

After the introduction of multi-party politics in Kenya in the early 1990s and especially after the general elections in 1997, Parliament is gradually emerging as a very active and independent institution, with rising significance in the country's policy-making process. Parliamentary independence has, however, to be seen in the context of the many hindrances it faces. In particular:

- Many MPs are still caught up in the country's patronage system, which has permeated the political system since independence. There is considerable evidence that a large number of MPs are pursuing vested interests and do not contribute substantially to the development of an issue-based political decision-making process.

- The political parties, which play an important role in the Parliament, are, in one way or another, still related to ethnic issues (on this dimension in Kenyan politics, see Murungi, 1998: 423-42). The executive arm of the government has tended to treat Parliament as a subsidiary institution and still continues to exercise enormous control over it.

During the period of our study, there were several signs of the maturing of Parliament. A major breakthrough on its way to becoming a more issue-oriented and independent institution was the establishment of the Parliamentary Service Commission in late 1999/early 2000. This commission has since then taken several steps to strengthen Parliament's role and independence and it plans to enhance these efforts in the future. An example of Parliament's greater assertiveness is that for the first time in the country's history, Parliament began rejecting or changing some government bills. While it is debatable whether these decisions were all based on sound economic and political arguments, what they tell us about the rising strength of Parliament is positive. In the medium term, it could lead to a more effective system of 'checks and balances' and a more institutionalised participation of Kenyan society in national decision making.[1]

Kenya has many vibrant and active civil society organisations (CSOs). In part, their development is a by-product of donor relations with the government. CSOs, especially the internationally based NGOs, became major recipients of development assistance from the late 1980s onwards, and their significance increased as many donors shifted funds from government projects and programmes to NGOs in the late 1990s. CSOs have traditionally been active in poverty reduction projects in local-level programmes. As a result of widening political space following the introduction of multi-party politics (see Nyang'oro, 2000: 91-108), a large proportion of Kenyan CSOs are increasingly involved in advocacy work for more reforms, which are regarded as important for improving the enabling environment for their service delivery.

Within government, some people are increasingly uneasy about, and in some cases openly opposed to, the rising capacity of NGOs to attract resources from the donor community. The volume of foreign exchange brought in through NGOs is significant enough to effect macro balances and there is concern, among other things, to be able to collate the information on these inflows and ensure that funds are used transparently by all recipient organisations.

---

1. In 2001, this process seemed to be jeopardised by the move to bring the National Development Party (NDP) led by Raila Odinga into the government, which significantly reduced the strength of the opposition parties in Parliament. In March 2002, NDP and KANU merged, but subsequently KANU defections and the restructuring of the opposition into the National Rainbow Alliance altered the short-term political panorama once again.

Previous poverty plans

Poverty featured prominently in Kenya's policy discussions in the 1990s. A National Poverty Eradication Plan (NPEP) was prepared by the Poverty Eradication Commission in the Office of the President in 1998 and launched in 1999. It describes the extent of poverty and sets poverty reduction targets. The NPEP was developed using relatively progressive participatory elements. Representatives from NGOs, the private sector and donors were included in the four governmental led committees that drafted papers on: poverty, social integration, employment and the enabling environment for social development. The results, together with the findings of a Participatory Poverty Assessment Study (GoK, 1997) were discussed in several workshops with a broad range of stakeholders. The draft NPEP was discussed in several workshops with representatives from civil society, private sector and the donor community before it was finalised.

The poverty reduction strategy advocated in the NPEP builds on the project approach that has characterised the poverty reduction interventions in the country. It calls for a bottom-up approach to poverty planning and policy implementation, combined with more attention to social sectors and a Charter for Social Integration that defines the rights and responsibilities of various Kenyan stakeholders in promoting social integration. An Anti-Poverty Trust Fund was set up to mobilise contributions from government, donor agencies and the private sector, and to finance locally determined poverty projects at the district level. However, as discussed below, it has had limited support as the majority of donors prefer a 'mainstreaming approach'.

3.3   The PRSP process in Kenya

Basic facts

The MTEF and the iPRSP came on stream in Kenya at the same time, leading to considerable overlap in their development. The Macroeconomic and Sectoral Working Groups formed for the MTEF also contributed to various chapters of the iPRSP. In June 2000 the first MTEF Budget was produced and the iPRSP was completed the following month. For the full PRSP, the government launched an ambitious consultation process in November 2000, with the PRSP Secretariat in the Ministry of Finance and Planning as the lead agency.[2] The PRSP consultation process was implemented at both national and regional levels.

---

2. With respect to the PRSP consultation process, the Government notes: 'Participation happens when we value people's ideas and knowledge, and power is given to them to make decisions independently of external agents whether governmental or non-governmental. When people take a lead role in analysing

Nine Sector Working Groups[3] were maintained for production of the full PRSP, which was scheduled for completion by April 2001. There were also eight Thematic Groups,[4] whose input supplemented the work of the Sector Working Groups. Box 3.1 (overleaf) presents the organisational structure for the PRSP consultation process.

District consultations took place between January and February 2001. These were organised in three categories, namely, comprehensive consultations conducted in 25 districts with an average of 200 participants in addition to participants in sub-district-level meetings; general consultations held in 45 districts with an average of 150 participants; and in-depth community-level consultations carried out in the form of Participatory Poverty Assessments (PPAs) in 10 districts and coordinated by an NGO, AMREF.

Participants in the district consultations were drawn from all sectors and interest groups in the various districts, with a representative target of at least 30 percent women, 10 percent youth, 20 percent government, 10 percent private sector, 10 percent disabled and 20 percent community leaders. A district secretariat drew up the guidelines for the selection. The actual selection was done in some cases by the local administration officials, such as District Officers and chiefs, and in some cases by the district secretariat or local authority councillors on the basis of the guidelines. Most of the districts selected participants from already existing participatory-based institutions such as self-help groups, churches, women's groups and other community-based organisations.

A more bottom-up procedure was followed in some districts. For example, in Kilifi about 100 of the 500 villages in the district elected Village Development Committees (VDCs). These VDCs sent their representatives to the divisional consultative fora. A comparable approach was adopted in Busia

---

their situation, and then plan to change it, then we can say that meaningful participation is taking place' (MoFP, 2000: 8). The paper mentions the following official objectives of the consultation process: to facilitate an intensive and wide ranging consultation process; to promote participation of all, especially the poor and vulnerable; to increase transparency and accountability to the public from the planning to delivery stages; to reach consensus/agreement with various stakeholders on policies and priorities for poverty reduction; to develop a gender responsive poverty reduction strategy; to enhance ownership of the PRSP; to reach agreement of monitoring and evaluation plan for the PRSP; to develop an action plan on poverty reduction; to seek support from development partners on the implementation of PRSP.

3. The nine SWGs were Agriculture and Rural Development; Human Resource Development; Information Technology; Public Administration, Public Safety, Law and Order; Physical Infrastructure; Tourism, Trade and Industry; National Security; and Macro.

4. The eight Thematic Groups were Gender, Governance, HIV/AIDS, Media, Pastoralists, Youth, Finance and Disability.

Box 3.1 Structure of the consultation process at the national level

The broad-based institution in charge of the process was the **National Consultative Forum (or National Stakeholder Forum)**. A first three-day forum took place in March 2000 with about 300 participants discussing the iPRSP. A second one-day forum was held in March 2001 (for information dissemination), and a final forum to discuss the PRSP draft was held in June 2001, shortly before the 2001/02 Budget. The **National Steering Committee** was responsible for steering the process and finalising the PRSP draft (on the basis of a draft written by the PRSP Secretariat). The government strongly dominated this committee: Apart from the government representatives – the Permanent Secretaries – there were several institutions that are either government institutions (e.g. the Central Bureau of Statistics) or KANU-dominated (e.g. *Maendeleo ya Wanawake* or COTU). NGOs were represented by one delegate from the NGO Council. The private sector had two representatives. A **PRSP Secretariat** within MoFP was created to support the Steering Committee and to conduct the process. The Secretariat consisted of the MoFP staff members responsible for the MTEF design as well as two delegates from the NGO Council, one academic representing the private sector, and one UK DFID staff member representing the donors that funded the consultation process. Time constraints meant that the Secretariat's role was enhanced relative to the Steering Committee.

---

district. In both districts donor-supported programmes had been working to revitalise and reform the VDCs.

It was not possible to assess all the district reports, but in the view of some donors, several of them were more or less 'wish-lists'. The PRSP Secretariat then had the task of drafting the national PRSP based on the key sectors identified in the iPRSP.

The full PRSP was finalised in May/June 2001. It was supplemented with an implementation action plan in December 2001, and some thought was given to its integration with previously existing planning instruments. The government identified three key stages of the planning process: the National Poverty Eradication Plan – the long-term (15-year) strategy implemented by the Office of the President; the National Development Plan – the 5-year strategy implemented by the Ministry of Finance; and the PRSP – a relatively short-term strategy to implement the NPEP in 3-year rolling plans using the Medium-Term Expenditure Framework as a link. However, at this stage little progress had been made in harmonising this planning process.

At the end of the Moi presidency, there was still no agreement between the government and the IMF, and the IMF and World Bank were not willing to take the PRSP to their Boards. The PRSP will, however, have to be presented to the Boards before lending under the PRGF and related World Bank instruments can be resumed to the NARC government. On the basis of the IMF's disbursement plans, the PRSP was expected to go to the Boards in the second quarter of 2003, but this has proven over-optimistic.

Features of the consultation process

Positive features of the consultations that were noted include: the frank and open nature of the discussions; the improved working relations of communities and NGOs with local government in some districts; the integration of cross-cutting issues and specific themes (for example, gender, disability, youth, street children, pastoralists), which were voiced very effectively in some consultations; and the identification of actions in some communities which can be taken forward immediately with recourse to existing institutions and funds. The consultation process also had important positive effects on the participating NGOs, for example giving them experience of engaging with national and sectoral-level policies in poverty reduction work, and identifying needs for capacity-building around advocacy on national policies and processes.

Several weaknesses in, or constraints on, the PRSP consultative process were also identified. In some districts the tight time schedule is thought to have limited the level and quality of participation. Introductory information on the iPRSP and PRSP was only available just before the one-day workshops. 'Meeting-dominated' consultations limited the participation of some population categories. Despite the fact that the consultation was broad-based, its domination in some districts by government officials was said to limit the space for the common people to air their views freely.

Another notable weakness was the limited involvement of Members of Parliament. The launching of Kenya's consultative process towards a full PRSP was marked by a boycott of the process by sections of the country's MPs. This partly reflected inadequate efforts to involve the country's politicians in, or sensitise them about, the process. The boycott revolved around arguments that the Ksh 140 million pledged by the donor community for the district and community consultative seminars should have been used directly for poverty reduction projects; that the government still lacked serious commitment to poverty reduction; and that the country's poverty issues were well known and did not require more seminar discussions. In a few cases, Members of Parliament organised parallel poverty discussions in their constituencies.

Despite these weaknesses, we found many participants and observers expressing a positive and fairly optimistic view of the PRSP consultation process. While there had been previous experiences of consultation at the national level (for example, the NPEP process) as well as at district/local level (the PPAs), there had been no effective institutional link between the two, such as the PRSP framework promised.

Stakeholder perceptions

Since the breakdown of relations with the IMF and the donor community in 1997, increasing poverty, recession and poor macroeconomic management have had the effect of uniting many actors from the private sector and civil society in support of an agenda of far-reaching and fundamental reform. The appointment of the Economic Recovery Team in 1999 was seen as a major signal that the government was willing to implement reforms and improve governance. One of the first tasks of the team was to undertake the work necessary to be able to resume IMF borrowing, which entailed preparing an iPRSP.

The PRGF agreed (on the basis of the iPRSP) in July 2000 had the dubious accolade of being the lending agreement with the toughest conditionalities ever imposed by the IMF Board. However, most government, donor, academic and private sector stakeholders seemed less concerned about the implied challenges to national sovereignty than about whether the ends would eventually justify the means. In any case, the government's eventual inability to complete the agreed actions on corruption that were conditions of the PRGF agreement prompted the IMF to suspend its lending in December 2000, with other donors following suit.

The PRSP process (and, to a lesser extent, the PRGF agreement) received widespread support from a cross-section of the nation, making it seem qualitatively different from many of the previous externally-imposed 'solutions' to poor economic performance. However, there were some sectors of government (including the Office of the President) and some sections of the NGO community that held back support for the PRSP or were openly opposed to it. An important source of criticism of the approach was parliamentarians, some of whom saw the exclusion of Parliament from the preparation of the PRSP as an affront.

NGOs have had mixed reactions to the conditionalities accompanying the PRGF and World Bank/IDA lending. Some see them as a continuation of the externally imposed adjustment and liberalisation measures that have led to rising poverty or, at best, done little to mitigate the impact of economic crisis on the poor. Others support those conditionalities aimed at improving governance and curbing corruption but are more critical of other liberalisation measures. Many of the NGOs implementing the consultation process outside Nairobi were unaware of the link between mainstreaming poverty and regaining structural adjustment lending, and had limited understanding of the macro constraints facing the government and the magnitude of the consequences for government spending if concessional lending was not available.

Knowledge of the PRSP process and its goals was weakest among the stakeholders linked to ongoing donor-financed poverty projects. At the district level, several of the implementing NGOs encountered confusion as participants and community leaders struggled to differentiate between the PRSP consultative process and the recent initiative by the Poverty Eradication Commission which had instructed local and provincial government officials to set up committees to work on community plans for poverty reduction projects. In some cases funds had already been received and projects started.

This, combined with the much-politicised issue of the allocation of Ksh140 million to fund the consultation process, led people to think and expect that the PRSP was directly related to the distribution of funds for poverty projects in the country.

The high-level commitment to reform, heralded by the appointment of the Economic Recovery Team in 1999, was withdrawn in April 2001. In the final stages of the PRSP preparation process, leading members of the team were dismissed. In the aftermath of this, observers gave, on balance, a highly positive assessment of the team's achievements for the short period it had been in office. However, a year later strong doubts existed about whether the impact of the ERT would be able to be sustained. A test of this today will be whether a reform-oriented government (if that is what President Kibaki's government turns out to be) can quickly and convincingly restore momentum to the reform agenda previously being pursued.

Government plans, approach and capacities

In many senses, government capacity in Kenya is stronger than in the majority of low-income sub-Saharan African countries. The government enjoys one of the largest revenue takes in sub-Saharan Africa (24 percent of GDP). The provincial administration system controlled from the Office of the President extends the reach of central government down to the district and, through the appointment of chiefs, to the community level. Plans and policy documents are well designed and donors operating projects through line Ministries report that they are efficiently administered.

In the dominant culture, however, government offices are the site of rent-seeking activity. This extends from mismanagement of parastatals to widespread corruption and mismanagement of government funds, from central government down to provincial and district administration. Government activities are strongly linked to patronage politics at all levels, which permeates the activities of the small-scale and large-scale private sector and impacts negatively on policy and plan implementation, affecting both domestically and donor funded projects. The Kenyan Government has been strongly top-down and, until recently, non-transparent and substantially closed to independent opinion and non-partisan influence.

Despite severe macroeconomic instability and recession, and the prospect of budget support from donors like the UK Department for International Development, the European Union and the World Bank, the government's incentives to ensure that the PRSP is endorsed by the Bank and IMF Boards were overridden by the political imperative to keep donors at a distance through the election period. Once the new government settles in, the incentives to regain access to concessional borrowing, arising from financial necessity, will be strong. The past record, however, leads to widespread scepticism that the political elite, including sections represented in the new government, will be seriously committed to the implementation of the PRSP once the short-term goal of accessing donor funding is achieved.

The prospects remain, in this sense, quite bleak. Nevertheless, the introduction of the PRSP did result in a considerable opening up of government, with the consultation meetings and national stakeholder fora creating a dialogue among key stakeholders and facilitating more effective dissemination of information.

Donor plans, approaches and capacities

Most of the donor representatives interviewed were aware of and supported the key objectives of the PRSP initiative. Their views were, however, split with regard to whether these objectives were implementable in the prevailing economic and political situation in Kenya, characterised as it is by lack of transparency in the management of public affairs.

At the time of our initial study, one of the strongest supporters of PRSP implementation, based on the 'mainstreaming' principle, was DFID, UK. By early 2001, however, fears were expressed by some DFID officials that the PRSP had to some extent weakened the MTEF process, as some Treasury officials were required to work on the PRSP as well as the MTEF. This had tended to reduce the time and focus devoted to developing the MTEF. The World Bank, another strong supporter of the PRSP approach, has tried to improve donor co-ordination in this context through the Economic Governance Group (EGG).

A more sceptical view was taken by the German GTZ, which argued that, in a highly corrupt and non-reform-oriented environment, it is not possible to effectively mainstream poverty reduction through the national budget. Instead, GTZ prefers a bottom-up approach, starting with district institutional reforms. These should be accompanied by poverty reduction programmes financed by a transparent and non-government-monitored Anti-Poverty Fund, a key component of the NPEP approach (see Box 3.2).

One year after the study's first phase, in April 2002, none of the donors thought mainstreaming possible under the current political circumstances. Neither DFID nor other supporters of mainstreaming were giving aid in the form of direct budget support, though some of their funding was going into projects and programmes. Work on the MTEF was still ongoing in 2002, though the links between the PRSP and the MTEF remained only partially developed.

The corruption issue (reflected during the Moi regime in the tension surrounding the Kenya Anti-Corruption Authority, the Economic Crimes Bill and the Code of Conduct Bill) was foremost in donors' concerns about the viability of the PRSP approach in Kenya. Furthermore, doubts about the efficacy of the implementing institutions (especially at district and sub-district levels), and the strong control exerted by the Office of the President over sub-national constitutional issues, considerably reduced donors' willingness to buy into the process.

Box 3.2 The Anti-Poverty Trust Fund

The National Poverty Eradication Plan, launched by the government in early 1999 as Kenya's long-term poverty reduction strategy (to 2015), includes the establishment of an 'Anti-Poverty Trust Fund' Some in the government see the APTF as complementary to mainstreaming – an instrument 'to channel funding for small-scale projects'. The plan to establish the APTF was confirmed by the cabinet in 2000. Minister of State Sunkuli (Office of the President) repeated the confirmation in a speech in March 2001.

Supporters of the Anti-Poverty Trust Fund (e.g. GTZ and the African Development Bank) argue that an APTF could:

* contribute to poverty reduction; provided proper mechanisms for independent scrutiny of its use are in place, experience from several other countries suggests that such a fund can deliver much needed resources and services to the poor, and so play a vital role in developing and implementing pro-poor public policies;
* bridge the gap until a mainstreamed poverty reduction strategy really works (GTZ assessment: 4-5 years); corruption and lack of government commitment limit the extent to which mainstreaming poverty reduction through the budget will deliver improvements to the poor in the short and medium term;
* help to mobilise public as well as private funds for independently controlled poverty reduction programmes;
* contribute to institutional reforms at district level and strengthen the capacity of institutions to implement pro-poor policies – a necessary pre-condition for a successful mainstreaming of poverty reduction policies; and
* quickly respond to the expressed needs of people at district and sub-district levels, avoiding frustration and disenchantment among those who participated in the PRSP consultation process.

Other donors (e.g. DFID and the World Bank) are opposed to the APTF, as it could:

* undermine the necessary medium-term structural reform process, harming or derailing the processes and institutional developments that favour poverty reduction;
* undermine the shift in instruments of public policy towards meeting the needs of the poor better and empowering the poor to influence how their needs are defined and met;
* close the openings for political coalitions and alliances which benefit the poor that are beginning to emerge in Kenya;
* continue with the old-fashioned project development style, with little impact on the countrywide poverty situation;
* support projects that cannot be replicated or sustained once the development organisations (NGOs, donors) withdraw;
* be used to strengthen the patronage system and ethnically-based politics, especially in a pre-election phase, as the APTF is identified with the Office of the President;
* not be safeguarded against misuse by politicians and other politically connected power brokers; the critics do not believe in the possibility of establishing independent decision-making and monitoring rules and regulations within an APTF structure; and
* undermine efforts to de-politicise poverty reduction programmes.

Despite the compelling reasons for concern about the viability of the PRSP in Kenya, as the process moved from the Interim to the full PRSP many donors engaged actively with it. A group of donors provided finance for the consultations, which, in view of the fact that the government had failed to allocate any of its budget to the process, was a critical factor in its success. In addition to financing the consultation process, some donors (DFID, GTZ and UNDP) became actively involved in developing monitoring strategies, and others (including GTZ, Sida and DFID) supported government capacity-building in pro-poor planning and budgeting. But the PRSP has now been on the table since summer 2001, and, up to December 2002, none of the donors saw any immediate prospect of supporting its implementation.

3.4   What difference has the PRSP made?

The politics of poverty reduction

Kenya's political system can be loosely defined as a minimally institutionalised state (Moore and Putzel, 1999). In spite of the introduction of multi-party politics in 1991 after more than two decades of a single-party regime, the country has not yet established a strong democracy with effective checks and balances. For the entire post-independence period, the Kenyan political system has been strongly influenced by the personal rule of the first two presidents.

Both Kenyatta and Moi were able to dominate the political scene, partly through deft manipulation of ethnic politics, which made the opposition parties ineffective agents of institutionalised democracy. Nonetheless, more than a decade after the establishment of a multi-party political system, there is some small evidence of increasing space for competitive political parties (though these are still dominated by ethnic affiliations). Civil society, NGOs, the private sector and other pressure groups have also become better organised. This has allowed them to make more effective demands for improved government services and increased participation in national decision-making. This has, in turn, facilitated stronger articulation of pro-poor measures.

Kenya's PRSP process culminated in an environment dominated by the country's 'political succession' issue, which significantly distracted the attention of policy-makers from poverty reduction efforts. The extensive political patronage network has over time used government development funding to sustain certain pro-establishment politicians who are seen to be more 'development conscious', and to weaken political rebels by making them seem unable to bring about development projects in their areas of jurisdiction. This is clearly one of the factors underlying the ongoing debate on the use of poverty funds in the country's poverty reduction efforts and mainstreaming poverty financing into the budget.

A related dimension is the silent struggle between the Office of the President

(OP) and the technocrats in the Ministry of Finance, over who should take charge of the poverty reduction process. The National Poverty Eradication Plan (NPEP) was prepared under the auspices of the OP through the Poverty Eradication Commission (PEC). The introduction of the PRSP saw a shift of control over poverty eradication activities from the OP to the Ministry of Finance, which introduced considerable tension between the two arms of government. Whether the net effect will be to strengthen national commitment and political will to focus on poverty reduction (by putting it in the Ministry of Finance, further from the grasp of patronage-based politics) will depend on whether the new government takes steps to resolve this tension.

A particular issue is the way the political system operates at the local-government level. The politicians' desire to retain control of the grassroots is an obstacle to current efforts to reform the District Development Committees (DDCs) to make them more effective instruments of poverty reduction. The DDCs and the provincial administrative system have served as a key tool of political control by the executive in the country since the colonial period. The current pressure to reform the DDCs by having elected chairmen of DDCs instead of District Commissioners is largely interpreted as an effort to weaken the political control of the executive and to some extent, the ruling party, in the countryside. This partly explains the haphazard and *ad hoc* manner in which the changes in DDCs are being implemented in various parts of the country. Reports in 2000-1 that the President had directed that districts with ruling-party Members of Parliament would not need to change the format of their DDCs, are indicative of the close links that have existed between party politics and the operations of the DDCs.

The rising role of the NGOs and civil society institutions in socio-economic and political development activities among the communities, and the increasing competition for donor resources between these organisations and the central government, is another political dimension in Kenya's poverty reduction debate. As already noted, there has been a marked shift by donors in recent years to channelling resources through NGOs and civil society institutions, which are perceived as more effective and less corrupt. Because of the fear that NGOs and civil society activities could undermine the power of the politicians at the grassroots, there has often been considerable friction between the politicians, the civil service and the NGOs and civil society organisations. It took a long time for the government to begin to accept these other actors in the development process. Only now are there are indications that attitudes are changing.

Possible second-round effects

Despite the short time allocated to the PRSP process, there are indications that it initiated changes that are likely to have a long-term impact on national institutions and on the attitudes and activities of a wide cross-section of actors in the development process. More than any other national programme in the post-independence period, the PRSP has elevated public participation in the debate on poverty and wider socio-economic development issues.

The PRSP process significantly enhanced media coverage of poverty and related issues. After the launching of the iPRSP in a national consultative forum in March 2000, the mass media carried more articles and discussions on poverty. This played an important role in raising awareness of the problem among the general public, one of the spill-over benefits being a move by some NGOs and civil society groups to revise their programmes to devote more attention to poverty reduction. The process thus seemed likely to attract more financial resources to poverty-related programmes, as the government, donors, NGOs, civil society and other stakeholders push poverty up their list of priorities.

Some of the actors in the consultative process suggested that broad-based stakeholder participation had strengthened the communities' sense of self-determination. This had led to a shift in their attitudes to initiation of their own development activities towards poverty alleviation, with or without government and donor support. The consultative process at the national, district and community levels also provided a good opportunity for the various stakeholders to work together. It enabled them to share information and to appreciate better each other's capacities, weaknesses and methods of operation, helping to reduce the prejudices that tend to exist among them.

At the same time, it generated an enormous amount of community-level data, which, if effectively processed, could radically change the country's planning in terms of priorities and new insights. Government officials in some districts agreed that, in some cases, the community participation was able to bring dimensions and insights which were radically different from those that inspired past district development plans.

The Kenyan PRSP consultation process may thus have contributed to a number of longer-term institutional spin-off effects. First, it seems likely that it added force to the call for more democratic and participatory elements in Kenyan politics. The openness the government showed towards debate on general policy issues set a precedent. Kenyan governments may now be expected to meet the rising public demand for more open discussions on all poverty-related decisions, for example in the context of the annual budget.

Secondly, the most important institutional changes may not have been at national but at regional level. The broad consultations at district and divisional levels all over the country may have raised the demand for more community participation in the decision-making process.

Third, the institutional exclusion of Parliament from the PRSP process may have increased the demands for its *inclusion*. If so, this could mark the beginning of a more systematic involvement of Parliament in poverty reduction politics, an important manifestation of which could be its greater engagement in the budget process, which has been dominated by the executive arm of government.[5] At present, Parliament's first contact with the budget is when the Minister of Finance delivers his budget speech ('budget day'), only hours before it comes into effect. A first step to overcome this institutional constraint could be the establishment of a parliamentary budget office supporting the MPs in their work. There are initiatives within Parliament to create such an institution.

Fourth, the relatively well-developed NGO community in Kenya used the PRSP process to improve its organisation with respect to economic and poverty issues, and this may lead to more institutionalised advocacy work on poverty issues in future. This would naturally have secondary effects on the governance framework. NGOs have been demanding more involvement in the budget process, for instance.

Fifth, the PRSP process may also have had an impact on public debate on poverty issues. An indication of this is the fact that the PRSP was widely discussed in both the print and electronic media, in sharp contrast with the experience in many other countries.

The system of public financial management

Poverty projects in Kenya have a long history of being used as vehicles for patronage politics, with little attention to the overall pattern of public action for development. Up to 2000/1, the budget was not linked to planning, and out-turns diverged substantially from allocations as a result of political influence. Allocations were in general little known among the public, particularly at the district level, while corruption and mismanagement have been endemic.

One important trend precipitated by the PRSP process is that poverty reduction is beginning to become less vulnerable to partisanship and patronage and more issue-based, with a general shift to assigning responsibility for poverty reduction and emergency relief to technical Ministries.

Some examples of the institutional changes that occurred as part of the PRSP process include:

- stronger partnership between the government, local and community leaders and NGOs in activities related to poverty alleviation programmes;
- a shift of the main poverty focus in the central government to the Ministry of Finance (Planning/Treasury) and other technical Ministries;
- greater openness on the part of central government to the advice and participation of non-governmental stakeholders in planning and budgeting;
- increased awareness in the Ministry of Finance and other Ministries of the role that a bottom-up approach can play in budget prioritisation for poverty alleviation.

---

5. Greater parliamentary engagement with the budget could, of course, also be used to effect anti-poor changes in the budget.

However, there is still considerable resistance to these institutional changes. The successes achieved during 2000-1 in reforming and institutionalising poverty reduction were not sustained in the run-up to the general elections during 2002.

The key constraint to reforming Kenya's public financial management remains lack of strong commitment from political leaders who wield immense power and influence in the country. Further down the ladder, parliamentarians are divided in their support for the reform process. Voting in parliament in the recent past has led to enactment of anti-poor measures or blocking, obstructing and undermining of pro-poor processes and measures.

There are various reasons why parliamentarians oppose reform. In some cases there are valid reasons to object to the way that legislation has been drafted, although in some cases, reforms have been resisted as a result of misguided belief that a return to the control regime of the past is an important way to restore economic growth and reduce poverty. Others oppose changes due to the fear that reforms could weaken the position of those with vested interests in the present regime.

The effectiveness of the MTEF and PRSP in delivering services to the poor will depend on the capacity of various district and local government institutions. There has been no clearly agreed reform programme for provincial, district and local government that enjoys strong political backing and the commitment required to drive such a process through. The current highly centralised provincial and district government structure is strongly linked to the political patronage system and is thus difficult to tackle. Following the removal of Dr Leakey and some other key personalities in the Economic Recovery Team in 2001, the push for reforms did not continue to feature prominently in the national agenda during the run up to the elections in 2002.

Evidence from the district consultations suggests that there is no single democratically accountable institution that works consistently well at the local level. In some districts it was thought that with reforms, District Development Committees could be made accountable and democratic. In other districts it was thought that county councils are likely to utilise that potential once the Local Authority Reform Act is implemented. National and international NGOs have an agreed strategy to resuscitate the Village Development Committees in districts where they work.

VDCs were constituted under the progressive District Focus for Rural Development programme initiated in 1980, though they were subsequently discredited due to widespread mismanagement and corruption. By reinstating VDCs, a participatory planning process with a wide degree of ownership has been successfully started in several districts. Kenyan NGOs have in the past successfully promoted other democratic pro-poor institutions in some districts. In some districts, donors have introduced new participatory village-level institutions with varying degrees of success in terms of their ownership and potential sustainability.

In short, there is no easy way to by-pass the problems experienced with management of poverty expenditures at the national level by going straight to the local level. Donor dependency is high in much of rural Kenya and years of attempts to implement poverty projects have produced a complex set of conflicting and cooperative relationships between donors and recipients. High-level political commitment is needed to change attitudes and the quality of recipient-donor relations. Champions are needed to push through measures that empower poor people and change embedded attitudes among government people and donors alike.

So what difference does the PRSP make?

In a relatively short period, the PRSP made a considerable impact on the management of the national economy. The 2000/1 and 2001/2 budgets laid more emphasis on the theme of poverty reduction than previous ones. They were the first budgets to be prepared under the MTEF, a three-year rolling plan for fiscal years 2000/1-2002/3, and they provided an opportunity to translate the first two years of planning under the PRSP into some annual estimates.

For the first time, the 2000/1 budget specifically identified 'Core Poverty Programmes', from which no re-allocation of budget resources was allowed, in an attempt to ring-fence key poverty reduction programmes. The ring-fencing was tested when the IMF suspended the disbursement of funds in December 2000. The resulting shortfall meant that 50 percent cuts were required across the board, but efforts were made to protect priority poverty reduction expenditures. The 2001/2 budget presented in June 2001, soon after the full PRSP draft had been presented at the national stakeholders' forum, made greater efforts to incorporate poverty issues in the budget.

The intended close link between the PRSP and the MTEF was expected to have other advantages. First, it was hoped that it might prove an efficient way of quickly achieving key initial steps in poverty mainstreaming. Second, it included all central and line Ministries in the poverty dialogue. Its main disadvantage was its failure to provide effectively for analysis of the links and feedback mechanisms between macroeconomic performance, meso and micro institutions, and sectors. It was for this reason that the iPRSP was unable to link successfully the sectoral and the bottom-up approach to poverty reduction proposed in the NPEP. Current indications are that the full PRSP may not do much better in this regard.

Institutionalising sustainable poverty reduction policies in Kenya implies not only consulting all stakeholders but also ensuring the appropriate participation of all relevant democratic institutions, especially the Parliament. While Kenya's Parliament is weak, bypassing it is no solution in the long run. There is need to work out a creative solution to overcome this dilemma.

3.5 Monitoring the PRSP: a second chance?

An evolving agenda

Our first impression, in November 2000, was that the capacity for poverty monitoring was very weak, since:

- the Central Bureau of Statistics (CBS) is unable to produce timely and accurate macroeconomic and poverty data;
- analysis of past poverty, macroeconomic and social trends and establishment of benchmarks is hampered by low quality data and inconsistencies;
- the demand for poverty data has been donor-driven and has not paid due regard to the need for the CBS to fulfil its core functions; and
- there has been no effective co-ordination of donor experience in district and other local-level projects on which the government can draw.

The government shared the above concerns and, by the time of our second phase of research, had taken steps to address them by appointing a new head of the CBS with a proven track record of delivering change. Plans had been made to address the limited analytical capacity of the CBS by mobilising teams to package proposals for analytical work that could then be undertaken by national institutions with the appropriate capacity, such as the Kenya Institute for Public Policy Research and Analysis (KIPPRA), the Institute for Policy Analysis and Research (IPAR) and the universities. Success in one area of weakness, the ability to get the data out, had already been achieved with the delivery of the Census in January 2001; internal reforms in CBS working practices proved capable of addressing this problem. Improving data quality was judged to be a longer-term exercise, involving not only the CBS in the case of national accounts statistics, but other government departments with data-collecting responsibilities.

One of the challenges we identified for the full PRSP process was to inform stakeholders about the role poverty monitoring can play in increasing the credibility of the PRSP and providing the right incentive structure to achieve its goals. Another was to draw up a short, strategic list of input, outcome and process indicators of progress towards poverty reduction goals, which is appropriate to the existing national capacity. New systems and institutions (inside and outside government) might need to be introduced to provide process and outcome indicators. The PEC and CBS would need technical assistance to co-ordinate this process effectively.

By the time of our second mission, the initial steps had been taken to address these issues. In contrast to the iPRSP where monitoring had been grafted on to the document, for the full PRSP monitoring had been integrated into the process as a cross-cutting issue for the thematic groups working on its production. The vision was for monitoring not to be confined to government alone, but to bring in national institutions such as the Monitoring and Evaluation Association of the University of Nairobi and work with donor partners, as, for example, with the GTZ technical assistance provided to the Ministry of Finance.

Demand

There is a massive demand for poverty-related data in Kenya. Welfare monitoring surveys were undertaken in 1994 and 1997, and people are now turning to the need to widen the understanding of poverty to the regions and to think and plan how to best go about this. New techniques are being introduced, for example the Ministry of Health has started to use Geographical Information System mapping as a planning aid for their efforts to roll back malaria.

Demand comes from a number of national sources in and outside government and from donors. Parliament has become engaged and has asked for discussion about town council statistics. Sections of civil society are playing a new and active role in the demand for data and monitoring. For example, the gender thematic group stressed the need for monitoring; and organisations for disability made a powerful case for the need for basic information on the numbers of disabled people in Kenya as a prerequisite for voice and impact in national planning processes during the PRSP consultative workshop.

The role of information in a PRSP was weakly conceptualised at the iPRSP stage, and there was no discussion of the role that various types of indicators, input, process and outcome, could play in the PRSP. Technical constraints included the lack of capacity in Treasury to introduce several reform instruments like MTEF and PRSP simultaneously. This has tended to limit the capacity to design and implement monitoring schemes. However, these limitations were later recognised and steps were being taken to address them. The inclusiveness of the proposed institutional arrangements looked promising, but there was little or no progress in implementing this vision during 2002. It remains to be seen whether the proposals will be taken up again now that the pre-election uncertainties have been resolved.

Donors and national institutions

Donors have traditionally been involved in funding data collection work in Kenya. More recently donor support has been used for upstream work. For example, DFID supported an initiative to publish the results of the 1993/4 urban household survey. Donors have also supported the development of indicators (UNICEF) and technical innovations to improve the timeliness of data production. A key shift that may help these efforts to lead to a strengthening of national institutions is the recognition of the importance of information and monitoring by the government, reflected in the appointment of a senior and highly respected official to head CBS.

Donors have also supported the independent think tank, KIPPRA. This organisation is close to government, which for some is a weakness, but it means that it has the ear of government and is consequently effective in promoting a shift towards evidence-based policy making. This shift was noted with approval by several sources in the Ministry of Finance.

3.6 Towards a new aid relationship

One of the most marked changes in donor behaviour we observed during our fieldwork was the shift towards a broader engagement with the PRSP process. At the start, justifiable doubts about its viability led many donors to hold back from active engagement. Later, a large number shifted to active support of the consultation part of the process, despite harbouring doubts about the initative as a whole.

While many donors had supported the development of the NPEP, launched in early 1999, most of them had shifted to the PRSP approach by the end of the year; that is, within a few months. For some stakeholders, this was because the PRS approach offered a genuinely new opportunity to bring together a broad coalition of reformers – private sector, NGOs, government and civil society – to implement the reforms needed to address corruption and secure sustained poverty reduction and economic growth. Others, more cynically, held that this confirmed their view that the PRSP process was 'just another donor conditionality', which should not be taken seriously in the long run.

The institutional by-passing of Parliament led to many MPs perceiving the PRSP exercise as an issue largely for donors and the executive. This perception has contributed to Parliament's growing assertiveness with regard to important decisions about institutional changes such as the Economic Crimes Bill, and the reluctance of many MPs to support the process. In recognition of this, donors have started engaging in dialogue with Parliament. For instance, an IMF mission met members of the Parliamentary Finance Committee in January 2001 to discuss reform issues. However, in terms of the 2000-1 PRSP process, this gesture was seen by some MPs as 'too little, too late'. And with only 93 members of the previous Parliament and 106 new members, it is hard to predict whether the new Parliament will have the inclination or capacity to engage with PRSP issues.

The rivalry between the two poverty strategies within the Kenyan Government (the PRSP and NPEP) is one of the unresolved problems. Under the Moi regime indications were that, as long as the PRSP was not placed under the NPEP and controlled by the Office of the President, influential stakeholders within the government would resist it. On the other hand, there were fears that a stronger role for the Poverty Eradication Commission, under the Office of the President, would weaken the role of the Treasury, lead to less donor support for the process and leave poverty reduction still vulnerable to the partisanship and patronage that have afflicted it in the past. It is as yet too early to tell whether political power will remain so highly centralised under the NARC government.

Related to the rivalry between the PRSP and NPEP is the divergence among the donors between poverty mainstreaming (through the MTEF and the budget) and poverty funds (including support for district reforms) as the optimal instrument for implementing poverty reduction policies. This is a divergence that is likely to remain as some donors judge the best opportunity to support reform as being early commitment to budget support, following an IMF agreement, and others want tangible proof of improved performance before altering their aid disbursements. Depending on how the Kenyan context evolves, the Ugandan example (Poverty Action Fund *within* the budget) could become a way of harmonising the two ideas.

Donor behaviour and the need for dialogue

In some important respects donor coordination improved during the PRSP process. Positive steps included:

- support for a donor representative on the PRSP Technical Committee;
- greater coordination of donor support for monitoring through UNDP;
- creation of a donor consortium to fund the consultation exercise; and
- donors retiring into the background or reducing their representation as the PRSP preparation took shape, with more nationals driving the process.

Regarding the Anti-Poverty Trust Fund, however, more dialogue would have been desirable, and at an earlier stage. The issue is by no means resolved satisfactorily yet. Overall, our conclusion is that greater effort must be made to recognise the fact that the PRSP is operating in a multi-donor environment, where different donors have different ways of working at the local level. Programmes at district level will continue, with a multiplicity of poverty reduction-related goals. This is desirable in the Kenyan context where poverty is high, the MTEF is at an early stage and government expenditure is extremely limited. The effects of budget and other reforms will inevitably take a long time to result in tangible improvements in service delivery and economic opportunity for the poor.

Unfortunately, we found several donor representatives in April 2002 taking the view that donor coordination had weakened recently. Reasons could be because, as of then, there was no PRSP implementation, aid inflows had decreased further, there was no IMF agreement in place, and the overall reform process had slowed to a crawl (in other words, there was relatively little work to coordinate). This suggests that donor coordinating fora need to review current activities and engage in constructive dialogue at the beginning of a PRSP process, with the aim of making sure that interventions at all levels are mutually supportive.

In the context of a corrupt government, agreement or consensus needs to be reached on what forms of development assistance can minimise the opportunities for the diversion of funds for political purposes or to support patronage relationships and, of course, mismanagement of funds generally. All donors share the goal of poverty reduction. Ways must be found to accommodate these efforts within a framework that is consistent with, and can build support for, national ownership of a poverty reduction strategy as the central plank of government policy.

3.7 Conclusions

A question our study aimed to address is whether the Kenyan PRSP has introduced a new aid dynamic, different from the older approaches of the IFIs and bilateral donors. Past donor-government relations exemplify the problems that the PRSP is trying to address – nominal compliance with reform conditionalities accompanied by massive institutional dependence on aid. Is there any evidence that the PRSP has induced greater ownership in Kenya?

At the time of completing this chapter, the future of the PRSP was uncertain. IMF lending was suspended after Kenya failed to meet key conditionalities. The IMF had indicated that revision of the PRSP and the passage of anti-corruption legislation are prior actions that the government must take in order to start discussions on a new programme. The NARC government came to power on election pledges which include regaining access to donor lending, and the domestic debt build-up, combined with the recent recession, means that there are huge incentives to gain access to concessional finance. The past record, however, leads to widespread scepticism that the political elite, including sections represented in the new government, will be seriously committed to the implementation of the PRSP once the short-term goal of accessing donor funding is achieved.

In the final months of the Moi regime, after IMF lending had been suspended, lack of political will and domestic ownership of poverty reduction goals and the PRSP process, extending to all quarters of government, especially the top echelons, was, more than ever, clearly evident. However, it had seemed for a while that the PRSP had introduced changes into the donor-recipient relationship and that domestic ownership had increased. We sum up below our findings on these points and identify some recommendations from Kenya's experience that may be relevant to its PRSP process and that of other countries in future.

Some important new dynamics have been introduced into the movement for economic reform and poverty reduction in Kenya as a result of the PRSP process. While the process was under way, poverty had never before been so high on the agenda or given so much media coverage. For several sections of civil society, national ownership of poverty reduction efforts was thought to have increased considerably. This laid down important pre-conditions for broader commitment by government, politicians and civil society to plans and strategies that are poverty-focused. It was creating the prerequisites for new partnerships between the government and donors.

These dynamics were suspended in the run-up to the elections, and it cannot be taken for granted that they will be resumed. Moreover, even if the PRSP is endorsed and becomes the basis for a renewal of concessional lending, it will not be worth having, unless the reforms needed to restore growth are implemented. Nevertheless, we think it worth underlining the achievements of the PRSP to date in Kenya, however ephemeral they may turn out to be.

Successes and failures of the PRSP process: how to do it better

On the negative side, unnecessary resistance to the PRSP was induced by failing to include Parliament as an institution in the process. While some parliamentarians might always criticise the PRSP as donor-driven, others could have been won over sooner if appropriate measures had been taken earlier. In future, PRSP processes should include deliberate measures to involve Parliament as an institution and to enable support for capacity-building efforts aimed at the dissemination to MPs of the PRSP's aims and intermediate outputs.[6]

More positively, Kenya's experience shows that, even where there is no high-level commitment to poverty reduction, participatory consultation processes are valuable in themselves. Key to the Kenyan experience was the involvement of NGOs in both the implementation of the consultation process and throughout the institutional structure of the PRSP. Under these arrangements, in-depth consultations were held in 25 districts. By no means all were an unqualified success in terms of their engagement with or representation of the poor; nevertheless, a large number of districts reported several positive features. These effects are important enough to justify the time, effort and cost that the exercise involved in the districts. It follows that broad, comprehensive consultations should be considered even where little commitment to poverty reduction exists at the top levels of government.

The question of how to maintain the momentum of a PRSP consultative process and to institutionalise an ongoing dialogue among the stakeholders should be very high on the agenda. Interim measures that bring universal benefits to poor communities should be identified in order to meet expectations raised by the consultation process and should be quickly implemented as part of the PRSP. The removal of school fees served such a purpose in Uganda and Tanzania, and it is noteworthy that the first policy implemented by the NARC government was to abolish primary school fees.

---

6. A cross-sectoral committee on poverty reduction policies should be established. As the PRSP is by concept an ongoing process with a regular cycle, such a parliamentary committee could function as a forum for debate on related issues and as an institution to monitor government policies in this area.

Donors, politics and 'ownership'

Politics has emerged at every stage of the PRSP process in Kenya. In every country, poverty reduction depends as much on political as on economic changes. It follows that donors need to seek to understand the nature of the political environment in which they operate. In particular, they should not underestimate the strength of opposition to the PRSP by those who see themselves, or their vested interests, undermined by the process.

Donors supported significant elements of the PRSP process in Kenya. Some of the particular forms of technical assistance used increased ownership and had generally good results. Examples include: financing technical assistance in areas such as the Economic Recovery Team, members of the Technical Secretariat, and NGOs as consultation implementors; funding the consultative process through NGOs and the Treasury; and funding the employment as technical assistants of skilled Kenyan nationals with a good understanding of poverty and/or international aid and economics. Our conclusion on this is that the support was consistent with building up ownership, and that donors should not hold back from financing elements of the PRSP because of fears about ownership.

References

Central Bank of Kenya (2002) *Monthly Economic Review*, Nairobi, September.*East African Standard* (2003) 'IMF to Resume Aid from July', 18 January, Nairobi.

Government of Kenya (1997) *The Second Participatory Poverty Assessment Study – Kenya*, Volume I (report prepared by AMREF and the Human Resources and Social Services Department of the Office of the Vice-President and Ministry of Planning and National Development for the Government of Kenya). Nairobi.

Ministry of Finance and Planning (2000) 'A Facilitator's Guide: Facilitating the Consultative Process for the PRSP'. Nairobi, Nov.

Moore, Mick and Putzel, James (1999) *Thinking Strategically about Politics and Poverty*. IDS Working Paper No. 101. Brighton: Institute of Development Studies at the University of Sussex, October.

Murungi, Kiraitu (1998) 'Ethnicity and Multi-Partyisim in Kenya', in Kivutha Kibwana (ed.), *Constitutional Law and Politics in Africa: A Case Study of Kenya*. Nairobi: Claripress Limited for Faculty of Law, University of Nairobi.

Nyang'oro, Julius E. (2000) 'Civil Society, Structural Adjustment and Democratization in Kenya', in Bensabat Kleinberg and Janine A. Clark (eds), *Economic Liberalization, Democratization and Civil Society in the Developing World*. Basingstoke and New York: Macmillan.

Chapter 4: Malawi

by Rob Jenkins and Maxton Tsoka*

There are few grounds for believing that the implicit hypothesis contained within the PRSP approach – that PRSPs will change the nature of conditionality, leading to enhanced ownership of the strategies themselves, and therefore more effective implementation – will hold true in the case of Malawi. This is despite the fact that the PRSP formulation process has been among the country's most participatory policy-making exercises to date, with civil society engaging in both policy dialogue and co-ordinated protest. Key constraints are an absence of high-level political commitment to serious reform and the lack of a thoroughgoing overhaul of conditionality by the IFIs.

4.1 Introduction

Malawi is one of the poorest countries in the world – whether judged by GNP per capita, the UNDP's Human Development Index or its Human Poverty Index. What combination of policies would be most effective in addressing this huge challenge is a vital question. It is not, however, the immediate concern of this chapter. As in the rest of the volume, our emphasis is on the *process* by which a Poverty Reduction Strategy Paper has been developed in Malawi, and what this indicates about the usefulness of the PRSP *approach*. In particular, what likelihood is there of the PRSP process effecting a transformation in the relationship between donors, governments and local civil societies, such that public action becomes more sharply focused on reducing poverty?

Factors unique to Malawi's economic and political trajectory, including the history of its relationship with external donors, have played a major role in shaping the PRSP process to date, and will continue to do so for some time. Therefore, we begin in Section 2 by identifying key features of the political and economic context that have a bearing on the prospects for the PRSP approach to yield the hoped-for benefits. Section 3 then examines the process by which the PRSP concept has been introduced in Malawi and the way in which the document itself has been formulated, bearing in mind that there is, as yet, only limited experience of trying to *implement* it.

Section 4 is the core of the chapter. It addresses the question of how much difference the PRSP initiative has made. It analyses the prospects for the

* Birkbeck College, University of London, and Centre for Social Research, Zomba, Malawi.

PRSP process to institutionalise poverty reduction as a central focus of public action (particularly with respect to public-expenditure management and larger issues of governance). The issues of performance monitoring, and the informational requirements thereof, are dealt with in Section 5. Section 6 explores the conditions under which the PRSP might become the basis for better coordination between government and external donors. Section 7 summarises the implications of the Malawian case for the 'ownership hypothesis' that underlies all the studies in this volume.

4.2 Poverty reduction and the policy context

The political context

Malawi emerged from thirty years of one-party rule in 1994, when the country's first multi-party elections were held. The United Democratic Front (UDF) won those elections and Mr Bakili Muluzi became Malawi's first democratically elected president, pushing the Malawi Congress Party (MCP) into opposition. The other main political party, AFORD, emerged as a third force in parliamentary politics.

While at the level of formal constitutional structures, Malawi became a democratic system, liberal politics is only slowly taking root, and has received setbacks at various points since 1994. Malawi took a large step in the direction of democratic consolidation in 1999 when it held, on schedule, its second round of multiparty elections. President Muluzi was re-elected, though not without charges of vote-rigging and other electoral irregularities from opposition parties and independent observers. The catalogue of questionable practices involved the full range of electoral activities: the demarcation of constituencies, voter registration, the composition and role of the electoral commission, media coverage, the use of donor funds, and the announcement of the election results (Patel, 2000). This has made opposition rhetoric since 1999 perhaps more vitriolic than it might otherwise have been. And, in turn, the failure of the MCP to accept the legitimacy of the electoral verdict has arguably increased the sense of defensiveness on the part of the president and other senior members of the ruling UDF. This, along with deep and continuing divisions within the opposition MCP, has made constructive relations between government and opposition on issues of policy and governance extremely elusive.

Partisan conflict has been accentuated by regional divisions. Each of the three main parties is associated with a support base in one of Malawi's three regions – north, central and south. While the regional divide is perhaps the main cleavage shaping the nature of the party system, it does not correspond (or rather corresponds very imperfectly) with tribal or linguistic divisions. This form of regionalism has been characterised as 'atypical because it did not dovetail closely with ethnicity' (Reynolds, 1999: 148). There have nevertheless been consistent complaints from opposition leaders that the government has distributed a disproportionate share of the benefits from development schemes to the southern region, the ruling UDF's political base.

An important institutional variable that has shaped the nature of political debate over policy issues is the cabinet system of government. Malawi's constitution allows the president to choose ministers – as in the American system – from non-parliamentarians. This theoretically has the advantage of insulating ministers from the day-to-day pressures of patronage politics based on servicing electoral constituencies, and (again, in theory) could have served to neutralise complaints of partisan bias in government policy making and execution. In practice, neither potential benefit has been realised.

The press – and the right to free expression – is without doubt less subject to government restrictions than it was under the period of one-party rule. Still, journalists and editors who criticise the actions and policies of the government continue to receive direct and indirect threats from government representatives.[1] The state-run Malawi Broadcasting Corporation (MBC) is notoriously biased in favour of the government, and is said to ban its reporters from conducting interviews with certain members of civil society known to be critical of government. Some private radio stations have taken on more controversial topics in phone-in programmes, which provide an outlet for criticism, if not fully informed and moderated debate.

Coverage of poverty and related issues in the press is relatively frequent. During the period of the field research for this chapter the World Bank-Government of Malawi Public Expenditure Review (PER) meeting was reported in great detail. But much of the coverage consisted of long direct quotations from the documents, with reports of this one-day meeting spread out over two weeks. This suggests a lack of investigative energy on the part of journalists as much as a genuine commitment to analysing the relevant issues in depth.

One of the key issues that dominated politics in recent years was President Muluzi's desire to run for a third term in office. (The next national elections are due in 2004.) This would require a constitutional amendment, as under the current dispensation a two-term limit prevents the president contesting again. Malawi's two main church groups – by far the largest and most respected organisations in civil society – both pleaded with the president to respect the current constitutional term-limit, and are said by some to have given their blessing to the creation of a new political formation, the Malawi

---

1. One example is found in *The Chronicle* (20 August 2001, p. 1), according to which the President's Press Secretary issued a letter to Mr Chinyeke Tembo, Managing Editor of *The People's Eye*, stating that 'you will be held responsible for all the personal articles contained in *People's Eye* Newspaper in which His Excellency the President Dr Bakili Muluzi is continuously being personally attacked for reasons best known to yourself and your sponsors'. This was one of the more low-key incidents of which the study team was made aware.

Forum for Democracy, partly out of a desire to rein in the President's ambitions.

In general, Malawi is progressing towards a more open, representative form of politics. Nevertheless, the tendency for government to over-react to expressions of democratic protest has remained something of a hangover from the previous political order.

Moreover, many of the government's efforts to improve governance have clearly involved ulterior political motives. 'Tough action' on high-level official corruption has been, extremely selectively, directed mainly at political opponents of the ruling circle. 'Anti-defection' laws (coupled with restrictions on the freedom of elected officials to participate in non-party groupings) further reinforce the image of a ruling clique preoccupied with choking off internal party dissidence.

The economic context

During the 1990s agriculture constituted 33 percent of Malawi's GDP. Three-fourths of this is produced by smallholder farmers, mostly for subsistence. The manufacturing and mining sectors contributed only 17 percent, on average, to GDP, and services 27 percent. Agricultural products constitute the bulk of Malawi's exports, while the manufacturing sector contributes less than a fifth. In the period 1997-2000, agricultural crops accounted for 85 percent of the value of all exports, tobacco alone contributing 63 percent.

Malawi's exports barely cover current imports. For example, in 1998 exports covered just 93 percent of imports. In the period 1994-2000, the current account deficit averaged 6.9 percent of GDP. The economy's narrow, undiversified base also limits its revenue-generating capacity. As a result, locally generated revenue covered only about 56.1 percent of public expenditure during 1994/95-1999/00, despite a high revenue-to-GDP ratio of 16 percent over the same period.

Grants assist in narrowing the gap between expenditure and revenue. However, it is foreign loans and domestic borrowing that close the gap fully. In fact, in difficult years when even external inflows are not enough – for instance, the democratic transition period of 1993/94 and 1994/95 – and when inflows are slower or simply low, as in 1997/98, domestic borrowing helps to make up the difference.

The World Bank is, by far, Malawi's largest creditor, accounting for as much as 73 percent of the multilateral debt. Japan is by far Malawi's biggest bilateral creditor, holding roughly 85 percent of the country's debt to the Paris Club of bilateral creditors and 11 percent of total debt. Commercial debt was only two percent of the total debt stock and this was mainly contracted with UK commercial creditors. Since the HIPC2 Initiative only covers debt contracted from multilateral donors, the structure of Malawi's debt means that Malawi stands to gain from the initiative.

Previous poverty reducing efforts and plans

Prior to the PRSP, Malawi had no history of serious (prioritised, costed, outcome-oriented) poverty plans. The policy documents of Hastings (Kamuzu) Banda, Malawi's first President, bore no resemblance to a poverty-reducing plan. World Bank and IMF structural adjustment programmes came to Malawi in the 1980s. These policies were enshrined in Policy Framework Papers (PFPs) that were littered with 'poverty reduction' objectives.

After the World Bank's 1990 *World Development Report* on poverty, both the Malawian government of the time and its main aid donors stepped up their rhetoric on poverty and poverty reduction. Policy discussions began to focus on the social dimensions of adjustment and the need for safety nets. However, it was not until the change of government in 1994 that concrete steps began to be taken with the launch of the Poverty Alleviation Programme (PAP).

As part of this initiative, the government established Technical Working Committees (TWCs) to develop plans for reducing poverty, and a Poverty Alleviation Programme Coordinating Unit within the Ministry of Economic Planning and Development (as it was then known). Over time, the unit has oscillated between being an important locus of long-term planning and a 'dumping ground' for non-performing or out-of-favour ministers and civil servants. The TWCs did some preliminary work that helped in producing a policy framework for the PAP. The policy framework did not have concrete plans on how, how much or when poverty would be reduced, and the PAP Coordinating Unit did little or nothing to rectify this situation, despite always having a Minister of cabinet rank. The main thing the framework accomplished was to identify groups that were disproportionately poor and policies that were considered more pro-poor.

Starting in 1996, the country went through a long-term perspective exercise that produced the Malawi Vision 2020, which was drawn up after extensive public consultations. However, like the PAP, it was not followed by fundable action plans. Thus, neither the PAP nor the Malawi Vision 2020 was operationalised.

With the introduction of the PRSP concept, the policy framework of the PAP and the Malawi Vision 2020 are both now considered 'source documents'. This is mainly a face-saving gesture and no thematic working group has seriously used these two documents as inputs. The failure of the government to implement its very own, home-grown, Poverty Alleviation Programme or the even more high-profile Vision 2020 has left serious doubts as to whether the poverty-reducing plans within the PRSP stand much chance of being operationalised.

4.3   The PRSP process in Malawi

Stakeholder perceptions

The PRSP concept is, at best, imperfectly understood in Malawi, though, when compared to the situation in September 2000, by late 2001 we found huge improvements. This headline statement requires further disaggregation for a more complete picture to emerge.

First, there was a good deal of variation between different stakeholders in terms of the degree of understanding of the general purpose of the PRSP. Government officials were, for the most part, more informed than civil society. Within government, officials in the Ministry of Finance and Economic Planning (MoFEP) were, unsurprisingly, best briefed, while in the line ministries there was quite a bit of uncertainty as to what the PRSP ultimately will do – a consequence, to some degree, of the proliferation of poverty planning exercises in recent years.

Within civil society, there was slowly emerging a core of reasonably well-informed people and organisations capable of acting as interlocutors with both government and donors on the extent to which Malawi's PRSP is conforming to the conceptual and operational approach outlined in the documentation produced by the World Bank and the IMF. Access to documentation on the experiences of other PRSP country cases had assisted this learning process, and the use of internet-based resources such as the publications from EURODAD and the Kenyan and Zambian NGO networks were particularly cited in this connection.

Second, the extent of understanding varied considerably across three key issues associated with the PRSP concept: 1) its relation to HIPC debt relief; 2) its role in present and future IFI conditionality; and 3) its links to other ongoing processes such as SIPS, SWAPs and reforms to systems of public expenditure management.

How the Malawian PRSP is connected to the HIPC initiative was for the first year of PRSP preparations a source of fairly widespread confusion. Though the confusion eventually waned, especially among senior officials, there remained a lingering sense that the multilateral agencies were, in certain matters, conforming to earlier patterns of non-transparency. According to one informant in MoFEP, it was not until the latter part of 2001 that the President himself fully grasped that the PRSP was more than a method for deciding how to spend resources freed up through HIPC debt relief. Another common misconception in the early stages was that the *preparation* of the PRSP was simply a condition (some thought the *only* condition) for obtaining debt relief under the HIPC initiative.

Slowly, the message that the PRSP will, ultimately, constitute something of a national development plan, from which annual budgets will (in theory) be derived, began to get through. And civil society organisations were taking concrete actions to increase the chances that this linkage between planning and budgeting indeed takes place.

As of late 2001, there remained significant scepticism that the policy priorities outlined in the PRSP would be translated into reality. During the final phases of completing the Malawi Poverty Reduction Strategy (MPRS), however, certain improvements were noted. During the budget preparation for 2002-03, for instance, ministries were sent the sections of the MPRSP that pertained to their sectors as a guide for budget preparation.

The link to IFI conditionality was an area of even greater confusion. As stated above, the tendency to see the PRSP as just a document that must be submitted in order to qualify for HIPC funds was on the wane. But the route from the HIPC Decision Point (the decision by the Bank and Fund that Malawi is eligible for debt relief, at which point limited relief is in fact granted) to the Completion Point (when the annual debt-service savings become locked in for twenty years) was imperfectly understood. The concept of the 'floating completion point' (which means that the final decision on debt-reduction 'lock in' can be put off indefinitely until the Bank and Fund executive directors are satisfied that realistic poverty-reduction plans are in place) blurred the picture even further.

In late 2001, the government stepped up efforts to clarify matters a bit. At an Economic Association of Malawi workshop, attended by a number of civil society organisations, presentations were made by officials from the MoFEP and the Reserve Bank of Malawi (RBM).[2] This helped to spread the message among the more articulate sectors of civil society – advocacy NGOs and the newly formed Malawi Economic Justice Network – that a successful year of PRSP implementation would be required for the HIPC debt relief to be 'locked in'. But what constitutes a successful year was less obvious. Moreover, the link to *future* conditionality – i.e., what kinds of strings would be attached to future non-HIPC resources – had not been adequately explained by either the IFIs or the government. This was at least partly because no decisions had yet been made.

The PRSP formulation process

The development of Malawi's PRSP got off to a slow start in the latter part of 2000, hamstrung initially by the extremely non-consultative nature of the process by which the country's Interim PRSP was developed. Shortcomings of the iPRSP process included its almost complete exclusion of civil society (and indeed bilateral donors as well), turf battles between the National Economic Council and the MoFEP, and reliance on previous Policy

2. Leslie Mkandawire (RBM), 'The Effects of HIPC Initiative on the Social Sector: Experiences with the Highly Indebted Poor Countries (HIPC) Initiative in Malawi' (paper); and Patrick Kabambe (MoFEP), 'HIPC Debt Relief: Implications for Public Expenditure Allocations' (presentation), both delivered at the Economic Association of Malawi Workshop, Lilongwe, 3 August 2001.

Framework Papers, which were fairly crudely assembled into an iPRSP under the direction of a small group of officials working with World Bank staff members.

Some of the worst fears expressed by excluded stakeholders at the time of the iPRSP – for instance, that the full-scale PRSP process would be as closed an exercise – did not come to pass. On the other hand, the worry that HIPC Completion Point triggers would be derived from the Bank-orchestrated iPRSP, and that on this basis they would be publicly justified by the Bank as Malawian-owned and therefore a reasonable constraint on the development of the full PRSP, turned out to be reasonably well-founded.

Institutional architecture

Against this backdrop, it was always going to be difficult for the IFIs and the GoM to sell the PRSP process as a new form of participatory development planning. When the government began the PRSP preparatory process in September and October 2000, it ran into resistance from civil society almost immediately. The organisational architecture for developing the PRSP was perceived as government-dominated, and unnecessarily concentrated in the MoFEP and NEC. Indeed, the consultation process was designed originally as a series of one-day workshops, to which various 'sectors' of civil society would be invited so that they could voice their views.

The PRSP Technical Committee (TC), whose job it would be to oversee the creation of the document, was to be chaired by a senior member of the National Economic Council, once Malawi's key planning agency. The Technical Committee was to report to the National Steering Committee – a committee of Principal Secretaries from a broad array of ministries – with the post of Coordinator being held by the Principal Secretary (Economic Affairs) in the MoFEP.[3] The role of the National Coordinator was to act as a link between the Technical Committee and the National Steering Committee, which was empowered to make recommendations to the PRSP Ministerial Committee that would table the report before cabinet.

PRSP Thematic Working Groups (TWGs), formed to draft sectoral and issue-based components for the PRSP, were launched in January 2001. The TWGs included representatives from civil society and donors (but only after a major campaign for inclusion by civil society – about which more later). Some TWGs included Members of Parliament from relevant parliamentary committees.

The background documents distributed to TWGs in January 2001 contained a reasonably clear statement of the key objectives of the PRSP approach. Compared with previous documents issued by the government, a sharpening of the focus on implementation was evident: 'the key feature of

---

3. The PS (Economic Affairs) is subordinate, in MoFEP, to the Secretary to the Treasury, the Controlling Officer for the Ministry as a whole.

the PRSP will be that it will be an implementable, prioritised plan of action'. The diagram outlining the linkage between the PRSP and Sector Investment Programmes, the MTEF and the annual budget was supplemented by a box indicating the place of implementation and monitoring, and highlighting their connection to the annual PRSP progress review.[4]

District consultations

The arrangements for the district consultations were planned by the PRSP Technical Committee, with input from the National Steering Committee (that is, the committee of Principal Secretaries). Coverage of Malawi's 31 districts was divided among three teams. Some members of local civil society were involved in the district consultations, having been invited, but in general the workshops were dominated by local officials (district councillors, the police, district health officers) and Traditional Authorities, as well as what the PRSP Technical Committee's Report on the process termed 'other influential people within the districts' (2001a: 3).

As part of our fieldwork, we visited two districts where consultations had been held. Those participants interviewed by us were in general reasonably satisfied with the way the consultations in their districts had been conducted. The major concern expressed was that there had been no follow up by the PRSP Technical Committee. Though the TC stated that they had circulated the report on the outcome of the district workshops to Chief Executives of the District Assemblies, the Chief Executive of Balaka claimed not to have received one, nor had his Director of Administration. The district officials interviewed in Dedza had not seen a copy of the report either, and they keenly reviewed the copy we showed them.

The list of names for each District Consultation, found in the Annexe of the report, did not include their positions or organisational affiliations. Inquiries in Balaka and Dedza – which involved identifying the affiliation of each name listed in the Annexe – revealed that the vast majority of participants were district officials, elected representatives of the Town and District Assemblies, and Traditional Authorities (or Chiefs). Civil society representation was minimal, consisting in each case of two or three NGOs. District Chief Executive Officers were responsible for determining the list of invitees.

Stronger guidance from the TC – which funded and facilitated the consultations – could have resulted in a more representative cross-section of participants. Nevertheless, an NGO representative in Balaka (one of only four invited to the meeting, and just one of two to attend) felt that the encounter had been beneficial. Issues raised in the consultations were taken

---

4. The revised version, distributed as part of the Terms of Reference for the TWGs, was entitled, 'Poverty Reduction Strategy Paper: Questions and Answers' (mimeo), January 2001.

up later in the District Executive Committee, a useful forum provided within Malawi's Local Government structure to improve coordination between elected representatives, district officials and key non-governmental stakeholders.

Thematic Working Groups: operation and outputs

The first drafts of reports from some, though not all, of the TWGs were submitted to the TC in February 2001. Others were late. Some TWGs appear not to have met at all, or very rarely, with irregular attendance reported in almost all groups. A few groups appear to have been highly dysfunctional (PRSP TC, 2001b: 2).

At a key review meeting, held in 2001 at the lakefront resort of Salima, each TWG presented its draft to a panel made up of the Technical Committee, members of TWGs dealing with related or cross-cutting issues, and experts in each of the fields. The Report on the Salima Meeting indicates a good deal of thought going into the detailed and highly relevant comments from the Panels. On the other hand, the nature of some of the comments directed to other TWGs indicates that a number of the 'drafts' under discussion were of extremely low quality.

The Salima Meeting was criticised by some stakeholders as poorly facilitated, though most found it highly useful. The biggest complaint came from (some) donors, who felt that the length and expense of the meeting, held in a relatively up-market leisure venue, represented all that was wrong with the process – unconnected to the reality of the lives of the poor. One donor and a number of NGO representatives said that this was symptomatic of the process as a whole, 'where no meeting takes place without everyone being paid their DSA' (Daily Subsistence Allowance, or 'sitting fee'). The reluctance (or outright refusal) of officials and others to take action in the absence of such payments is, however, something that long predates the PRSP, and the hope that somehow this exercise would lead to a change in this aspect of the 'DSA culture' was probably unrealistic to begin with.

Interim action and review

An important milestone in the PRSP process was the creation of a 'PRSP Findings to Date' document, designed to provide input into the 2000/01 national budget. As the full PRSP would not be ready for the budget cycle, it was nevertheless felt that some of the interim findings should be used as guiding principles. The Findings to Date document was discussed in a workshop, and in fact became significantly revised as a result of the discussions. The incorporation of the thrust of this document in the Budget itself was an issue of some debate in Malawi, but the fact that it was mentioned at all in the Finance Minister's Budget Speech to Parliament was an indication that the idea of the PRSP as an *operational* document meant for *practical* application was taking root.

The Technical Committee provided an admirable display of self-criticism at the 29 May 2001 Findings to Date workshop, capturing many of the *leitmotivs* of our interviews with stakeholders. These criticisms were tepid in comparison to those levelled by one civil-society-initiated review of the PRSP process, which was the subject of a report issued a month earlier (April 2001). However, the very existence of this civil society critique was itself a good indication that the PRSP process had become high-profile enough actually to spur such a thoughtful and coordinated response (MEJN, 2001a).

Another display of self-criticism by the Technical Committee was contained in its August 2001 review of the process, which was submitted to the Finance Minister and the Minister for Poverty Alleviation (2001b). This document highlighted the TC's own problems of coordination, admitting that 'interest in the PRSP Process has been reduced and the quality of debate damaged by the poor flow of information'. It also admitted that 'the media have not been used effectively' adding that 'newspapers continue to consistently misreport PRSP events and there has been limited radio coverage'.

The TC's report, however, was also adamant that it alone could not be held responsible for the manifest shortcomings in the process, assigning some of the blame to the TWG chairpersons, and more importantly to the two 'higher' decision-making tiers: the PRSP National Steering Committee (consisting of Principal Secretaries), and the PRSP Ministerial Committee. 'Blame for the current impasse has been passed between the Technical Committee and the National Steering Committee', said the TC's report.

According to the TC's report, the ultimate source of the problems outlined above was the lack of 'official and political commitment', meaning that the two upper tiers (senior civil servants and members of the cabinet) were not treating the PRSP as an urgent priority. Part of this, according to the TC's report, was a result of 'widespread misunderstanding of the process'. The importance of this issue to assessing whether the PRSP itself is likely ever to be implemented warrants quoting from the report at length:

> many senior officials and politicians see PRSP only as the key to increased resources through HIPC, rather than as a means of improving policy and public expenditure planning and management. Thus several Ministries are being encouraged to expand their programmes rather than rationalising them, and *commitment to the fundamental reforms implied by the implementation of the PRSP is absent in many cases* ... the PRSP has not become a priority within the Ministry of Finance let alone the Line Ministries ... without demand for the PRSP from the Ministers and senior officials in each ministry, the PRSP will always be seen as a side issue (ibid: 3, emphasis added).

Thus, we can see that the TC's criticisms were, in fact, directed more at ministers and the top echelons of the civil service than towards itself. This is, in fact, a pretty fair assessment. The lack of support and commitment at the highest political levels goes a long way in explaining what some donor informants have called a 'lack of urgency' among many officials in line ministries. Most of all, it does not bode well for future implementation.

The PRSP endgame

An abundant source of anxiety for civil society and donors throughout the PRSP formulation process was the lack of clarity about the arrangements for finalising the document. Two questions had been asked almost from the outset, with no clear response from the key government decision-makers. First, through what mechanisms would TWG findings be filtered and amended in the process of compiling the final composite PRSP? Second, through what means would the prioritisations agreed in the TWGs themselves be integrated into a master matrix that would spell out what was commonly referred to as 'overall prioritisation'.

This is an absolutely critical element in the process of formulating a national poverty reduction strategy, and it seemed to the key civil society organisations that it would be done under pressure of time and by a relatively small group. The main concern of civil society groups was that the detailed analytical work, in which they had invested so much time, could be undermined by a hasty completion process, and that the resulting dissatisfaction with the final product would in turn seriously harm efforts to impart a sense of national 'ownership'.

The Malawi Economic Justice Network (MEJN), which was the most coordinated voice of protest on this issue,[5] lobbied to have four non-government members (one of whom would be a parliamentarian) included in the drafting team – their participation to be paid for by MEJN. The first government response was that they would take only one (paid for by government). After further discussions, a further member was agreed, to be paid for by government. Much effort went into government vetting of the individuals to be included. Government on its own included other 'non government' members. One of them was from the Malawi Investment Promotion Agency, a parastatal agency; another was the Executive Director of the government-controlled NGO-coordinating body CONGOMA.

The drafting team's first version of the MPRS was circulated to all stakeholders and presented to ministers, parliamentarians, civil society organisations, top civil servants and donors. Civil society and donor representatives submitted, in some cases, substantial written comments. The most substantial were those from Washington-based IMF and World Bank

---

5. MEJN played a large role in pressing the government to involve civil society all the way to the concluding stages of finalising the document. It had established 'shadow committees' earlier, to examine the TWG drafts, and attempted to do something similar for the document as a whole.

staff, the recommendations from the Bank being particularly hefty. The Malawi-based staff of DFID and the Norwegians were notably vocal as well.

The major criticism was on the alleged absence of a sound macro-economic framework, linked to poverty reduction, and prioritisation. Overheads and other areas considered 'non-PRSP' still appeared within the MPRS, and consumed much of the resources. Aware that powerful interests benefited from these categories of expenditure, the drafting team was not bold enough to trim them. Instead they were stacked 'on top' as 'necessary expenditure'.

Because of problems of costing the programmes and retaining consistency within the prioritisation model, the drafting team circulated the second draft to the TWGs. Ultimately, however, the drafting team re-worked the cost estimates to ensure they were realistic and the macro-economic framework was similarly adjusted.

It is worth noting how large a role donor relations played in this phase of the MPRS's development. First, the macro-economic framework for the MPRS was required, under the terms of continued conditionality, to rely on the already agreed IMF/World Bank framework. This was unrealistic in a variety of – sometimes contradictory – ways. Not least of these was the inclusion of (very high) growth and trade projections, which were needed to help show that Malawi would expand and export its way out of indebtedness if it were granted the recommended level of debt relief.

Second, there was at the time a large amount of uncertainty – even larger than usual, that is – concerning the likely level of support from the bilateral donor community. This was due to charges of corruption and accounting irregularities levelled by some agencies (e.g. DANIDA, EU), and disappointment at the government's failure to fulfil policy commitments on the part of others (e.g. USAID). When it seemed likely that there would be a significant shortfall due to certain donors taking action, the drafting team was finally forced to cut some previously prioritised activities and to scale-down others.

The April 2002 launch of the MPRS was well attended. A speech by one official re-emphasised an issue raised, in fact, in the initial background document submitted for TWGs when the formulation phase was being launched: that developing a national work-ethic (doing away with what the document had called 'the laziness of Malawians') was the necessary first step on the road to poverty reduction. The lead donor spokesperson stressed capacity constraints and HIV/AIDS, both of which could hinder implementation. The Minister of Finance and Economic Planning committed himself to using the MPRS in constructing the budget.

4.4   What difference has the PRSP made?

This section analyses the effects of the PRSP process in Malawi, and assesses whether it is likely to result in the establishment of new institutional relationships capable of supporting the objective of poverty reduction. It consists of two parts. We begin by considering the potential for the PRSP process and public-sector reforms to become mutually reinforcing – that is, for the PRSP process to contribute to improvements in the system of poverty-focused planning, budgeting and expenditure management, and for these improvements to create an environment in which the PRSP itself can be implemented. We then examine the potential for the PRSP process to institutionalise new relations among the main actors that influence the ability of governance to contribute to poverty reduction.

Public expenditure reform

Malawi, like many other countries, has in recent years undergone a series of overlapping reform efforts designed to improve the effectiveness of public expenditure. These have sought to rationalise the entire cycle of expenditure-related activities – the identification of priorities, the costing of activities, the allocation of resources, and the creation of systems for effective implementation and review. Two key ingredients have been efforts to institute the elements of a Medium Term Expenditure Framework (MTEF) and to develop Sector Investment Programmes (SIPs) or Sector-Wide Approaches (SWAPs).

Both initiatives have been underway since the mid-1990s. Each has been subjected to continuous refinement and review. Though reforms to systems for sectoral policy planning are intimately bound up with the fate of the *general* system of public expenditure management (including the functioning of financial controls), for the sake of analytical convenience they are treated separately.

The attempt to institute an MTEF in Malawi – that is, to use an MTEF as a tool for managing the entire budgeting process – is widely viewed as having failed to meet its objectives. This was the conclusion of each of the two major reviews of the MTEF process conducted to date – the most recent submitted in late 2000. Activity-based budgeting has been only partly practised, and even then has been undermined by other flaws in the budget process. The result has been the reassertion of line-item budgeting.

While there are many ways to assess progress in what is inevitably a learning process, one review (while careful to highlight some of the achievements of the Malawian experience with MTEF) gave the clear impression of unsatisfactory performance. The key MTEF stage of setting ceilings was 'an area where the MTEF has not really functioned'.[6] Moreover, 'the integration of the Recurrent and Development budgets has not been achieved'.[7] The

---

6. Seth Anipa, Felix Kaluma, and Elizabeth Muggeridge, 'MTEF in Malawi and Ghana', presented at a DFID Seminar on Best Practice in Public Expenditure Management, May 1999, p. 9.
7. Ibid: 10.

Government of Malawi's own MTEF review, produced with assistance from a UK-based consultancy firm, Oxford Policy Management, was similarly self-critical, but with (again) a gloss emphasising the government's determination to redouble its efforts at fixing the main problems (GoM, 2000).

The most important of these shortcomings, in terms of its potential impact on PRSP implementation, is that patterns of actual expenditure often bear little resemblance to the budget itself. Virement between expenditure categories is a frequent occurrence. Expenditure ceilings are violated with impunity, and on a regular basis, by line ministries and other government agencies. This is by now very well known throughout government and non-governmental circles. As one bilateral donor put it, 'that the budget is largely a work of fiction is now an accepted reality'.

As these problems have persisted, proposals to rectify them have become increasingly radical. Reforms that delve deep into the institutional substructure of financial management were proposed in Malawi's 2001 Public Expenditure Review (MoFEP, 2001a). These include performance contracts for senior civil servants that would link personal emoluments to the ability of individual officials to adhere to high standards of financial management. Another World Bank proposal is to expand the role of the Malawi Public Service Commission as a way of insulating senior officials from political pressures exerted by powerful ruling party voices within the cabinet. Government officials, including the finance minister, have openly embraced the need for such changes and have agreed to implement some of them as part of Bank and Fund lending arrangements. But will the political incentives and distribution of decision-making authority within government make this possible?

This is, indeed, the central question, as a key concern of this chapter is whether the PRSP approach is likely to contribute to such efforts. There can be no categorical answer to this question, for a variety of reasons. Still, it is possible to assess the potential implications of current trends.

One clear trend is the inability of key reformers to control decisions at the highest levels of government. While former Finance Minister Mathews Chikaonda possessed a refreshing style, and a good deal of reformist zeal, it was hard to escape the conclusion (even before he left the cabinet) that his personal qualities alone would be insufficient to overcome the many (politically related) shortcomings identified by so many perceptive observers over the past half decade. One early indication of whether government words would be matched by deeds came when the Malawi Confederation of Chambers of Commerce and Industry (MCCCI) conducted an evaluation of the Finance Minister's Ten Point Plan for prudent financial management. The plan had been launched with great fanfare in March 2000 (that is, during the process of preparing the iPRSP), receiving extremely favourable press coverage and hearty endorsement from IFI staff. The MCCCI's report, however, confirmed the conclusions reached by most casual observers – that the plan had virtually no impact on the behaviour of officials, who viewed it as a publicity stunt staged for the benefit of donors.

However, the most damning indictment of the government's commitment to fundamental expenditure reform came in a letter (dated 24 July 2001) from the Deputy Chief of the IMF's Africa Division to Malawi's Finance Minister. The IMF's letter stated grave concerns about the viability of the government's revenue and expenditure forecasts for the financial year 2001/ 02, which began operation on 1 July 2001. The letter drew attention to the revenue-losing impact of tax cuts announced by the government. The IMF letter also detailed the continued profligacy of ADMARC, the parastatal government agency for agricultural marketing.

While the tone of the IMF letter was polite and couched in terms of 'recommendations' for positive action, the list of government commitments abandoned and disciplines violated was long and detailed. Interestingly, the IMF voiced some of the exact same concerns as did Malawian civil society in its critique of the budget (see the next sub-section below): 'the budget lacks the prioritisation of pro-poor spending and a safeguard system for monitoring and controlling such spending. Thus priority spending is not sufficiently safeguarded and the additionality of HIPC Initiative funds cannot be ensured' (MEJN, 2001b: 1).

On a more positive note, virtually all people interviewed for this chapter felt that the budget process had become more participatory in recent years. Pre-budget consultations for the 2000/01 budget, in part organised by the Malawi Investment Promotion Agency but with attendance at some sessions by a more representative cross-section of civil society (beyond business interests), was the turning point. The turn towards openness thus preceded the PRSP process, but clearly gained momentum in the run-up to the presentation of the 2001/02 budget. The 2002-03 budget consultations continued the trend towards official openness. The PRSP process is credited with some of this – both by normalising the idea of widespread consultation and by raising awareness of budget issues among a broad array of constituencies, including parliamentarians, who are usually bit players in this exercise.

SIPs and SWAPs

In recent years donors have insisted on the need to scale down project-based aid in favour of supporting either components of jointly developed Sector Investment Programmes or the national budget as a whole. The purpose is to reduce the costs (and unnecessary duplication) associated with individual donor projects, which often maintain parallel administrative structures. PRSPs are intended to further this movement towards greater complementarity between the operations of individual donors and also to ensure that the efforts of *all* donors are clearly focused within national priority areas. The mechanism for implementing a jointly defined SIP is for donors to adopt Sector-Wide Approaches (or SWAPs). This is likely to change the composition of aid across sectors, and may affect its total volume (if sufficient accountability mechanisms are perceived to have been put in place).

Compared to our rather downbeat assessment of the potential for the PRSP approach and general public expenditure management reforms to become mutually self-reinforcing, a substantially more positive story can be seen in the impact of the PRSP formulation exercise on sectoral policy planning processes. The high-profile nature of the PRSP has given a much-needed boost to efforts to a number of SIPs that were already in progress.

All three categories of stakeholders interviewed for this report were of the view that the development of a Policy and Investment Framework (PIF) for the education sector had benefited from the PRSP process. The Education TWG used the existing PIF (which was explicitly referred to as 'a living document') as the basis for preparing its paper. But the influence went both ways. As one government official remarked, the PRSP TWG process in Education sharpened the poverty focus of the PIF and identified a number of more realistic indicators.

More work needed to be done on the costing side, but even donor representatives pushing fairly narrow agendas in this sector found that the TWG process had brought on board a larger array of personnel from the Ministry of Education than had earlier been involved with the PIF. Some participants in the October 2000 joint donor-government review of the education sector[8] – itself an indication of the increasing movement toward some form of modified SWAP arrangement – felt strongly that the PRSP process had increased the momentum for the creation of joint funding mechanisms (even if some donors would be unable to permit a 'commingling of funds').

In the agriculture sector, the picture was a bit more complicated, as the Malawi Agriculture Sector Investment Plan (MASIP) had its own secretariat, separate from the Ministry of Agriculture. There are some indications that the PRSP TWG in agriculture suffered, to some degree, from ongoing rivalry between MASIP and the planning division within the Ministry. It was unclear to some donors and MASIP officials whether the PRSP approach had watered down the considerable work that MASIP had already undertaken over the previous two to three years. At the same time, by putting pressure on donors to buy into national priorities for poverty reduction, the PRSP approach has invested some urgency in the MASIP effort that was otherwise lacking.

In the health sector, the PRSP process was also seen to have had a beneficial effect, according to stakeholders from all three categories. Above all, it provided an opportunity for donors and government (along with the Christian Health Association of Malawi, whose members account for about two-thirds of health service provision in rural areas) to collectively define what would constitute an Essential Health Package (EHP). A huge number of technical

---

8. Hopes for this sort of development were expressed in the 'Review Report' of the Joint Review of the Malawi Education Sector (Lilongwe, October 2000).

issues are involved – pitting the conceptual frameworks of economists and health professionals against one another in some cases – but the process of defining an EHP had been assisted by the broad-based membership of the Health TWG, which appears to have been more active than many of the others. Key bilateral donors were upbeat about the ability of the work undertaken by this TWG (which benefited from targeted technical assistance from UNICEF) to influence the process of generating a full-fledged SWAP.

In general, then, the combination of the PRSP *formulation process* injecting momentum into the preparation of these three SIPs, and the PRSP *concept's* stress on promoting donor coordination, has increased the chances (somewhat) that future interventions could conform to a modified SWAP framework in at least some sectors. This could, potentially, reduce duplication and the burden on government to respond to diverse donor pressures on what should constitute national priorities for public action to reduce poverty. Crucially, however, putting these priorities into action will face the same financial management constraints mentioned above.

Institutionalising participatory governance

Participatory governance is the second area in which this chapter assesses potential institutional effects of the PRSP process. The analysis addresses two aspects of governance: voice and accountability.

The intense partisanship that has infected public institutions in Malawi in recent years has also stunted the development of an independent civil society capable of contributing effectively to policy debates. Criticism of government is often interpreted (sometimes correctly, of course) as motivated by partisan interests. This 'culture of loyalty and paranoia' has been remarkably resistant: when civil society groups *do* exploit opportunities for genuine policy dialogue, and thus refrain from public criticism of government during the process of negotiation and discussion, they are vulnerable to accusations from other non-governmental actors (and opposition politicians) that they have 'gone over to the other side' – a charge that carries more weight precisely because of the government's reputation for dealing almost exclusively with friendly, predictable civil society groups.

As a result of these and other tensions, including legitimate fears that nominally independent accountability institutions have been subjected to partisan intervention, not only has policy dialogue between civil society and government been less than constructive, until recently there has been, in many areas, little substantive interaction at all. The culture of bureaucratic secrecy and closed-door decision-making has relegated policy debate to fairly general issues.

This is slowly changing, and the PRSP process must be accorded at least some of the credit. Indeed, the coming together of a civil society network to engage with government and donors on issues of economic policy is perhaps the most promising development to have emerged from Malawi's PRSP process. That it was spurred initially by the non-inclusive nature of the government's approach to PRSP formulation makes it no less noteworthy or beneficial.[9]

The emergence of the Malawi Economic Justice Network (MEJN) can be traced to a November 2000 meeting of 23 civil society organisations in Mangochi. The event produced a statement of principles concerning how the PRSP formulation process should be conducted that was later termed 'The Mangochi Declaration'. In addition to committing themselves to creating a taskforce that would focus on advocacy in relation to economic issues, the groups resolved to 'organize Civil Society involvement in the formulation of the PRSP process', 'organize the training and awareness raising of Civil Society, to give them the economic literacy to make a positive and ongoing contribution', and 'scrutinize and analyse the implementation of the PRSP, including government budgeting and expenditure'. With the last of this troika of objectives, the MEJN committed itself to taking a lead role in 'participatory auditing'.

It was in the aftermath of this declaration that the MEJN was officially constituted. The PRSP formulation process initially envisaged by the Technical Committee encountered two main objections from MEJN: the non-inclusion of civil society in the substantive deliberations that were expected to produce drafts on relevant sectoral and cross-cutting issues; and the specification of an extremely condensed time-frame for public consultations and drafting of the PRSP.

Malawian civil society mobilised on both of these issues with more vigour and coordinated action than it had on any occasion in recent years, with the possible exception of the 1999 national elections. Following negotiations between the MEJN and key members of the PRSP Technical Committee and National Steering Committee, the process of formulating the PRSP began to open up beyond the ranks of government and donors. By early February 2001, the focus of civil society engagement shifted to the Technical Committee's schedule for preparation of the PRSP. After much discussion within government, this plea was heeded, and the time-frame for developing the PRSP was extended, including extra time for public consultations. Similar pleas for extra time were heeded during the finalisation stage of the MPRS.

MEJN, and a number of its constituent parts, were critical in establishing links to other parts of the governance structure, particularly parliamentary committees. Through the US-funded National Democratic Institute, a handful of members of parliament's Budget and Finance Committee became more active players in both the PRSP and annual budget processes. Both the MEJN

---

9. It should also be noted that a clear statement of suggestions for how to promote substantive civil society engagement in the PRSP process, drawing on international experience, was communicated from Oxfam-Malawi to the government as early as August 2000 (letter from Andrew Fitzgibbon, Malawi Programme Representative, to Henry N'Gombe, PS of NEC, 22 August 2000).

and the PRSP Technical Committee made presentations to parliamentarians on the linkages between HIPC, the PRSP and the national budget, as well as outlining some of the steps that would be required to improve the MTEF as a tool for more poverty-focused planning (MoFEP, 2001b).

It would be stretching the point to claim that this made it possible for Parliament to play the central role envisaged for it in Malawi's constitution. But the PRSP process has clearly given greater voice to a wider range of stakeholders. The question is whether these voices will be heeded, and whether they can cohere once the initial PRSP hype fades, and the effort gets underway to hold the government to account for policy and expenditure commitments.

Longer-term impacts of the PRSP approach on the accountability side of the governance equation are particularly difficult to gauge at this point. While the reaction of Malawi's civil society to the PRSP process has been encouraging – in that it has formed structures for engaging in both policy dialogue *and* coordinated protest on issues of substance and process – it is extremely unlikely that this will result in the emergence of domestic political leverage sufficient to hold government (or donors) accountable for commitments undertaken in the PRSP formulation process. Civil society remains extremely weak and fragmented, and government highly suspicious of the more vocal elements within its ranks.

The connections between the PRSP process and governance issues in the *formal* arena – i.e., state accountability institutions – are similarly mixed. The PRSP provided a vehicle for a small group of parliamentarians to get involved in substantive questions of oversight, but the numbers committed and capable enough to engage in these sorts of processes over the longer term is tiny. Budgets for parliamentary committees remain miniscule. The resources for other state accountability institutions have increased, but they are nowhere near the levels needed.

More importantly, the work of these state accountability agencies is still highly constrained by political interference by the executive. Fairly clear-cut cases of corruption have been put on hold because of executive intervention, and the partisan behaviour of the speaker of Parliament (who hails from the ruling party) further undermined confidence in legislative oversight as a tool of accountability. The Public Accounts Committee of Parliament, which in 2001 compiled its first serious reports on the misuse of government funds, did not see its findings acted upon by the relevant enforcement agencies. It is not clear how the creation of a PRSP would help to rectify these fairly fundamental problems.

The Budget for 2001/02 highlighted both weaknesses and emerging areas of improvement in the quest for more accountable governance for poverty reduction. The shortcomings of the budget were played up by the MEJN in a series of briefings produced in the wake of the Finance Minister's Budget Speech to Parliament. In a report for Members of Parliament, the MEJN highlighted a number of key issues of relevance to the PRSP process.[10] These concerns were then supplemented by further consultations held by the TC with a broad range of stakeholders. As a result, twelve separate Priority Poverty Expenditures (PPEs)[11] were identified as critical to poverty reduction, and these were detailed in the pre-budget report submitted to Parliament. In addition, detail was given on the mechanisms required to ensure that the money was actually spent on these priorities.

To ensure that these would be safeguarded, the MEJN, working alongside Parliament's Budget and Finance Committee, determined that (at a minimum) they required: 'A detailed outputs based summary of each PPE in the budget documents'; 'a comparison with last year, and a breakdown of the sources of funds (HIPC, Donor or Government)'; 'a commitment to the timely release of information on each PPE as the year progresses'; and 'a guarantee that money allocated to PPE's will not be diverted without Parliamentary approval'.[12]

When these were *not* included in the Finance Minister's budget for 2001/02, the MEJN wasted no time in criticising the government for its failure to place accountability-enhancing procedural reforms at the centre of its strategy for linking the PRSP to public expenditure priorities. That the MEJN and the IMF – which otherwise differ on many aspects of policy – were both pressing for the same sorts of informational prerequisites to support implementation of the PRSP helped to motivate the MoFEP to take at least some corrective action. In particular, the MoFEP's Budget Division began the task of identifying which line items from the budget constituted expenditure in the priority areas, something that is by no means obvious from the budget documents themselves. This on its own will not bring about accountability, but the process of demands generating at least some informational supply-side response is cause for slightly greater optimism than the larger picture might otherwise indicate.

Monitoring arrangements are likely to involve civil society in some sort of central role – either officially (in a partnership with government machinery) or unofficially (through a parallel process independent of the state-operated system for tracking progress on PRSP indicators). Given the current weakness of civil society, the latter option, though it requires more capacity than civil society currently possesses, will likely prove the more effective mechanism over the long term, given civil society's need to develop independence from

---

10. MEJN (2001b). It is worth noting that by August 2001 the MEJN was claiming a membership of '69 Civil Society organisations, including the Church, Trade Unions, Professional Associations, Academics and NGOs' (p. 1).

11. Rural roads, bridges and essential infrastructure; safe water supply; security (especially community policing); teaching and learning materials; training new teachers; paying teachers a reasonable salary; purchasing and distributing essential drugs; training more health workers; paying health workers a reasonable wage; expanding the Starter Pack programme; providing credit for rural smallholder farmers; increased allocation to agricultural extension.

12. MEJN (2001c: 3-4).

the state, even as it continues to rely on external assistance for a large proportion of operational funds.

4.5   Monitoring the PRSP: a second chance?

Government has in the past established various mechanisms to monitor and evaluate the implementation of national development plans, projects and programmes. Economists, employed under a common service managed by the National Economic Council, were responsible for the monitoring and evaluation exercises. All key ministries and departments have monitoring and evaluation units. At the national level, monitoring and evaluation was the responsibility of the erstwhile Ministry of Economic Planning and Development, most of which has been absorbed into the National Economic Council.

Since 1994, a dispersed form of monitoring and evaluation has been practiced. Staff responsible for monitoring and evaluation, along with others responsible for national development planning and aid coordination, were transferred out to the Ministry of Finance. This was after the abolition of the Ministry of Economic Planning and Development – and the creation of the National Economic Council (NEC) in its place – and the renaming of the Ministry of Finance as the Ministry of Finance and Economic Planning (MoFEP).

The Poverty Monitoring System (PMS) was designed to undertake three types of monitoring of government development endeavours. These were input, output and poverty-impact monitoring. Input monitoring would entail tracking specific policy, project and programme implementation by checking whether action plans were followed as stipulated. This would also involve expenditure tracking. The output monitoring would entail checking whether policy, project and programme outputs, as stipulated, were achieved. The outcome or impact monitoring would then concentrate on indicators that directly reflecting poverty status.

So far, the PMS has managed to undertake mainly impact monitoring. It has not been able to undertake serious input monitoring, whether regarding policy implementation or expenditure tracking. On impact monitoring, the PMS has conducted two qualitative impact assessments of poverty projects and programmes and conducted the Integrated Household Survey (IHS), which provided the basis for impact analysis.

A review of the PMS undertaken in 2001 revealed numerous problems. One of the most important was that the system was not part of the normal government monitoring and evaluation system, but a parallel mechanism. As a result, the output of the PMS had not informed policy as much as originally hoped. On a more positive note, the analysis of the IHS, when it finally did begin to emerge in late 2000, provided up-to-date information on the poverty situation, and the PRSP process was able to use the results extensively. Some (though not all) Thematic Working Groups, most notably the Poverty Profile and Monitoring Working Group, incorporated the results of the analysis into their draft reports.

The Poverty Profile and Monitoring Thematic Working Group (PPM-TWG) originally proposed a system for the monitoring of the MPRS once implementation commenced. However, the donor-funded PMS was being reviewed even as the PRSP formulation process was underway, and the PPM-TWG finalised its work before the completion of the review. As the MPRS was coming into being, it was generally assumed that monitoring of PRSP implementation would use a system similar to the current PMS, despite the latter's recognised deficiencies. In its analysis of the 'status of the current system', the PPM-TWG's draft stated that the PMS does not function efficiently, and yet there was no statement on why this was the case and what could be done about it. Most likely the PMS will fail to deliver so long as there is no consensus on this question.

The PPM-TWG draft suggested that the PRSP monitoring system would use integrated household surveys and sector-specific surveys conducted by the National Statistical Office (NSO); administrative records; and qualitative impact assessments. In its report to the PRSP Technical Committee, the TWG also proposed that the collection and reporting of administrative records be decentralised. Each district would have statisticians responsible for collecting district-level administrative records on education, health, water, sanitation and so forth. The NSO would be the apex coordinating body; district-level administrative records and statistics would be passed on to the NSO for compilation and storage in a central database.

The TWG on PPM proposed that Malawi's existing Poverty Monitoring System monitor in closer detail, and with more regular frequency, a number of key poverty indicators. The indicators selected mainly covered impact monitoring. There was little emphasis on input and output monitoring. Monitoring of expenditures, for example, was completely omitted. Since inputs and outputs are critical in determining the impact of policies, projects and programmes, neglecting to monitor them risks repeating, although in a different form, the failings of the current system.

The proposed (highly complex) institutional structure that emerged in late 2001 was criticised as almost bound to fail to produce the intended results. If the results of the PMS are to influence policy, they need to use mainstream government channels. The key committees should not be for technicians, but rather a forum where policy makers review key decisions in the light of evidence.

The MPRSP Final Draft tried to improve on this institutional framework. The Ministry of Finance was now expected to monitor inputs and outputs. The NEC was to conduct poverty analysis and to keep track of poverty outcomes and impacts and also house the Secretariat of the PMS. This would bring together the TWC, the MPRS Monitoring Committee and the Cabinet Committee on the Economy. Moreover, it was to be an inclusive TWC, involving government officials, donors, civil society, researchers, media, district representatives and parliamentary committee members. The NSO was assigned the task of managing the poverty database and conducting surveys.

But after the poverty monitoring and evaluation workshop held in July 2002, this structure was radically modified. The TWC and the MPRS Monitoring Committee were merged, but with limited membership. The battle between NEC and MoFEP continued. The issue concerned where the Secretariat would be based. The question was asked: how could MoFEP have an MPRS Unit while the NEC was the institutional home for the Secretariat? Would the DG (the political head of the NEC) present the PMS results at the cabinet? Would MoFEP (in the form of the Finance Minister) not be a better salesman to political colleagues? Yet, if the salesman is the Minister of Finance, is it not logical that the Secretariat be in the Ministry of Finance? These highly political questions are likely to be resolved only in the medium or long term.

What is missing in both the current and proposed systems is a strong institutional link to accountability bodies like the National Audit Office and Parliament's Public Accounts Committee and its Budget and Finance Committee. A formal link between the PMS and the Treasury's Budget Department and the Accountant General's office could, if properly nurtured, be the cornerstone of a successful PRSP monitoring system. Without a link to the financial accounting system being developed in the Treasury and Accountant General's Office, monitoring of expenditures will not be possible.

4.6   Towards a new aid relationship

Part of the attraction of the PRSP concept to stakeholders of various types is its promise to contribute to a new kind of relationship between governments, donors and civil societies. One element is the idea that conditionality will be streamlined, replaced by relations of partnership. Many government and non-governmental observers in Malawi feel that the potential for this type of relationship to emerge has been undermined (though perhaps not fatally) by the tendency of IFI officials to continue operating with a command-and-control mindset.

One frequently cited example is the HIPC Decision Point Document. This was prepared in late 2000 by World Bank staff for endorsement by the Bank's Executive Directors. It identifies a list of 'triggers', or conditions, that would have to be met by the government in order for Malawi to reach Completion Point (the point at which debt relief becomes irreversible).[13] By the time of the second round of field research for this chapter in August 2001 there was

---

13. The following discussion is based on IDA/R2000-234 (2000). The Completion Point Triggers are summarised in Box 2 of that paper.

greater awareness that there were such things as triggers. The very existence of triggers raised concerns among members of civil society and even, in some cases, among government officials, as the idea of HIPC conditionalities seemed to contradict the portrayal of the PRSP as an alternative to IFI-imposed conditionality. Most importantly, non-negotiable and previously agreed policy commitments appeared to pre-empt the PRSP formulation process.

Beyond this objection in principle, three specific triggers found in the HIPC Decision Point Document were the subject of considerable consternation.

'Progress in the implementation of the National Safety Net Strategy'

The NSNS was at the time it was developed (during 1999-2000) a source of some controversy, particularly because of the extent to which it appeared to bear the heavy imprint of certain staff members of the World Bank. While it was appreciated by most observers that the PRSP process (which includes a Thematic Working Group on Safety Nets) was not intended to 'reinvent the wheel' – that is, it would 'build upon existing policy documents' – the inclusion of the existing NSNS as the basis for one of the conditions for HIPC Completion appeared to pre-determine the content of the section of the PRSP on Safety Nets. Stakeholders asked to participate in the PRSP's Safety Net TWG wondered whether they had been invited merely to legitimate policy decisions that had already been taken.

'Achieving performance indicators in HIV/AIDS and Education'

Government officials referred to the triggers in these two areas as 'a bit random', in addition to (once again) seemingly pre-empting the PRSP formulation process. The requirement/trigger that '75% of all condom outlet points [have] condoms in stock at any given time' struck one Treasury official as arbitrary, and possibly even perverse: stockrooms brimming with condoms could as easily indicate that no one is using them.

In Education, there was some questioning of the requirement/trigger that there be a 'yearly enrolment of 6000 students for teacher training and institution of in-service training for primary teachers (at least once each year)'. As Bank staff indicated when queried about this, this condition was drawn from the existing Policy and Investment Framework (PIF) for Education (the 'living document' on which the Education SIP is ultimately to be based). But, as both donors active in the sector and Ministry staff complained, this figure had not yet been fully costed and capacity constraints in meeting it had not been adequately assessed, as the process of developing the PIF had run into a number of problems.[14] So, they asked, why was this suddenly seized upon as a non-negotiable condition?

---

14. See, for instance, Kadzamira and Rose (2000).

The feeling among informants who were critical of HIPC Completion-Point triggers in these sectors was that they had been selected 'in a rush' to meet the Decision-Point deadline in late 2000, and were biased towards the sort of quantitative indicators that would appeal to the Boards of the IFIs. This has dented confidence in the belief that the PRSP represents a genuinely new form of national ownership.

'Submission of draft Land Law to parliament'

This trigger, which falls in the category of macroeconomic and structural reforms in the HIPC Decision Point Document, was another that came in for criticism – in this case, mainly from civil society, but also (reportedly) from officials in the Ministry of Gender and Community Affairs. Again, the issue is one of pre-empting the nationally owned PRSP-formulation process: if the purpose of the PRSP is to identify a comprehensive national development strategy in which policies are focused on poverty reduction, why should the promulgation of a prefabricated Land Law, which may or may not be focused on poverty reduction, be a condition of HIPC Completion?

Suspicions were further heightened by the fact that land policy was conspicuous by its absence from the Thematic Working Groups established as part of the PRSP process. When asked about this omission, and whether it might be linked to the fact that the existing Land Law had been stipulated in the HIPC triggers, World Bank representatives (as well as a member of the Technical Committee, responsible for organising the PRSP Thematic Working Groups), stated that land policy was simply an area that was overlooked when establishing the TWGs. It was not, they stated, a deliberate omission.

Either way, the *impression* remained that another (politically sensitive) policy domain, of direct relevance to the economic prospects of the poor, had been defined out of the consultative PRSP process – in effect, pre-determined by the existing land policy. This, unfortunately, reinforced the suspicion the PRSP process was designed to overcome.[15]

Other conditionality concerns

Making widespread comprehension of the relationship between IFI conditionality and the PRSP even more difficult was the inclusion in the HIPC Decision Point Document of a detailed breakdown of the 'Indicative Use of HIPC Resources: 2000/01-2002/03'.[16] Though the document repeatedly stressed that these are 'potential' uses for HIPC debt relief, the legacy of suspicion surrounding the nature of the agreements between the IFIs and the

---

15. It should be noted, however, that one donor interviewed for this chapter argued that the current land policy document is 'quite solid' and that there was no need to reopen the issue.
16. The breakdown is found at IDA/R2000-234 (2000: 21).

government created the impression that the distribution of HIPC debt relief outlined in this document had been decided upon *in advance* of the PRSP formulation process.

Ironically, the belief among informants in all three stakeholder categories – government, civil society and other donors – that the World Bank's Decision Point Document predetermined the allocation of HIPC savings had generated a new (mis)perception that is, in a sense, the mirror image of one of the earlier misperceptions. That is, if the distribution of HIPC resources had been decided in advance of the PRSP-formulation process, then far from the PRSP being *exclusively* about how to spend the debt relief funds, it would actually be devoted to *everything but* how to spend the HIPC resources.

While some civil society groups were concerned that debt-relief resources had been pre-assigned to the categories identified in the Bank's HIPC Decision Point Document, others were more concerned that they would *not* be spent according to this formula. (The table of 'indicative uses' does in fact prioritise such clearly poverty-focused expenditures as drugs, primary health care, nurses' training, rural roads, teaching materials, borehole construction and maintenance, and agricultural extension.) This latter complaint stemmed from the belief that the first tranche of HIPC funds had largely been earmarked, without public notification let alone debate, to repayment of domestic borrowings incurred during financial year 2000/01.

The 'folding in' of the Fund's PRGF conditionalities within the HIPC Completion Point triggers was another source of worry for some stakeholders, particularly in the donor community: How inviolable would the PRSP be as the centrepiece of national policy when the IFIs continued to possess the leverage contained in other lending instruments? While less of a concern than it had been at the time of the scoping exercise for this study (in September 2000), this remained a significant theme in the perceptions of all three stakeholder categories. Civil society representatives were concerned at the lack of clarity on how the monitoring indicators identified for the PRSP would be used in whatever Bank Poverty Reduction Support Credit (PRSC) arrangement ultimately emerged. And Treasury officials were worried that any future adjustment operation would impose *additional* conditionality burdens.

At the same time, for those who wonder whether there will be sufficient incentive for the government to remain committed to the PRSP priorities after the HIPC savings are locked in – that is, after the first year of successfully implementing the PRSP and adhering to the other HIPC triggers – the fact that IFI conditionality will continue to exist in one form or another is a source of some comfort. For those of this view, the primary concern is that HIPC funds should be used to create *additional* expenditure on poverty priorities – that is, above and beyond what was being spent in these areas prior to the introduction of HIPC relief. Bank staff stated that the first annual review of the implementation of Malawi's PRSP – i.e., the review that would determine whether Malawi had passed its Completion Point tests and locked in debt relief – would examine not only the use of the HIPC funds themselves, but also the *overall* levels of expenditure on anti-poverty priorities.

This aspect of the PRSP review was not formally stated in the Decision Point Document. Bank officials stated privately that it would be based on 'an informed judgement call' by the Bank review team. The discretion this afforded IFI staff was a source of concern to some observers, especially those who worried that it could be used to undermine commitment to PRSP objectives that did not conform to Bank/Fund priorities.

The MASAF factor

Perhaps the most substantiated fears about the future of the PRSP – shared by at least some in each of the three stakeholder categories – concerned the Bank-funded Malawi Social Action Fund (MASAF), reportedly a favourite of President Muluzi. This programme, which among other things supports (mainly) infrastructure-related community development projects at the local level, has been criticised as highly politicised – meaning that the selection of projects is allegedly skewed towards localities that support the ruling party.[17]

In addition to concerns about partisan implementation and outright corruption[18] (and more importantly from the perspective of the PRSP), officials in line ministries fear that poverty-reduction priorities identified in the PRSP will, in practice, get squeezed out of future budgets because of the tendency for MASAF projects to have unplanned-for recurrent cost implications. These limit the pool of resources available for other discretionary spending, which may be of more direct relevance to the poor. That Phase III of MASAF was being negotiated before various evaluations (from inside and outside the Bank) had been submitted raised further suspicions about the Bank's (and the government's) commitment to ensuring that MASAF is both functioning well and geared towards the poverty priorities identified in the PRSP.

4.7   Conclusions

The ownership-effectiveness hypothesis

There are few grounds for believing that the implicit hypothesis contained within the PRSP approach – that PRSPs will change the nature of

---

17. According to press coverage, the President himself was reported to have made fairly direct statements in public meetings, warning local people that they would stand little chance of gaining access to MASAF funds if they supported opposition parties.

18. The PRSP Consultation workshop held in Dowa District revealed complaints from members of the district assembly 'that some MASAF projects claimed to have been undertaken in November 2000 in the MASAF report were never undertaken' (PRSP TC, 2001a: 10).

conditionality, leading to enhanced ownership of the strategies themselves, and therefore more effective implementation – will hold true in the case of Malawi. Indeed, currently proposed prescriptions for the shortcomings in public expenditure management are (rightly) premised on the belief that ownership at the highest political levels is not likely to emerge any time soon, either on its own or as a result of another poverty planning process.

The central explanation for the failure of expenditure-management reforms to date has been the absence of high-level political commitment. The primary objective of reform proposals has been to install systems that can bind politicians to their expressed commitments, and to existing legal prohibitions, largely based on the assumption that high-level political commitment simply cannot be conjured through external exhortation.

It is therefore not surprising that all informants interviewed for this study – *especially* those in government – were extremely sceptical about the viability of the conditionality-ownership-effectiveness equation. The reasons for the scepticism varied. One donor argued that the then Finance Minister, though universally praised, was 'not really at the centre of political power'. This view was echoed by a government official who stated that the Finance Minister's cabinet colleagues were more than capable of having him overruled on matters of fiscal discipline. In fact the government's own Public Expenditure Review all but stated this outright when it discussed the breaching of Credit Ceiling Authorities (CCAs) and the chronic non-priority expenditures incurred by parastatals.

So even if the Finance Minister and Principal Secretaries in a large number of line ministries were to feel that they 'owned' the PRSP, the real stumbling block would be the lack of seriousness among the President and senior political heavyweights in the cabinet. The replacement of Mr Chikaonda in early 2002 as Finance Minister by someone noted above all for his loyalty to the President seemed to confirm many of these views.

Another commonly expressed reason for pessimism on the question of ownership, voiced mainly by civil society representatives, was the continued existence of various forms of conditionality. Elected and bureaucratic officials, it was argued, have an instinctive understanding that 'with or without the PRSP, money will keep coming with lots of strings attached'. Those of this view pointed to the IMF's PRGF, the negotiation of new adjustment loans, and AfDB financing conditions. It was not uncommon for this belief to be stated alongside an assertion that government officials are also aware of the strong incentives for donors not to enforce conditionalities. This was expressed by one donor as 'the worst of both worlds: no ownership, but no responsibility either'.

Prospects for long-term and broad-based ownership will be determined mainly by the fate of accountability initiatives (including participatory monitoring) outlined in previous sections of this chapter. But Malawi has rather a sad history of lack of effective monitoring and evaluation, and as we have seen, the current stage of the PRSP process does not furnish much hope for the emergence of a dynamic poverty monitoring system.

Policy messages

There are obvious limits to the general recommendations that can be generated from a single-country study. But when assessed in the context of reports emerging from other countries engaged in PRSP processes, the Malawian experience to date does suggest a number of important findings that could inform the approach of donors. These fall into two broad categories: the PRSP formulation process, and the reform of conditionality.

The PRSP formulation process

Compared with Malawi's earlier policy-development processes – with the exception of the Vision 2020, which was an open process but focused more on general principles than specific policies – the PRSP formulation process was among the country's most participatory policy-making exercises. It nevertheless had some serious shortcomings. Some of the key lessons to have emerged are the following:

- Bilateral donors should not be shy about seeking inclusion in all aspects of the formulation process. The desire to allow a 'nationally owned' document to emerge is commendable, but in countries where foreign assistance amounts to a considerable portion of public expenditure, donors are de facto stakeholders. There are several benefits from donor participation in the substantive development of the PRSP.

- Their presence, somewhat paradoxically, increases the potential for a broad and serious form of non-government involvement (ownership being a slight misnomer) by signalling to other stakeholders that this is an important process with practical implications for future expenditure patterns.

- Donor participation not only gives government and civil-society stakeholders a more nuanced understanding of donor objectives within individual sectors. It also helps donors to get a clear picture of the nature of disagreements within government and between government and civil society.

- The constraints on changing the modalities of Country Assistance Strategies can be more readily communicated in the context of discussions on substantive policy questions than in other, less focused forums.

- Existing Sector Investment Programme documents and briefing papers should be used as the starting point for Thematic Working Group deliberations.

- The key, day-to-day coordinating body for preparing the PRSP should include civil society representatives, including both advocacy organisations and more conventional development-oriented groups.

- The entire process – including the 'endgame' – must be mapped out in fairly detailed terms at the *outset* of the process. In Malawi, the arrangements for drafting the PRSP, and the extent to which it would rely upon the papers produced by the Thematic Working Groups, emerged only slowly near the end of the process. This led to huge disappointment (and suspicion) from many stakeholders involved to that point.

- Involve parliamentary committees, including members of staff (where these exist), rather than just *individual* MPs, in the Thematic Working Groups.

Overhauling conditionality

The HIPC/PRSP concept claims to be a new approach to conditionality. To the extent that it changes *some* elements of conditionality, this is by definition true. But it is a rather piecemeal reform of conditionality, when what is required is a complete overhaul. The focus on 'national ownership' is welcome, but is only partly observed in practice. Either way, it is insufficient. To have any significant impact – on policy design, expenditure priorities, service-delivery patterns and, ultimately, economic performance or human development outcomes – other key elements of conditionality need restructuring. Donors should seek to do at least three things in their own assistance strategies, as well as encouraging their representatives in the IFIs to institute similar practices.

First, make conditionalities on all *external assistance completely transparent.* As things stand, in Malawi (as in many other countries) only some conditionalities are publicised. Even those that are nominally 'public' are not disseminated widely enough. There is no reason why any agreement into which an aid-recipient government enters should be confidential (with the exception of those that might directly and immediately affect financial-market behaviour). The 'sensitivities' of aid-recipient governments are insufficient grounds for the failure of donors to publicise the nature of aid programmes, including the conditions imposed and undertakings agreed.

Not only is secrecy unwarranted in principle; it is damaging in practice. Until thoroughgoing transparency is a standard feature of aid agreements, 'national' ownership (that is, beyond senior government officials) will be unattainable. Suspicions of donor-government collusion – which are often well-founded – will undermine the ability of either party to establish effective working partnerships with domestic civil societies.

Second, insist upon civil society involvement in all *aspects of monitoring adherence to conditionalities.* Once conditionalities are agreed and publicised, it is also necessary to stipulate with some precision the nature of the performance criteria against which compliance will be judged. Publicising these widely is part and parcel of making conditionality transparent. Details of what governments must do are insufficient if not coupled with an explanation of the methodology by which their actions will be assessed. Involving a cross-section of civil-society representatives in the process of arriving at this methodology is an important part of involving a wider range of stakeholders in the process of monitoring adherence to conditionalities. Where conditionalities include performance targets on financial probity, this provides scope for civil society groups to be directly involved in output monitoring.

Third, enforce (disaggregated) conditionalities strictly. Conditionalities are rarely enforced. Where agreed actions are not taken, new conditionalities insisting upon re-doubled commitment to taking these actions in future are often added to subsequent lending instruments. This undermines the belief that conditionalities are serious.

There are many reasons why donors do not enforce conditionalities, and Malawi's politicians are more than aware of these, as are political leaders in other aid-dependent countries. The legacy of non-enforcement may turn out to be the biggest constraint on effective implementation of PRSPs. In the case of Malawi, the somewhat encouraging impetus given to civil society's engagement with the state – on both policy dialogue and the question of monitoring – is an inadequate basis for expecting local pressure to substitute for hard external conditionalities linked to financial accountability and specific performance targets.

If conditionalities are to be enforced, they must of course be more finely tuned. That involves disaggregating instruments of financial support into smaller components that can be assessed separately. One of the major lapses of the early phases of the PRSP process was that while it identified performance targets for each policy intervention, it did not specify what would constitute an aggregate 'passing score'. Could great success in one policy area offset dismal failure in another, leading to continued funding across the board in future? This was a question many people were asking, but not one could answer.

Conditionalities that, if enforced, would lead to the withdrawal of *all* funding contained within a large programme of support are unrealistic – because of the understandable desire to avoid throwing the baby out with the bathwater. Such all-or-nothing forms of conditionality are unlikely to create adequate incentives for changed official behaviour and performance improvement. The strict enforcement of disaggregated conditionality may also need to be supplemented by instruments that lead to *increased* funding for performance on those criteria that exceed minimal requirements.

References

Government of Malawi (2000) 'MTEF Phase Two – Consolidation Revitalisation: Overview and Plan of Action'. Lilongwe: MoFEP, October.

Government of Malawi (1997) *Statement of Development Policies 1987-1996*. Lilongwe: Department of Economic Planning and Development.

Government of Malawi (1995) *Policy Framework for Poverty Alleviation Programme*. Lilongwe: PAP Coordinating Unit, Ministry of Economic Planning and Development.

International Development Association/R2000-234 (2000) 'Malawi – Enhanced HIPC Debt Initiative: President's Memorandum and Recommendation and Decision Point Document'. For consideration at the Executive Directors' Meeting of 21 December 2000. 8 December.

Joint Review of the Malawi Education Sector (2000) 'Review Report'. Lilongwe, October.

Kadzamira, Esme and Rose, Pauline (2000) 'Educational Policy Choice and Policy Practice in Malawi: Dilemmas and Disjunctures'. Paper presented at the Social Policy Workshop, Capital Hotel, Lilongwe, 29-30 March.

Malawi Economic Justice Network (2001a) 'PRSP in Malawi: Progress Report and Recommendations'. Lilongwe, April.

Malawi Economic Justice Network (2001b) 'Comments on the Proposed Malawi Budget 2001-2002: Report for Members of Parliament', Lilongwe, 8 August.

Malawi Economic Justice Network (2001c) 'Presentation on Priority Poverty Expenditures (PPEs) to HIPC Discussion Forum', 3 August 2001, Capital Hotel, Lilongwe.

Ministry of Finance and Economic Planning (2001a) 'Malawi 2000 Public Expenditure Review'. Lilongwe, August.

Ministry of Finance and Economic Planning (2001b) 'The National Budget Process: Measures to Protect its Integrity and Improve Effectiveness – Paper for Parliamentarians'. Lilongwe, June.

National Economic Council (2000) *Profile of Poverty in Malawi 1998*. Lilongwe: NEC.

National Economic Council (various) *Economic Report 1996-2001* (various issues). Budget Document Number 4. Lilongwe: NEC.

National Statistical Office (2001) *Demographic and Health Survey 2000*. Zomba: NSO.

Patel, Nandini (2000) '1999 Elections in Malawi: Challenges and Reforms', in Martin Ott, Kings M. Phiri and Nandini Patel (eds), *Malawi's Second Democratic Elections: Process, Problems, and Prospects* Blantyre: Kachere Series.

PRSP Technical Committee (2001a) *Malawi Poverty Reduction Strategy Paper (PRSP) Preparation Process: District Consultations Report*. Lilongwe, 14 March.

PRSP Technical Committee (2001b) 'Malawi PRSP Progress Report'. Presented to Minister of Finance, Lilongwe, August.

Reynolds, A. (1999) *Electoral Systems and Democratization in Southern Africa*. Oxford: Oxford University Press.

United Nations Development Programme (2000) *Human Development Report 2000*. New York: UNDP

Tsoka, M.G. and Kutengule, M. (2001) *Fiscal Sustainability of Social Policy in Malawi*. Zomba: Centre for Social Research.

Tsoka, M.G. (1998) *Review of Development Policies and Use of Research Findings in Policy Formulation*. Zomba: Centre for Social Research.

World Bank (2000) *World Development Report 2000*. Washington, DC: World Bank.

Chapter 5: Mali

by Idrissa Dante, Jean-François Gautier, Mohamed Ali Marouani and Marc Raffinot*

In Mali the process of preparing a PRSP was relatively long-drawn-out, partly because of the way it interacted with the timetable of political change in the country. This chapter explains how this had some benefits in terms of a maturing of government, NGO and donor attitudes in a nation that has been both highly aid-dependent and the focus of DAC-led efforts to improve aid coordination. It is argued, however, that significant constraints remain to transforming this good will into effective anti-poverty action, including weak policy-making capacities and incentives in government service, the slowness of public finance reform and uneven progress in eliminating supply-driven aid and lending, and the use of parallel funding channels.

5.1 Introduction

Initially, the preparation of the PRSP in Mali was widely seen as nothing more or less than World Bank/IMF conditionality to obtain debt relief. The pace was rapid and the motivation largely instrumental. However, during the two-year period between the completion of the Interim PRSP (iPRSP) and government agreement on the final document, stakeholder perceptions evolved progressively. There is now a more widespread acceptance of the PRSP as involving a permanent process rooted in the country with the aim of poverty reduction. Some institutional issues that undermined national identification with the PRSP in the early stages have been resolved.[1]

---

* University Paris Dauphine, DIAL, Paris. Gautier, Marouani and Raffinot dedicate this chapter to the memory of Idrissa Dante, who tragically died before the final results of their collaboration could be published. The report on which the chapter is based benefited from the comments of Howard White, Günter Hornung (GTZ, Bamako) and an IMF team. We would like to thank them for their comments. We have taken into account the factual critiques and some of the remarks based on their opinions. We would like to acknowledge that the remaining errors are ours, and that the opinions expressed here are those of the authors.

1. Notably, the existence of a previous UNDP-driven National Poverty Alleviation Strategy (SNLP) created problems at the start of the process. The World Bank rejected the use of SNLP as a basis for elaborating a PRSP. In due course, however, the SNLP was accepted as one of the inputs to the PRSP. Until the SNLP expired in 2002, both processes continued, the lead institution for the PRSP being the

An iPRSP was completed in July 2000 and endorsed in September 2000, and an ambitious timetable was set by the government for the preparation of a full PRSP. However, the subsequent process was much slower than expected, with deadlines being extended several times. Cabinet eventually approved the full PRSP on 29 May 2002. By this time, attitudes to the PRSP process had changed significantly. This chapter analyses and assesses this process. It is largely based on three missions to Mali by different members of the DIAL team, in September 2000, April and July 2001, and July 2002.

There are seven sections. The next two set out the country context and the main features of the PRSP process, while the third assesses the degree to which the institutional framework governing poverty reduction in Mali has been changed. The last three sections discuss the monitoring arrangements of the PRSP, the challenges to aid donors and overall conclusions from the study.

5.2   Poverty reduction and the policy context

Growth and poverty

During the period from 1992 to 2000, Mali enjoyed a period of sustained economic growth. The average growth rate of 4.6 percent was higher than the rate of population growth (2.2 percent). However, the devaluation of the CFA Franc made a large difference: the average annual growth rate was only 1.1 percent between 1989 and 1993, but it was 5.6 percent between 1994 and 2000. The growth rate has also been more regular since the 1994 devaluation, but remains linked to rainfall (agriculture represents 40 percent of GDP).

The relationship between growth and poverty is very controversial in Mali. Results of the various surveys can barely be compared. The Poverty and Human Development Monitoring Unit, ODHD (ODHD, 1999, 2000), reported that poverty increased significantly between 1989 (41 percent) and 1996 (72 percent) and then decreased between 1996 and 1999 (64 percent). The most astonishing result concerns an increase in poverty in the period 1994-96, which was characterised by sustained growth. The evolution of poverty between 1996 and 1999 is intuitively more acceptable if we suppose that growth induces poverty reduction. However, the latest results are controversial since they do not come from survey observations, but rely on mere extrapolations of incomes and the poverty line.

A study conducted by DIAL (2000) on the evolution of urban poverty shows a significant increase in poverty in Bamako. With a poverty line of $2 (at Purchasing Power Parity), the headcount poverty index rose from 33

Ministry for Economy and Finance (which includes the former Ministry of Planning).

percent in 1989 to 57 percent in 1996 (4.7 percent to 16.2 percent with a $1 poverty line). Nutrition indicators for children also deteriorated between the two Demographic and Health Surveys (DHS) of 1987 and 1995/96. The analysis covered Bamako alone, because the 1994 survey covering the whole country is unreliable (it uses a questionable methodology to assess household consumption), whereas the 1996 survey covers only Bamako.

Sahn and Stifel (2000) used a new methodology to assess the evolution of poverty in Africa. They use DHS information about assets (not incomes). For Mali, the result with this approach is a sharp decrease in poverty (and the poverty gap) between 1987 and 1995. The headcount falls from 23 percent to 16 percent, using the 25th percentile of 1987 as the poverty line – and from 43.3 percent to 30.8 percent using the 45th percentile of 1987. According to the authors, a reduction in poverty is observed in both urban and rural sectors.

In short, the evolution of poverty and the analysis of its causes and links with the evolution of GDP are far from clear in Mali. A new DHS has been undertaken, and a new income survey took place in 2000/2001, but results were still not available in July 2001, and were not able to be used for the full PRSP. They will provide a benchmark for monitoring.

A little history

Mali proclaimed its independence on 22 September 1960. The *Rassemblement Démocratique Africain*, led by Modibo Keita, opted for a socialist regime, and increased ties with USSR. The regime encountered tremendous difficulties on account of the hostility of the West (especially France) and this was compounded by its poor economic performance.

This experience ended with a military coup in November 1968. The coup leader, Moussa Traoré, dissolved Parliament and forbade political activity for ten years. A new constitution was adopted, leading to the creation in 1978 of the country's only political party, the *Union Démocratique du Peuple Malien*. However, the regime remained dominated by the military, which controlled the economy and strengthened their political basis by distributing rents. A popular revolt backed by a part of the army led by General Amadou Toumani Touré (ATT) put an end to this regime in 1991.

A transitional committee was established, to introduce a pluralist political system. The first general election, in June 1992, was won by the *Alliance Démocratique du Mali* (ADEMA), led by Alpha Oumar Konaré, in coalition with other political parties grouped in the *Pacte Republicain*.

From an institutional point of view, Mali respects most of the rules of a modern democracy. It is characterised by a plural political system, freedom of the press, separation of powers, existence of all the institutions we find in a modern democracy, plural trade unions and the emergence of various NGOs and a civil society. Human rights are respected and a political dialogue has been initiated by the government of Alpha Konaré, which permitted the end of the Touareg conflict and allowed the implementation of a programme of normalisation of the Northern regions with the support of donors.

However, this young democracy has yet to overcome the patrimonial structure that is its political heritage. The main questions relate to the weakness of the opposition and concerns about the neutrality of the administration. In 1997, most opposition parties had strong doubts regarding the administration's impartiality, which led them to boycott the elections, resulting in a Parliament dominated by ADEMA (80 percent of the seats). The consequence was a weak Parliament, dominated by the executive. ADEMA leaders, who dominated the administration, occupied 90 percent of Directorships of ministries, as well as holding positions as managers of public enterprises.

The Malian Constitution does not allow for more than two Presidential mandates (five years each). Some attempts have been made to modify this rule without success, and President Konaré eventually decided to retire at the end of his second mandate (2002)

The general elections of 2002

The conflict between the opposition and the party in power, following irregularities in the 1997 elections, did not end until the dismissal of Prime Minister Ibrahim B. Keita. One of the main tasks of the new government led by Mandé Sidibé (February 2000) was to organise transparent and credible elections. A framework for dialogue between the administration and the political parties was established to debate the 2002 elections. The main agreements concerned the cancellation of the judicial proceedings against opponents and neutrality of the administration.

An electoral census (RACE) was undertaken to ensure reliable electoral lists. Opposition parties decided to participate in these elections whatever happened, since they understood that their previous boycott only served the political party in power, allowing it to dominate all the institutions.

The National Electoral Independent Commission (French acronym CENI) and the General Delegation for the Elections (DGE) supervised the 28 April polls, in addition to the Ministry of Territorial Administration. The 24 candidates included Amadou Toumani Touré (ATT), who ruled the country from 1991 to 1992, Soumaila Cissé of ADEMA, Ibrahim Boubacar Keita, a former prime minister backed by 16 parties, and Mandé Sidibé, Prime Minister 2000-01, who was running as an independent. The only woman candidate, Awa Sidibe Sanogo, was disqualified for failing to pay the required fee (about US$6,700).

The elections were considered fair, despite some irregularities and a low turnout. ATT eventually won. Even though he did not have a political party, he gained the support of most of the existing parties. One result was the election of a Parliament in July 2002 in which there was no real opposition.

Aid dependence

Because of its high dependence on aid, Mali was chosen by the DAC/OECD as a pilot country for an 'Aid Review' exercise in 1996 (OECD/UNDP, 1998). Official Development Assistance (ODA) to Mali amounts to $400-450 million per year. It represents 15-25 percent of GDP. ODA finances about 70 percent of the government investment budget and 20-30 percent of current public expenditures. However, these aid figures (provided by donors and published in OECD and UNDP Cooperation reports) are more a measure of their costs than an assessment of the sums actually injected into the country's economy.

In fact, according to a recent study conducted by the Club du Sahel/OECD, about $100 million of aid flowing to Mali in 1998 was not recorded in the national accounts (Naudet, 2000). There seems to be a problem both of information and of transparency in the reporting of aid flows, and some large questions about the uses to which they are put (e.g. the share accounted for by technical assistance and headquarters' expenditures).

From a civil-society perspective, although corroborating data are not available, it is generally accepted that international cooperation plays an important role in grassroots' development and the financing of social organisations. On the other hand, the NGOs' heavy dependence on official donor funding represents a risk to their autonomy.

During the Mali Aid Review process, the broad consultation organised by the Djoliba Centre found that the population has an ambivalent view of aid. People are critical of the distorting effect of external assistance and the dependency it creates. However, the need for aid seems to be widely accepted. In conclusion, aid seems vital to the economy, national institutions and society at large in Mali, although Malians consider that it has not produced deep-seated changes in society and has had a limited impact on poverty.

Previous poverty plans

In 1997 the Government of Mali launched a National Poverty Alleviation Strategy (*Stratégie Nationale de Lutte contre la Pauvreté*, SNLP) with the help of UNDP (Diallo and Raffinot, 1999). The process took 18 months and comprised the following steps:

- Studies and surveys on poverty (mostly qualitative, but with some quantitative studies based on the Consumption Budget Survey of 1994). A survey on the perceptions of the poor was launched.

- Evaluation of 30 anti-poverty projects undertaken across the country.

- A national consultation in November 1997 defined the main strategic axes and priority actions to reduce poverty. This consultation included: the public administration, civil society, the private sector, universities, development partners, community organisations, and elected bodies.

- The draft SNLP was validated through a series of consultations at the national and regional levels.

- Final examination and adoption of the SNLP by the Council of Ministers in July 1998. This final draft defined eight axes of the fight against poverty. Among the eight axes, several priority actions were proposed, with cost estimates, although the method of costing was not precisely explained in the document.

The SNLP was validated by Mali's partners in development at a 1998 round table. In 1999, the SNLP was transformed into an action plan, with an integrated monitoring and evaluation system. A network of 30 poverty focal points was mobilised, across all major ministries, national institutions and collective organisations. A new Ministry, the *Ministère du Développement Social, de la Solidarité et des Personnes Agées* (MDSSPA) was specially created to manage the projects elaborated under the SNLP process. At the same time, the former Ministry of Planning was merged with the Ministry of Economy and Finance (February 2000).

In 2000, we noted positive opinions about the SNLP among both CSOs and members of the administration (especially, of course, within the MDSSPA). However, Serra (1999: 38) reports criticisms from NGOs suggesting that the SNLP was not 'truly participatory'.

The arrival of the PRSP should not have been a real problem for the Malians as a process for elaborating an anti-poverty policy was already in place.[2] But when the PRSP was proposed, the World Bank considered the SNLP to be inadequate for the purposes of the PRSP. 'As a matter of fact, the work required to produce a PRSP was considered so important, given the timetable, that Mali was obliged to go through an interim PRSP phase before being able to propose a final PRSP' (Lok Dessallien et al., 2001: 8). This resulted in a conflict between the World Bank and UNDP. The reasons given by the Bank included:

- the lack of a recent household survey for the elaboration of the SNLP;
- the lack of macro and structural-adjustment elements in the first document;
- the length of time needed for the PRSP initiative, to allow for grassroots participation in the process; and
- the fact that the SNLP is only focused on a few points – that is, some sectors like energy, transportation and industry were only partially covered by it.

---

2. During our first mission (September 2000), the persons we interviewed often got the PRSP and the SNLP mixed up.

For these reasons, the Bank asked Mali to make a fresh start and elaborate a PRSP with a fully participatory process. This decision was widely interpreted as a lack of tolerance on the part of the Bank. People involved in the SNLP did not understand why they had to do the work again, and considered it a waste of time and money. Moreover, they knew that in some other countries, like Mozambique, previous anti-poverty strategies had been considered acceptable as the basic framework for the elaboration of a PRSP. In Burkina Faso, the process had been very fast, although the country circumstances were quite similar.

Civil servants concerned with anti-poverty strategy were generally working on implementation of the SNLP. Some civil servants told us that they judged the PRSP to be a 'political thing', an instrument of the government and the Bank. Furthermore, they felt that the Bank's attitude generated suspicion regarding the declared wish of the Bank to let the Malian authorities have ownership of the PRSP. It is worth noting, however, that these civil servants knew they were going to be partly excluded from the process since the Ministry of Finance (MoF) was the main partner of IFIs. This could have been a factor in their initial resistance to the PRSP process.

Subsequently, the government took a decision to use the SNLP as one of the main bases for elaboration of the PRSP, and as a result most of the tensions were resolved. The iPRSP incorporated the eight axes of the SNLP.

In our opinion, the main weakness of the SNLP was its lack of a macro framework guaranteeing the coherence of its different axes, assessing their feasibility and linking them with the management of the economy. Thus it is difficult to consider the SNLP as a strategy ensuring the mainstreaming of poverty into public policies, even if it was an attempt in that direction. Moreover the MDSSA, responsible for its implementation, was not sufficiently strong to attain this goal and did not have sufficient influence on the economic or budgetary variables to impose its anti-poverty views. The SNLP ended in 2002 and is now completely merged with the PRSP.

5.3 The PRSP process in Mali

Initial arrangements

The process of preparing a full PRSP began slowly in November 2000, and it was only in February 2001 that it really started. Eleven working groups were established to cover sectors (rural development, education, health, etc.) and cross-cutting issues (governance, culture, etc.). The working groups were led by representatives of the different Ministries but included representatives of bilateral donors, IFIs and CSOs. The Joint Commission that had been created for the Mali Aid Review was used for the dialogue on the PRSP. The Netherlands led the group of bilateral donors, because of its involvement in poverty issues, debt cancellation and aid reform.

The working groups submitted draft papers in mid-May 2001. However, the institutional setting was finally completed at the beginning of June 2001 with the establishment of a PRSP unit (*Cellule technique de coordination du CSLP*) to coordinate the drafting process.[3] This provided human and material support to the official responsible for the process. The unit was officially composed of the coordinator, two Malian consultants and an international consultant, the consultants being financed jointly by the UNDP and the French Cooperation Office. The EU, the WB and the ILO also financed international consultants to be at the disposal of the PRSP Unit.

A series of drafts of the full PRSP were elaborated by the consultants, and discussed by various committees. Each draft was submitted to the IFIs and donors, in order to get their reactions. But there was also wider discussion. For example, a forum took place in June 2001 in Bamako, to discuss the findings of various poverty studies in Mali. The forum was supported financially by the World Bank and the African Capacity Building Foundation (Harare). The Malian authorities turned it into an opportunity to present the results of the different PRSP working groups. The discussion was very lively. For many participants, it was the first opportunity to take into account the findings of poverty studies, the dissemination of which remains very limited.

At the beginning, the PRSP Unit wished to draft a very detailed PRSP (like the Bolivian one, with more than 180 pages), in order to have a reference document explaining in detail the strategies and their rationale. The IFIs opposed this view and pushed for a light document (about 60 pages) presenting a policy overview as was done in the former PFPs. The final PRSP contained 93 pages of main text, and substantial appendices (60 pages).

Institutional roles and responsibilities

The Prime Minister was made head of the Orientation Committee (in charge of managing the whole process). Operational management of the process was to be the responsibility of the Ministry of Economy and Finance (MoEF). This might be seen as a source of strength. However, the MoEF is not as powerful as one might imagine on the basis of experience in other countries. It does not arbitrate effectively between budget submissions taking into account internal and external resource constraints. Nor does it urge line ministries to respect budget constraints. The Ministry often responds positively to the financing requests of the sectoral ministries, disregarding financial constraints.

The National Directorate of Planning (MoEF) provided the technical secretariat of the PRSP. This was explicitly presented as a guarantee of the sustainability of the process. The Ministry of Social Development (MDSSPA), in charge of coordinating the SNLP, was allowed to lead just one of the

---

3. Décision No 01 00047/MEF-SG (01/6/2001).

eleven groups, the 'poverty analysis and monitoring and gender' group.

The Joint Staff Assessment of the iPRSP expressed the view that 'the different anchorage of the SNLP and of the PRSP is likely to create confusion ...', creating 'a potential for duplication and/or divergence of objectives, indicators and monitoring'. The UNDP, which was the main supporter of SNLP, has now fully joined the PRSP process. The SNLP expired in 2002, putting an end to the duality. But not all its achievements or planned activities (e.g. regarding monitoring) have been taken into account by the PRSP.

The organisational structure of the SNLP included identified persons or 'focal points' (*points focaux*) in the line ministries. The role of these focal points was supposed to be mainly concerned with monitoring and evaluation. They did not play as such any role in the preparation of the PRSP, which is surprising, given the difficulty of getting sectoral ministries involved.

The PRSP process encountered several coordination problems during the second quarter of 2001. A widespread complaint was that the working groups did not really know what they had to do. There were different views as to whether they were expected to prepare a synthesis of already-existing programmes and projects, or design a brand new programme.

The failure of the macro group to ensure coordination was behind the decision to create a PRSP unit in charge of that task. However, this unit had some difficulties on account of the lack of substance in certain group reports, the shortage of statistics and the lack of 'modern planning' capacities within the administration. There is an old-fashioned tradition of plan formulation in Mali. But this tradition is quite useless for elaborating a realistic strategy. The missing link is a firm connection with a reformed budgetary process, as discussed in the next section.

Questions of ownership and conditionality

After preparation of the iPRPSP, the government saw the need to internalise the final PRSP elaboration process, since it would have to assume responsibility for its implementation. In addition to getting debt relief, which was the main objective for the government, the authorities understood that the PRSP was a good opportunity to prove their commitment to fight poverty and to create a unified framework of cooperation with their development partners.

The IFIs limited their influence on the process voluntarily. In fact, their interventions were limited to participation in the various committees and meetings organised by the MoEF. The IFIs were members of the 'macroeconomic, competitiveness and growth' working group, but not of its 'core editorial team'. As the Malian authorities reported very frequently to both IFIs and donors, the IFIs had the opportunity to make a lot of 'remarks' on the different drafts. These 'remarks' were far from homogeneous, as the position of the Bank and the Fund differ on some topics, and within each institution, team leaders in Washington and in-country representatives had different points of view.

The room to draft the PRSP was, however, reduced by the existence of a recent Policy Framework Paper. The PFP was dated July 1999 but its macroeconomic framework had been revised in May 2000. It contained commitments by the government and an analysis of economic prospects. It was unclear whether these commitments were really 'owned' by the government. In the past, discussions with IFIs have usually been reduced to a very small group of high-ranking civil servants, who have often agreed with the IFIs' programmes. But this consensus has been very limited, and does not spread to the administration as a whole, and even less to civil society.

The IFIs still have their own programmatic lending instruments (PRGF, etc.), which allow them a substantial influence over public-expenditure patterns, even if their conditionalities are not included in the PRSP. Discussions with World Bank representatives made it clear that they do not propose to give up their conditionalities. They do intend to link conditionalities more closely with policy performance indicators geared to poverty eradication, but still do not know exactly how to do this. The IMF took the important step in July 2002 of deciding to use the PRSP as the sole reference document – meaning that there would not be a distinct 'PRGF programme' any more. But the PRSP was not precise enough for that purpose, so the IMF was proposing to 'operationalise' it.

Anyway, the full PRSP was expected to be close to the IFIs' orientations, for several reasons. First, the Ministry of Finance is close to their way of thinking. Second, the incentives of debt reduction and further financing would drive the Malian authorities to write a PRSP as close as possible to the will of the IFIs. By reading some already-accepted PRSPs (such as those of Burkina Faso or Mauritania), the Malian authorities believed they could obtain a clear idea of what the IFIs want. (In general, this possibility will surely induce some homogeneity between PRSPs, even if they are written in different countries and independently). The Joint Staff Assessment of the iPRSP also gave many recommendations as to what should be presented in the final PRSP (but not the content or the way to do it).

The full PRSP was in fact generally close to the IFIs' orientations, but diverged in some respects. Good governance, competitiveness, etc. were emphasised. Some points, like the introduction of graduated VAT rates (lower on products consumed by poor people) had been agreed in the Macro Working Group, but disappeared in the final version. The existing privatisation programme was endorsed, in very fine print, although it had been totally rejected by Civil Society Organisations. On the other hand, the PRSP proposed a general increase of public servants' wages and salaries, which could be expected to result in a substantial budget deficit.

Although initiated by the IFIs, the PRSP has received the increasing support of other bilateral and multilateral donors through funding, participation in various working groups and technical assistance. Indeed, the involvement of donors in the process has been so massive that it could endanger the ownership of the process by the Malians. This is a danger particularly because each donor seems to have a definite thematic or sectoral interest in projects being executed or in the pipeline. The tendency of each donor to support the related working group and promote its particular perspective may well have affected the coherence of the final PRSP.

Debt relief and allocation of additional resources

Mali was granted effective debt relief under both HIPC1 and HIPC2 in September 2000 following a positive Joint Staff Assessment of the iPRSP. At the same time, bilateral donors grouped in the Paris Club provided 70 percent debt relief until the completion of the full PRSP, awaiting the full PRSP to provide debt reduction in line with the Cologne terms (90 percent). Mali had then to negotiate bilateral arrangements with others creditors to make debt relief effective (some bilateral creditors like the Netherlands and the UK used this opportunity to cancel all outstanding debt). Since the relief was in practice already effective, its pressure on the PRSP elaboration process was reduced, although this does not seem to have made a large difference.

As the process of debt cancellation is complex and slow (negotiations with Russia, China, Libya, etc. had not been completed by July 2002), the real amount of debt reduction remained unclear. Debt relief amounts may seem low (disappointingly so, in the opinion of all the Malian civil servants we met), representing only about 10 percent of ODA, 9 percent of public revenue, and 4 percent of total public expenditures. But one has to keep in mind that the level of education and health expenditures is also very low. For instance, health expenditures outside Bamako (regional hospitals included) were only CFAF 6.3 billion in 1999. Debt relief corresponded more or less to the amount of total public expenditures for basic social services in 1998, and about 50 percent of total social expenditures.

Hence, an absorption problem arises, if debt relief is to be spent only in basic social services. At the beginning, the IFIs insisted that debt relief resources should be allocated to basic social expenditures, education and health only. They later softened their positions with regard to social spending, and accepted allocating the resources generated by the debt reduction to a broader range of expenditure expected to have an impact on poverty reduction (e.g. the fight against desertification).

The real incentive comes from access to future financing. Finalisation of the PRSP was presented as a condition for obtaining the PRGF, a PRSC and also bilateral funds. Some bilateral donors made it clear that they would not consider any new programme before completion of the PRSP. For example, donors refused to fund an employment programme proposed by the Ministry of Employment, pending presentation of the final PRSP. This turned out to be only a way to exert some pressure on the government. The PRGF as well as other loans or grants were in fact disbursed before the finalisation of the PRSP.

Government plans, approach and capacities

One of the most striking points we noted during discussions with different stakeholders is that they consider the PRSP more a medium-term development plan than a poverty reduction strategy. This may mean that poverty reduction is being taken in a broader sense than before. Certainly, the Malian PRSP adopts a longer time horizon than traditional IMF financial programming. However, this progressive transformation of the PRSP into an exercise of development planning poses the difficult issue of Malian administrative capacities.

The former Ministry of Planning and Integration (MEPI) disappeared as such, and its senior employees have been attracted by more rewarding opportunities in projects or bilateral or multilateral organisations. The long-serving executives of the Directorate of Planning in the MoEF have had difficulties in adapting to the new context. The former five-year plans (which lasted to 1991) did not take into account budget constraints, and did not really allow for the private sector and the market economy. There has been little serious thinking about the sources of growth in Mali.

From the institutional point of view, the creation of a PRSP unit is problematic. If the PRSP is to be a medium-term plan focused on poverty, technically the Directorate of Planning of the MoEF should lead it. Most people with whom we discussed this agreed that this Directorate was unable to do the job and to lead the process. Nevertheless, if the PRSP turns out to be a permanent process, the coexistence of the PRSP unit and the Directorate of Planning will be problematic.

The government's weak planning capacity poses two problems. First, there is a problem of timing, as shown by the delays in completing the PRSP. The way of doing things is different if you plan your work on the basis of six months or two years. Second, there is a serious problem of ownership by the Malian administration, since considerable external technical assistance has been needed for the elaboration of the PRSP. However, as stressed by one donor representative, the impact of technical assistance on ownership depends on the nature of the assistance. If the role of the expert is purely technical, the threats to ownership are limited. But if it interferes in the strategic choices made by working groups, the danger is obvious.

Stakeholder perceptions

There has been a broad consensus among stakeholders (especially the Malian ones) that debt relief is so important that everything should be done to obtain it. Therefore, most of them seem to have endorsed the time constraint on PRSP preparation, and even those who criticise it (mainly NGOs) play the game to avoid being sidelined. Since fresh money is available for financing the process, the incentive is quite strong for different actors (even within the government) to be involved in the process. The new status of the PRSP in

Mali as the sole framework for government action and external cooperation makes it a pole of attraction.

The CSOs considered the pace of PRSP elaboration to be too fast for them, and therefore decided to organise a parallel process. Despite this, it is worth noting that they still participated in the different groups, and the Steering Committee promised to include their proposals in the final PRSP. As the deadline was supposed to be near, the CSOs' consultation process was quite fast. Their contribution arrived in July 2001, but it was difficult to use because no precise proposals were included.

Malian stakeholders are so used to donor-driven initiatives, and cooperate so closely with the donor community in every programme that there does not seem to be a strong awareness of the concept of ownership. Bilateral donors also do not seem overly concerned about ownership. They are aware of participation issues and have encouraged the involvement of CSOs in the process (and exerted some pressure when the CCA-ONG complained of being sidelined). However, donors seem to ignore the risk that their strong involvement could endanger the coherence of the process and its ownership by the Malian people.

The IMF seemed satisfied by the quality of the participatory process. It declared in August 2001: 'the staff is encouraged by the authorities' effort to ensure participation of all segments of the population in the preparation of the full PRSP' (IMF, 2001). But the consultations in the regions were several times postponed. They took eventually place in January 2002 in eight regions.

Participation, stakeholders and political traditions

'Participation', in the Malian political tradition, is mainly a way to get people to endorse government policies. Texts prepared by officials are submitted to 'seminars' or 'workshops' and are approved by the participants (who are usually paid for their participation).

In Mali, civil society is not a traditional actor in the political arena. A political opposition party leader told us that he considers the introduction of this concept in the PRSP process as an 'artificial importation of an Anglo-Saxon concept'. The lack of legitimacy of many CSOs (meaning NGOs) is often emphasised by civil servants. The former President of the Parliament is quoted as having declared: '*La société civile, c'est moi*'.

However, the Parliament itself did not play any role in the PRSP process. There was not even any discussion of the PRSP in Parliament, or by the *Conseil Economique et Social*, a consultative assembly representing the interest groups of the country. The justification given to us by government officials was that Parliament would ratify the final version of the PRSP anyway. The Joint Staff Assessment of the iPRSP stressed that 'it will be important to include parliamentarians and elected representatives of the newly established communes', which is not exactly the same as a formal involvement of the Parliament as such.

A progressive upgrading of the human resources available to CSOs (and not only the NGOs which are the favourite partners of IFIs and some donors) could give them more influence in the decision-making process. This would allow them to develop their own alternative proposals, and prevent civil servants from criticising their 'weak technical capacities'. Also, the recent strike of the farmers in the cotton sector (Bourdet, 2001) shows that some groups are starting to structure themselves to protect their interests, even if they are not part of the 'official civil society arena'.

The main obstacle, however, lies in the lack of education of the general population. The educated elite of the country dominates all government, administration and non-governmental institutions. Even in the case of 'well-meaning' NGOs, it must be asked: do they really represent the interests of the poor? The close ties of some of them with the donor community may anyway reduce the range of positions they can adopt. A real democratisation of the country will take the time necessary for the improvement of educational skills within a significant part of the population.

The PRSP as a consultative process

The consultation process of the PRSP was open to all stakeholder groups (donor community, civil society and national and regional government representatives). The institutional apparatus set up to manage the PRSP process included all these stakeholders as members of the working groups (WG). An *ad hoc* committee (chosen from within each group) prepared the synthesis documents of each WG for discussion and approval. One can say that the participation process reflected the desire to include all the actors; however, the contributions of the various actors depended on the methodology adopted by the WG.

Concerning civil society, the only organisations involved from the beginning of the process were NGOs, and their involvement was limited, as already mentioned. Later on, the trade unions and the chamber of commerce joined the process and expressed their positions through a document delivered to the PRSP steering committee.

CCA-ONG, a co-ordination structure of NGOs, organised five regional workshops in May and June 2001 (Bamako, Koulikoro, Sikasso, Ségou and Mopti), and then a national workshop in Bamako (6-7 June 2001), to which the other regions (Kayes, Tombouctou, Gao and Kidal) were invited. They received support from USAID for this. The final declaration acknowledged that there was limited information about the PRSP, due to the fact that 'its elaboration did not involve a public debate nor an active participation of the broad social categories of the poor'. The declaration criticised IFI conditionalities as responsible for 'a decrease of consumption, of production ... decrease of the prices of cotton and gold, ... increase in taxes ... in prices of water, electricity and cereals ... increase in diseases like malaria, HIV/AIDS, crisis of education system, deterioration of traditional values, etc.'.

The declaration stressed that HIPC is not an effective way of fighting poverty in Mali, because debt relief is too limited. It added that the PRSP relies on the same principles as structural adjustment, and is likely to have the same disastrous consequences for the population. According to the declaration (rather surprisingly, considering the above), civil society does not reject the PRSP, but asks for:

- the organisation of a public debate;
- the fixing of the conditionalities of the PRGF by 'our country';
- a real involvement of grass-roots organisations, local elected bodies, MPs and civil society representatives in the conception of the document (with suitable timing);
- simple mechanisms and strategies for implementation, monitoring and assessment of the PRSP, easily understandable by everybody.

This report was given to the Minister of Finance at the meeting of the Steering Committee of the PRSP on 17 July 2001, with significant coverage by the media.

In our opinion, the NGO process has had a limited impact on the PRSP. However, in terms of institution building, the PRSP process was a good opportunity for civil society (or at least for the NGOs, which benefit from the most significant support) to discuss crucial issues for Mali. This represents an improvement for the long run, even if its short-term benefits are not obvious.

The media

Media in Mali enjoy a broad freedom. There are a large number of newspapers, but their impact is limited because of widespread illiteracy. More important is the number of free radio stations (Mali is one of the best-served countries in Africa). The Malian media feel free to criticise government and IFI interventions. For example, during each World Bank/IMF mission, they express their scepticism about the results of negotiations. There is often a juxtaposition of a press release by the IFIs (or articles directly inspired by them) and articles criticising them on an ideological basis, mainly by NGOs. However, the media seem to be unaware of the new instruments and orientations of the IFIs. They still criticise structural adjustment and old-fashioned conditionalities without apparent awareness that changes are supposed to be under way.

The visit of Köhler (IMF) and Wolfensohn (World Bank) to Bamako (19-20 February 2001) was a notable opportunity for NGOs and the media to express their opposition to the IFIs. *Info-Matin* (22/2/01, p. 4) expressed the view that 'Le Mali, il n'y a pas encore deux ans a été contraint, le couteau sous la gorge, de signer un PAS au termes duquel était écrit noir sur blanc la réduction des systèmes sociaux, condition de son accession au PPTE' – an affirmation not really in line with the HIPC process.

Earlier, an *Association des Journalistes pour la Promotion du Professionalisme* (Association to promote the professionalism of journalists) organised a press conference to oppose the IFIs as 'responsible for the African tragedy' (*Le Républicain*, 21/10/00, p.4). But other newspapers and journalists seem more favourable. The *Indépendant* (22/2/01) noted the changes in conditionality and the emphasis on country ownership and good governance. Surprisingly, the journalist G. Drabo provided a description of HIPC in *l'Essor* (20/2/01), but without mentioning the PRSP.

CSO *structures and capabilities*

In a society with the cultural heritage of Mali, traditional and customary chiefs, as well as representatives of the different confessions, have a significant influence on the authorities. Trade unions (especially the autonomous ones) are well organised and powerful. They often point out the contradiction between the declared objective of poverty reduction, and the lay-off of workers due to IFI-driven privatisations (e.g., the open letter of the railway trade union to the President, *Nouvel Horizon*, 05/05/2001).

Civil society has been increasing its influence since the end of the 1990s thanks to the support of donors. Until the end of the 1980s, the political, economic and social organisation of the country did not leave any room for civil society. Even existing organisations (*Union Nationale des Jeunes du Mali*, or the *Union Nationale des Femmes*) were brought under the control of the ruling party.

At the beginning of the 1990s, the change of regime, together with strong support from donors, resulted in a boom in civil society. There are currently between 4,000 and 8,000 associations in Mali, and 650 Malian NGOs (half of them active), while their number was less than 50 in 1990. The peasants' organisations are also progressively structuring themselves into larger entities (such as SYCOV in the cotton sector). In addition to providing financial support, donors are trying to push towards increasing the participation of civil society in the important choices facing the country. The SNLP and PRSP processes are good examples where participation of CSOs has been initiated by multilateral agencies, and encouraged by bilateral donors. Nevertheless, the heavy dependence of many NGOs on external funds poses a problem of sustainability and also of independence. The Malian newspaper *Le Républicain* (22/2/01) adds that 'one may fear the possibility of manipulation of civil society by politicians'.

Moreover, there is a consensus among stakeholders (even donors who strongly support them) that NGO technical capacities have been an obstacle to a deeper involvement of their members in the different PRSP groups. The persons supposed to be the most competent of the group always constitute the small committees within each group, and these are most of the time government or donor representatives. These people have a kind of technical legitimacy that gives them more influence on the process.

Results of district-level consultations

Until December 2001, the PRSP official process had not reached the regions outside Bamako. The consultation in the regions could have been faster and more effective if locally elected bodies had been involved in the process from the beginning. The problem is that while the legal framework of the decentralisation process had been recently set, financial transfers corresponding to the new powers of the communes had not yet started. Eventually, however, an official participatory process did take place, from December 2001 to March 2002, and covered eight regions (Kayes, Koulikoro, Ségou, Sikasso, Mopti, Tombouctou, Kidal and Gao), as well as the Bamako District. Three workshops were held in each place, on poverty analysis, axes of intervention and monitoring respectively.

The participatory process was much more effective than initially expected. There was wide participation at the local level by civil servants and civil society representatives. The result was a lengthy list of demands and proposals, including roads; incentive payments to civil servants in the regions; translation of the PRSP into the national languages; transfers to improve the resources of the poorest zones; improvements in security; the fight against animal pests and diseases, and so on.

The difficult task was to prioritise the demands. It is difficult to assess to what extent they were taken into account in the PRSP. Some of them, like the incentive payments, are quite contrary to the World Bank's standard prescriptions.

Donor responses

At the beginning of the PRSP process we noted that bilateral donors were in the position of 'wait and see'. Bilateral donors did, however, eventually join the process, following in some cases the adoption of new positions by their governments regarding the PRSP initiative as a whole. In France for instance, the Ministry of Foreign Affairs moved toward supporting the PRSP initiative, and its local representatives received clear recommendations in this regard. The German GTZ provided important support to launching the PRSP preparation in February 2001, mainly by financing moderators for the working groups.

The involvement of donors increased progressively with their perception of the effectiveness of the process. Funding followed. The MoEF presented the donor community with a budget amounting to 880 million CFA Francs, which is about $1.2 million. The donors requested a more comprehensive budget with the expected outputs, the sequence of activities, and a breakdown of the total between PRSP preparation, implementation and monitoring. This blocked the disbursement of funds by most development partners. The lack of funds induced a delay in the preparation process since some groups decided not to start working until they received the amounts promised. Finally the MoEF provided financial support to the groups from its own budget. In addition, some donors (France, UNDP, EU, WB, ILO) provided technical assistance to the PRSP unit.

The PRSP process and donor practices

Donors' funding of the PRSP process has been welcome, but it was not effectively delivered. Practical complications arose. Only donors with money already available (GTZ) were able to provide support in good time – consultants apart. As already mentioned, the result was that PRSP working groups delayed the start of their work. Till August 2001, the WG on 'Mines, natural resources and environment' did not get any support and did not work at all.[4] At the opposite extreme, some other groups received a lot of money from institutions like the ILO and submitted very detailed documents, reflecting sometimes the views of their sponsors. In some other cases (like health), consultants wrote the WG document.

Donors considered the quality of the WG papers to be very uneven. Some of them were progressively improved. Some did not provide figures, and contained only wish-lists. This complicated considerably the tasks of the macro group and the coordination unit. In addition, they often reflected the pet projects of their financial backers, rather than a genuine concern to mainstream poverty into the sector in question. This affected the final outcome.

5.4   What difference has the PRSP made?

The politics of poverty reduction in Mali

In Mali, where poverty is so widespread (with about 64 percent of the population under the poverty line), the fight against poverty has a different meaning from that in rich or middle-income countries where fighting poverty consists of a set of targeted policies for a small fraction of the population. People in Mali often say that everybody in the country is poor.

The theme of poverty reduction has not been historically dominant in Malian political debate. However, the need for new slogans to win support in the new democratic system has led the party in power (ADEMA) to use this concept as one of its main elements of propaganda. The main opposition political party considered therefore that any reference to the fight against poverty was liable to be interpreted as a support for the government. Since fighting poverty has also become the first declared objective of the

---

4. This situation was overcome later.

international institutions, the government could gain both external and internal support by focusing its policies on the eradication of poverty.

Countervailing powers are weakly institutionalised in Mali, and thus there are few effective controls on government activities. Transparency has hardly improved and the patrimonial system is still in vigour. Even with the advent of democracy, clientelism is still present. Until the 2002 elections, the administration was dominated by ADEMA members, and rent-seeking was still the rule in the private sector. A campaign against corruption through an ad hoc Commission to investigate irregularities in the use of public resources was launched in 1999. It was described by the press as a way to oust political opponents, or disgraced members of the party in power. Some changes may be under way, however. A well-known judge declared to the press he had proof against many members of the government (*Info Matin*, 15/2/2000). An opposition party leader told us that the judicial system is progressively getting some power, and trying to impose itself as an independent actor.

Moreover, it is a salient fact that Alpha Oumar Konaré was not a candidate in the 2002 Presidential election, and did not support any successor. He seemed to be investing in his image of democrat, especially at the international level.[5] The acceleration of the campaign against corruption during this time (with the arrest of the CMDT CEO and a high-level customs officer) may be partly explained by this factor.

Mali has initiated a number of reforms, among which are the decentralisation process, civil service reform and budget reform. Many of these reforms are intended to strengthen the managerial capabilities of the administration, to increase the effectiveness and efficiency of public expenditures, and to allow more transparency through the participation of various stakeholders in decision processes.

The difficult improvement of budget procedures

The link between the PRSP and the budgetary process is very important if the PRSP is to be more than just a policy declaration. The missing link with the budget was always a major weakness of old-style development plans in Africa.

The assessment of Malian budgetary procedures by donors is mixed. Some find them unreliable, while some declare them safe enough to be used for budget support. However, donors and IFIs bear some responsibility for splitting the Malian budgetary process. Most projects are off-budget. Also, some donors are keen to create special funds and agencies. After the CFA Franc devaluation, for instance, the World Bank persuaded the Malian authorities to create a special agency (ADS) to provide a safety net. Each year, ADS spent CFA F 10 billion (that is, more than the half of the projected debt relief) outside of the normal budget procedures.

---

5. Since July 2003, he is the new Secretary General of the African Union.

Budgetary procedures seem to have improved (one reason is the improvement of the liquidity of the Treasury after the 1994 devaluation). Parliament votes on, and has some control over the execution of, the budget through the approval of the budget after execution (with large delays). Parliament now wants to extend its control to the relevance, as well as the proper administration, of public expenditures. The Supreme Court is in charge of the verifications, but lacks human and financial resources.

At the request of Parliament, a system called programme budgeting was introduced in 1998. As adopted in Mali, the programme budgeting approach does not entail all the features of an MTEF process. In fact, as already indicated, the allocations do not respect some of the constraints and there is no clear indication of the priorities between the sectors. The MTEF is far from being implemented, even if the PRSP was an opportunity to work out a first attempt. Even in the two sectors where SWAPs have been established (education and health), the process is still only half-implemented. At a result, it was impossible for the PRSP to assess clearly what will be the budgetary ceilings up to 2006, at least until the first months of 2002.

The IFIs advocate greater transparency. But they do not yet channel all their loans through the Malian Treasury. The World Bank created a new Loan Administration Change Initiative (LACI) in order to get a local fund ready for the payments of expenditures for projects and programmes. This is progress in the sense that all payments were formerly made from Washington. But it also means that we remain a long way from direct budget support.

The situation is set to improve. Mali has joined the 'norms and codes' process of the IMF in order to strengthen its national budgetary procedures. This could give donors more incentives to move toward budget support. An assessment of the budgetary procedures of Mali by an IMF team in July 2001 suggested that Mali does not meet the standard in seven topics out of 15. Not only were investment expenditures of donors not integrated in the budget, but there was no clear identification of anti-poverty expenditures in the budget; no integration of medium-term projections in the budgetary process; no use of a functional classification of expenditures; no audit presented to Parliament within 12 months of the end of the budget period, etc.). But the IMF stated that the Malian budget system did allow for effective internal audit, and that the implementation of the budget reflected the forecasts. The World Bank's last Country Financial Accountability Assessment (CFAA) recommended an improvement of the budget information system and strengthening of the audit system.

One of the expected positive side-effects of the PRSP process is an increase in the transparency of public financial procedures. However, transparency is made difficult by the multiplicity of channels used by donor funds, and the poor reporting system of these loans and grants. So far, the PRSP process has not led to a greater integration of donor funds into national funding channels.

Integrating existing SWAPs

Two major SWAPs were already in place before the launch of the PRSP: PRODESS (Health) and PRODEC (Education), and a minor one named PRODEJ (Justice). Their implementation had started. The PRSP did not modify anything in this regard. PRODESS and PRODEC were simply integrated into the PRSP. The macro group did not include these programmes initially, but took them into account after criticism. Critics emphasised that the PRSP was a government document and, as such, had to take into account any previous government commitments.

Debt relief may be expected to ease the financing of the SWAPs, helping them reach the social targets agreed by the government. The main objectives were to increase the gross school enrolment rate by 25 points (from 50 percent in 1999 to 62 percent in 2002 and 75 percent in 2006). The literacy rate of adults was required to increase to 36 percent in 2008 from 31 percent in 2002.

What difference might the PRSP make to institutional development?

It is difficult to predict to what extent the PRSP process will affect institutional development. To start with, the whole process was designed to fit a specific one-shot need, to enable access to HIPC2 relief. However, because of the unexpected length of the process, the PRSP now seems for many more Malians to be a permanent process. However, if the PRSP is here to stay, this poses new problems. The PRSP unit has become a central institution. It will absorb the former Secretariat of the DAC/UNPD Aid Review. Donors consult it to know whether their programmes are in line with the PRSP. It has become a major partner of the IFIs. Its status as a mere staff unit in the cabinet of the MoEF no longer seems appropriate.

The planning processes of the PRSP and the budgeting system (allocation of funds to the various sectors) will have an effect on the behaviour of line ministries. One of the main innovations of the PRSP (compared with the former Policy Framework Papers) is that it calls for the Ministry of Finance to make a medium-term allocation of available funds. In principle, this should strengthen programme budgeting and give it more of a medium-term perspective. The difficulty lies in the weak links between the sectoral ministries and the budget office, which do not allow the latter to define the envelope of each ministry taking into account its objectives. However, this is a real change, since under structural adjustment programmes, the IFIs were mostly interested in the levels of public expenditures and not in their allocation.

The government has also increased the time-frame of the PRSP from three to five years, which corresponds to the length of previous development plans. It was intended to start in 2002 and run until 2006, but will now start in 2003. The new President and government were thus in office from the beginning of the implementation. At first, the new government was cautious about endorsing a strategy document that had been prepared by the outgoing government. However, it gave up the idea of redrafting the PRSP to avoid further delays.

What are the key constraints?

Mali is frequently seen as committed to reforms. For example, UNCTAD's 2001 Report (*Economist*, 12/05/01) presented Mali as an example of a strong adjuster from the financial point of view that did not achieve corresponding results in respect of poverty alleviation. Even the IMF has stated that 'in completing the first review (of the PRGF), Directors welcomed the measures taken by the new government and its commitment to push ahead with structural reforms' (IMF, 2001). In short, the commitment to reform seems high, but this does not have a positive impact on the welfare of the population.

There are three main points to stress in this regard. First, some reforms will have an impact only in the long run. Second, the fight against corruption is recent. Finally, the behaviour of the administration, which is supposed to implement the reforms, is at best questionable.

The preparation of the SNLP, which preceded the HIPC2 initiative, proves that there was political interest in fighting poverty before the start of the PRSP process. However, the complexity of the PRSP process, the difficulty of understanding what the IFIs really wanted, and the mixed signals they sent, weakened the commitment of the government. Former President Konaré publicly declared: 'For every programme, we are told it is necessary to take it into account in HIPC. I frequently wonder what it is exactly' (*Les Echos*, 14/07/2000).

The problem is even more complicated, because the PRSP is not the only programme the government has to take into account in its decision process. Regional integration, for instance, is the source of new constraints that are difficult to manage (like the new Common Tariff for West African Economic and Monetary Union, which is likely to reduce public revenues).

The resources that will be freed by the HIPC initiatives are welcomed by the officials, even if they have serious concerns about the relative modesty of the amount compared to what is needed to meet the international community's goals for 2015. Former president Konaré indicated this worry clearly in his speech during the FAO Summit in July 2001: 'The amount of $870 million over thirty years is certainly important but not enough to alleviate poverty in Mali'. Against this background, the choices made by the government are sometimes difficult to understand. For example, in the 2001 budget, CFAF 10 billion were allocated to the organisation of the African Cup of Nations 2002, while the HIPC resources in 2001 were not expected to exceed CFA F14.3 billion.

Commitment at the top of the government is important, but the PRSP process is highly demanding for the public administration. The PRSP begs the question of the willingness of civil servants to participate in the process.

Its preparation has shed light on the fact that even if the government is committed to the reforms included in the PRSP, success will depend on the capacities and the motivation of the civil servants in charge of implementing the policies. This suggests the importance of ownership of the process by the civil service as well as ownership by the government.

It is difficult to mobilise Malian administrators in support of a national programme. Because of the numerous opportunities for civil servants to receive supplements and per diems by working on donor projects, the time remaining for routine duties is limited. The elaboration of policies is an activity without direct financial interest for civil servants. Donors have tried to resolve this problem by financing special units (PRECAGED, CAFPD, ODHD and the *Cellule de Croissance Accélérée et Développement*). However, this strategy seems to be neither very effective nor sustainable. The *Cellule de Croissance* disappeared when the World Bank financing ended, and so did ODHD in 2002 when UNDP stopped its financing.

In addition, from the technical point of view, the Malian administration lacks tools such as sectoral and economy-wide models for analysing the impact of public policies on poverty. This reflects the inadequate response of donors to this need, the lack of capacity to make use of the available tools, and the intrinsic difficulty of the task – which is well reflected in the changes that have been necessary in the macro chapter of the World Bank's PRSP Sourcebook. The 'new Washington consensus' aimed at poverty reduction is far more complicated to implement than the former structural adjustment agenda, because the links between policies and poverty reduction are far from obvious and are often controversial (Klasen, 2001).

5.5 Monitoring the PRSP: a second chance?

Poverty information: supply and demand

The PRSP group in charge of 'analysis and monitoring of poverty, and gender' identified several problems in the Malian statistical system that may be expected to impede the monitoring process:

- The lack of institutional coherence due to the failure of the decentralisation of statistics collection. The *Direction Nationale des Statistiques et de l'Informatique* (DNSI) does not have the means to ensure the coordination of the supply of statistics.

- The lack of specialists able to design surveys, write questionnaires, and collect and clean data.

- The lack of funds to finance current and special statistical operations.

- The lack of appreciation of the data: There is low awareness of the available data, the dissemination is irregular and of bad quality, and analysis of the data by the DNSI is very elementary.

In our opinion, the weakness of the statistical information system in Mali (including poverty surveys) has three main sources. The first is related to technical capacities. The second deals with the reluctance of the statistical directorate to divulge the results of its surveys outside the administration. Finally, the Malian authorities do not seem to be interested in financing their statistical system. They rely on external financing for their surveys, which makes these surveys very irregular, and poses a serious problem of ownership. Overall, this creates a problem of commitment, since if the government is not able to assess the performance of its policies, it is not obliged to respect the commitments it makes.

The monitoring and information hole in PRSP planning

At the beginning of the PRSP process, the IFIs complained that there was no recent information about poverty in Mali. This was one of the main arguments against the SNLP. Therefore, the World Bank decided to support a national poverty survey and regional poverty mapping.

Thus, a new Consumption Budget Survey (CBS, or EMEP by its French acronym) was planned to provide fresh information for the preparation of the PRSP. It was delayed, but began in January 2001, and was completed in January 2002. By June 2002, only the results of the first CWIQ (QUID) survey were available. This sheds light on some issues, mainly the distribution of benefits of social expenditures among household categories. However, it was not enough to provide an accurate basis for an analysis of the trends in the poverty situation. Instead, an indicator has been computed on the basis of the supply of infrastructures (education, health, water, etc.) in each village. These data have been mixed to produce an indicator (Is) that varies between 0 and 20. If Is<10, the village is said to be poor. According to this definition, the poverty incidence was 64 percent in 1998.[6]

The PRSP targets for poverty reduction were set at the very end of the process (poverty is to decrease to 47.5 percent in 2006). Education and health are exceptions, given that specific targets had been set under PRODEC and PRODESS – but they have to be projected up to 2006. Furthermore, the relationship between targets and budget is still unclear.

It is still not yet clear which institution will be in charge of the monitoring process. The ODHD, in charge of the monitoring of the SNLP could have been a candidate for the monitoring of the PRSP. With the end of UNDP and

---

6. These data on poverty need to be completed by macro data-bases (input-output tables, social accounting matrices) that can help in modelling the link between growth and poverty reduction, and thus design effective pro-poor growth policies.

World Bank financing, this observatory disappeared at the beginning of 2002, but its rebirth with more realistic assignments is awaited. The working group on monitoring has only declared that monitoring will rely on the national statistical system. Will the National Direction of Statistics (DNSI) be responsible for that task? Is this realistic given its tremendous difficulties? Moreover, there has not been any costing of the monitoring process yet.

No participatory monitoring or assessment has been planned. Such a process would have the advantage of extending ownership of the monitoring process to a wider range of stakeholders. It would ensure greater transparency and fewer doubts about the outcome of the process. Concretely, the working group responsible for defining the monitoring strategy could play the role of a steering committee in charge of poverty-reduction assessment.

Concerning the indicators selected, some previous work has been done. The first is a report by an international consultant hired by the government with the support of the EU, which deals explicitly with the monitoring strategy. The second is the result of the work of the 'Poverty Analysis and Monitoring Group'.

The first report proposes three kinds of indicators:

- *impact indicators*, which will summarise the evolution of poverty in its different dimensions (medium- and long-term);
- *results indicators*, which allow the monitoring of the effects of the PRS in the short and medium term, and which concern the elements that most influence the impact indicators (e.g. vaccination); and
- *activity indicators*, which assess the evolution of inputs to the PRS (number of roads, of teachers per class, of doctors per inhabitant) and the quality of these inputs (number of effective hours taught, availability of medicines).

The second report presents a matrix indicating the type of indicator (monetary poverty, human poverty and life conditions, potentialities, and macroeconomics) and 78 sub-indicators, their periodicity, source and method of collection. Noteworthy is the will to extend the different indicators to the regional level. However, the intermediate results and activity indicators highlighted in the consultant's report are generally lacking (although they have an important place in the Education and Health SWAPs). Also, there is no costing of the different monitoring activities. It would have been especially relevant to estimate the cost of the new surveys that will be needed to ensure monitoring of the PRS.

The final PRSP presents two lists of indicators. The first list is a classic list of indicators in the health and education sectors. The second is a wider list corresponding to the main objectives, like institutional development, good governance, sustainable development, etc. The indicators are quite vague ('satisfaction rate of the users of public services', 'number of anti-corruption controls', for instance). No values for the base year or targets for 2006 are presented.

The PRSP unit stresses that the PRSP is work in progress and that a large workshop will be held to define more closely the monitoring and evaluation arrangements for the PRSP. Donors (Canada, EU) and institutions (CAFPD) are engaged in a non-coordinated way in supporting the design of a monitoring system (without taking into account what was done for the SNLP).

5.6   Towards a new aid relationship

Coordination between bilateral donors has improved as a result of both the DAC/OECD/UNDP Mali Aid Review and the PRSP process. The Netherlands has been the spokesman of all bilateral donors in the PRSP Steering Committee. This is to avoid a heavy representation of donors in the process. Co-funding of support to PRSP preparation is also a noteworthy development. France and UNDP provided a joint programme of assistance.

As already mentioned, the government and its development partners have agreed that the PRSP become the reference framework for all cooperation with Mali. The lack of such a framework was identified by the Mali Aid Review (UNDP, OECD, Club du Sahel, 1999) as a major obstacle to the coordination of aid to Mali. The lack of commitment of some PRSP working groups and the quality of their drafts strained the credibility of the process, as did the many shifts of the deadline for completion. Nevertheless, the PRSP has come to be seen by bilateral donors as a way to improve coordination between them, the IFIs and the Mali Government.

An interesting development is that bilateral donors have asked the IMF to allow them to be involved in the joint IMF/World Bank missions. EU members sent two formal letters in this regard. The response was twice negative, the IMF and the government each blaming the other for this refusal. However, it seems that this EU initiative was not strongly supported by the national donor agencies either, since some of them consider that their nominees on the Boards of the Bank and the Fund already represent them.

Another important point, raised by one of the bilateral donors, concerns the scepticism about the willingness of the World Bank to change its lending policy. The Bank has committed itself to develop its future activities within the PRSP framework. But some observers consider there is still a risk that the Bank will continue to be the 'lender of first resort' on account of the motivation of its employees to lend as much as possible.

A final noteworthy point is the complete absence of the African Development Bank from the discussions around the PRSP. This is surprising given the fact that AfDB is the second creditor of Mali, just behind the World Bank (IDA), for an amount equivalent to that owed to the whole Paris Club.

The World Bank faces important dilemmas. HIPC debt relief is supposed to be granted as budget support. But at the same time, the Bank's biggest success story in fighting poverty in Mali is PAIB, a grass-roots' initiative that avoids the government (and the new elected 'communes') as much as possible, using NGOs to identify and monitor public-infrastructure provision in the villages. As stated by Larry Summers in his letter to the Bank's Country Directors (2001), this strategy of the Bank 'weakens democratically elected governments'. However, the ability of budget support to produce comparable results is a long way from being established.

What difference might donor behaviour make?

Before the start of the PRSP process, donors requested the Government of Mali to elaborate a national development framework that would build on existing sectoral and thematic programmes. The arrival of the PRSP should help meet this need. The PRSP has the potential to be a bridge between short-term and long-term policies, linking existing strategies with costing, the setting of priorities and the fiscal framework.

In Mali all these conditions are well understood by the donor community. But the practices of donors during preparation of the PRSP were not particularly encouraging. So far, donors seem to perceive the PRSP as a general framework that does not constrain them very much in the preparation of their own programmes. There are also doubts about whether the longer-term changes in aid modalities that the PRSP invites will begin to occur in reasonable time.

One of the shortcomings of the aid system in Mali is recognised to be the poor integration of aid into existing national structures and procedures (OECD/UNDP, 1999). The aid system has a tendency to create parallel structures, decision-making channels, and financial and information systems. This has two major consequences:

- it weakens national institutions, which is in contradiction with the goal of strengthening local capacities and complicates the government's management of the economy; and
- it undermines the overall coherence of development activities.

If donors use the PRSP process as a national planning instrument and if they integrate their interventions into the final PRSP, the resource mobilisation process will benefit and the management capacity constraint at the national level will be eased. Fragmentation of donor interventions and the use of parallel structures will be reduced.

Moreover, if the PRSP process strengthens the executing instrument (the national budget system) and donors move towards budget support, overall coherence of programmes could be enhanced. This would allow the government to develop medium-term planning, which is not really possible so long as aid is project oriented. The corollary would be a limitation of the number of conditionalities and the use of a single set of conditions that all the donors will use for their own interventions. Ultimately, this would be the product of the same nationally-owned thinking that goes into the PRSP.

The PRSP seems to be welcomed by some donors partly because of its potential for increasing the integration of aid flows into public channels. Some of them envisage increasing progressively their budget support. However, the behaviour of the various donor agencies is not homogeneous in this regard. For instance, the Dutch are pushing strongly toward budget support, while others are still reluctant, even if their *discours* has changed.

The main argument of the latter group is based on the absence of transparency and continued mismanagement of the budget. However, it seems that some agencies also have their own preferences in terms of aid management. Indeed, it may be in the interest of staff in the field to keep control over the management of projects. Greater budget support might be resisted because it would reduce their influence over the decision processes. For this reason, it is possible that change will occur only if clear instructions are given by the agency's headquarters.

The personality and views of the agency head at the country level may make a difference in one direction or the other. In some cases, in-country representatives are able to decide the speed of implementation of the new policy. The issue of donor behaviour is thus linked to the degree of delegation (decentralisation) of power to the field level within each agency.

5.7   Conclusions

Even if it is still early to draw firm conclusions, it seems possible to sum up some points that are not likely to vary. The main focus is to assess to what extent the institutionalisation of the PRS process is under way.

1) The capacity of the Malian administration to work out policies is weak. Constraints on civil-service pay, coupled with extra salaries paid by donor projects, are responsible for many distortions in the Malian administration. A general move towards budgetary support would provide, among other things, an opportunity to break with these practices.

2) The capacity of civil society is also weak, and its role in the process is still unclear.

   • Civil society is composed of different bodies, with very different approaches, skills and involvement in the PRSP process.

   • Elected bodies did not play any role in the PRSP process.

   • The consultation with civil society in the regions eventually took place at the end of 2001 and beginning of 2002. Many demands were made, but it proved difficult to take them into account when the PRSP had reached such an advanced stage. Furthermore, there was no clear methodology for prioritising the demands.

3) The IFIs refrained from intervening directly in the process, but the weight of their previous programmes and projects, their close monitoring of the process, observation of the outcomes in other countries and their capacity to hire top civil servants heavily influenced the outcome.

- The IFIs did change their mode of operation. They did not write the documents themselves, as they did the former Policy Framework Papers. They also eased the budgetary constraint by providing early effective debt relief, although the magnitude of the debt relief remained unclear during most of the PRSP process.

- There were different interpretations of the PRSP process between the IMF and the World Bank and within the two institutions, notably between the representations in Mali and the teams in Washington.

- The World Bank initially refused to build on the former UNDP-driven SNLP, which resulted in delays and some discouragement in the Malian administration.

- Previous agreements (like the PRGF) reduce the ownership of the process. As they have been formally endorsed by the government, one may argue that these policies are 'owned' by the Malians. There is nonetheless a problem, because programmes like the PRGF have been in the past discussed with a limited number of top civil servants who share in the bulk of the old Washington consensus. These policies and their justifications are not widely shared by Malians. The IMF eventually agreed to have the PRSP as the sole reference document for the PRGF. For that purpose, the PRSP is supposed to be 'operationalised', but what exactly that means is unclear.

4) Mali is a very aid-dependent country. The previous DAC-UNDP donor-coordination initiative gave some substance to aid coordination. The PRS process has helped to speed the coordination measures.

- Donors have supported the PRSP with advice, participation in the PRSP Working Groups, financial resources and consultants.

- Most donors have agreed to use the PRSP as the reference document for their activities, programmes and projects. But it is not clear yet how much this will change the way they act, because of the high inertia shown by aid institutions.

- There remains a problem of coordination between donors and IFIs.

The joint missions of IFIs are not open to bilaterals (although they do share the results). The IFIs remain the sole judges of the acceptability of the PRSP.

5) The budgetisation of the PRSP has been very difficult. SWAPs exist in two sectors (education and health), but are hardly effective. Nevertheless, the PRSP has provided an opportunity to embark on an MTEF.

- The debt relief received is very limited, but it could enhance dramatically the funding of basic health and education – to such an extent that a problem of absorptive capacity arises.

- The link between targets and costs is still missing, so the MTEF remains a first attempt.

- The budgetary process is not very effective and corruption is widespread. Some donors put these elements forward to explain their reluctance to channel their funds through the Malian Treasury.

Policy messages

A number of clear action-implications follow from this analysis, and it is worth itemising them by way of conclusion:

- There is no need for a PRSP to contain the views of the government alone. It would enhance the sense of country ownership if the document were to include a clear statement of the positions and arguments of the opposition (whether political parties, NGOs or CSOs).

- It is not possible to build a PRSP on some sort of *tabula rasa*; that is, with no reference to existing policy commitments. Nevertheless, the preparation of a country's first PRSP should be an opportunity to break with analysis and policies that have proven ineffective, or have not been widely discussed and endorsed by elected bodies.

- A PRSP should capitalise on previous methods that proved useful (such as the participatory approaches used in programmes or projects). The scope and aims of the participatory approach adopted should be precisely defined.

- It is important to enhance the technical capacities of CSOs. Support should not be limited to NGOs, but also extended to trade unions, smallholders' organisations and so on, even if these do not share the views of IFIs (as during the cotton-sector crisis, for example). The challenge is to provide aid to CSOs and NGOs, but with restraint, because too much help is likely to be counterproductive.

- If ownership is to be taken seriously, then the national capacity for designing anti-poverty strategies is crucial. Reform of the civil service is a prerequisite for this, and it needs to be based on a broad approach, not only on budgetary considerations.

- It is important to avoid creating new institutions for the PRSP. As a national process, the PRSP should be managed by a senior body (such as the Prime Minister's Office). Any special unit at this level should only coordinate the work of the appropriate bodies (sectoral ministries, Planning, Finance, etc.). Planning and programming units in the sectoral ministries (CPS) should be reinforced and made attractive to well-qualified civil servants.

- Donors should avoid financing only short-term operations. They should invest in basic information – statistics at micro-level (surveys) and macro-level (e.g. social accounting matrices). The government has to show its interest in such basic information by investing in permanent macro databases. Developing the statistical system should be one of the government's priorities and, if poverty monitoring is intended to be a sustainable process, it should not be left to donors. A costing of the monitoring process should be performed so as to include it in the budget, and thus guarantee its effective implementation.

- Donors should integrate their interventions into the PRSP and re-design their policies in this regard. They should not merely use it as a general framework for already planned projects. Donors should use national instruments and procedures.

- Thus, the coordination between donors and Government of Mali initiated by the Aid Review process should be extended to a policy dialogue between the government, donors and IFIs. This dialogue would permit discussion of new conditionalities and strengthen the PRSP as the sole reference document for cooperation between Mali and its development partners. To this end, IFI missions should be more transparent, and should involve donors (or their representatives) in discussions between IFIs and the government.

- A move towards budget support is needed if the Government of Mali is to be able to undertake serious medium-term planning, and to strengthen the link between planning and the budget. A greater focus on the MTEF is needed, with links between targets and costs. The government should pursue its efforts to improve transparency and efficiency of the budget process, and encourage donors to move towards budget support.

- HIPC funds do not have to be managed in a different way from the other budget funds. The Malian budget is already complicated by the World Bank's desire to monitor priority expenditures by creating special accounts (like the 'safety net' fund) that become difficult to integrate later. More freedom should be permitted on the budgetary side, and more emphasis placed on ex-post audit and control.

- The IFIs should avoid introducing new instruments every two years. Assurance is needed that PRSPs and country ownership of the fight against poverty is not just another fad of the IFIs that will be soon replaced by something else.

References

Bourdet, Y. (2001) 'Mali, Coping with Adversity' Department of Economics, University of Lund, Sweden (mimeo)

DIAL (2000) *Etude de la pauvreté urbaine en Afrique de l'Ouest, Côte d'Ivoire, Mali, Sénégal*. Report for World Bank. Paris: DIAL.

Diallo, C. S. and Raffinot, M. (1999) *Evaluation du programme national de lutte contre la pauvreté au Mali*. New York: UNDP.

Diop M. (2001) *L'expérience du Mali, cadre stratégique de lutte contre la pauvreté. Groupe d'apprentissage africain sur les stratégies de réduction de la pauvreté.* Addis Ababa: Economic Commission for Africa, Sept.

Gouvernement du Mali (2002) *CSLP Final, Cadre stratégique de lutte contre la pauvreté*. Bamako, 29 May.

Gouvernement du Mali (2001) *CSLP Final, Cadre stratégique de lutte contre la pauvreté, version provisoire*. Bamako, 30 Nov.

Gouvernement du Mali (2000) *CSLP Intérimaire, Cadre stratégique de lutte contre la pauvreté*. Bamako, 19 July.

IDA (2000) *Mali: Interim Poverty Reduction Strategy Paper and Joint World Bank-IMF Staff Assessment of the Interim PRSP*. Washington, DC: World Bank, 17 Aug.

IMF (2002) *Mali: Report on the Observance of Standards and Codes – Fiscal Transparency Module*. IMF Country Report N°02/33. Washington, DC: IMF, Feb.

IMF (2001) *Mali: Second Review under the Poverty Reduction and Growth Facility*. IMF Country report N°01/130. Washington, DC: IMF

IMF-IDA (2001) *The Impact of Debt Reduction under the HIPC Initiative on External Debt Service and Social Expenditure*. Washington, DC: IMF, November.

Klasen, S. (2001) 'In Search of The Holy Grail: How to Achieve Pro-Poor Growth?'. University of Munich, Draft, May.

Lok Dessalien, Renata; Sanoussi Goune, Alissabatou; Diarra, Bakary; Larivière, Sylvain; and Martin, Frédéric (eds) (2001) *Poverty Reduction Strategy: The Malian Experience*. New York: UNDP and Québec: Université Laval, IDEA International.

MoEF (Ministère de l'Economie et des Finances) (2001) 'Programme pluriannuel de convergence, de stabilité, de croissance et de solidarité 2002-2004'. Bamako, Nov.

Naudet, J. D. (2000) 'La comptabilisation des flux d'aide au Mali'. Paris: Club du Sahel, OECD (mimeo).

ODHD (2000) *Aide, endettement, pauvreté*. Bamako: MDSSA, PNUD and World Bank.

ODHD (1999) *Croissance, équité et pauvreté, Rapport national sur le développement humain durable*. Bamako: Ministère de l'Economie, du Plan et de l'Intégration, UNDP and World Bank.

OECD/UNDP (1998) 'Mali Aid Review: Synthesis and Analysis'. Provisional Report. Paris: OECD and New York: UNDP.

OECD/UNDP (1999) *Improving the Effectiveness of Aid Systems: The Case of Mali*. SAH/D(99)502. Paris: Club du Sahel, OECD and New York: UNDP.

Petersen, K.H. and van der Hoeven, R. (2000) *Rapport sur la mission d'appui pour renforcer l'articulation entre le cadrage macroéconomique et la lutte contre la pauvreté au Mali*. Bamako: UNDP.

Sahn, D. E. and Stifel, D.C. (2000) 'Poverty Comparisons Over Time and Across Countries in Africa', *World Development*, 28(12): 2123-2155.

Serra, R. (1999) *Mali Country Study: Creating a Framework for Reducing Poverty: Institutional and Process Issues in National Poverty Policy in Selected African Countries*. Report to the SPA Working Group on Poverty and Social Policy. Brighton: Institute of Development Studies, Dec.

Société Civile du Mali (2001) *Point de vue de la société civile sur le cadre stratégique de lutte contre la pauvreté au Mali, atelier national de validation de la synthèse de ateliers régionaux (6 et 7 juin 2001)*. Bamako: CCA-ONG, May-June.

Summers, L. (2001) 'Remarks by Larry Summers at the Country Directors' Retreat'. Washington, DC, 2 May.

Chapter 6: Mozambique

by Hans Falck and Kåre Landfald, with Pamela Rebelo

The setting for the PRSP initiative in Mozambique includes continuing political tensions, extreme capacity constraints and financial shortfalls, and a policy process that is very far from a rational planning model. Nevertheless, this article argues, the initiative has improved the prospects for clear prioritisation in poverty reduction efforts by the government, and provides a focus for better coordination of international cooperation. Mozambique's PRSP – PARPA 2001-5 – builds on previous sector strategies but, unlike its predecessor (PARPA 2000-4), integrates sector plans within a common fiscal framework. Broad political ownership, encompassing the opposition and Parliament, is lacking, and this is a notable weakness. Government ownership of the plan is comparatively good, but observers doubt the government's capacity to implement it.

6.1   Introduction

The PRSP process in Mozambique has been distinguished by being able to build on an existing process incorporating at least some of the elements of the PRSP concept. When, in 2000, the preparation of a PRSP became a requirement for World Bank/IMF concessional loans and HIPC debt relief, Mozambique had recently prepared an Action Programme for the Reduction of Absolute Poverty 2000-2004 (PARPA). The PARPA 2000-4, with minor additions on the process of preparing a full PRSP, was able to be endorsed by the World Bank and IMF Boards as an Interim PRSP (iPRSP) in April 2000.

Consultations had been carried out during the preparation of the PARPA 2000-4. A further consultation process was, however, required by the World Bank/IMF for the full PRSP. This was carried out in the context of the preparation of a new version of the PARPA, covering the years 2001-2005.

*   Respectively, Lund University and Kristianstad University, Sweden; Oslo, Norway; and Maputo, Mozambique. We would like to thank staff both inside and outside the Mozambique government for their generosity in giving of their time and insight to this study. We are grateful to the staff of the Norwegian and Swedish embassies as well as staff of Norad Oslo and Sida Stockholm for their help in arranging for the study. We would also like to thank Per-Åke Andersson, Bruce Bolnick, Maimuna Ibraimo, Anton Johnston, Arnim Schwidrowski, Marit Strand and Maude Svensson for valuable comments and suggestions on earlier drafts of this manuscript.

The PARPA 2001-5 was adopted by the Mozambique Council of Ministers in April 2001 and endorsed by the Joint Boards in September of that year. Mozambique reached HIPC2 completion that same month, becoming only the third country to reach that point (after Bolivia and Uganda).[1]

The approach of the PARPA[2] is that of a broad development plan with a poverty focus, which encompasses most of the budgetary resources of the government. The key elements of existing sector strategies are integrated into a macroeconomic and fiscal framework. In addition, the document includes a description of the consultation process, and a monitoring and evaluation strategy.

This chapter describes and interrogates the PARPA process, paying particular attention to the potential for institutional change. Since the PARPA process is young but institutional change takes time, firm conclusions are not reached. Instead, we limit ourselves to identifying some trends, point to some strengths and weaknesses of the process so far, and present some hypotheses about likely future developments.

Section 2 places the PARPA process in its country context and section 3 is a description of the major elements of the process. On that basis, the following three sections explore the way the initiative has affected and been affected by other elements of the institutional framework for poverty-reduction planning in Mozambique, current plans for monitoring PARPA implementation and the potential for changing roles on the part of the country's external partners. Section 7 concludes.

6.2 Poverty reduction and the policy context

Governance

The governance system of Mozambique has been significantly strengthened in recent years, but is still marked by political tensions, severe financial short-falls and capacity constraints. There remains a large gap in capacity and a significant psychological distance between the central level and the provincial/district level.

Under the current Constitution the President is the Head of Government, with the power to convene and preside over sessions of the Council of Ministers, or to delegate this to the prime minister. He is the main political force and the key to political stability in the country. The Assembly of the

---

1. Mozambique was also one of the few countries where completion was not made conditional on the endorsement of its first annual review of PRSP implementation. A favourable Joint Staff Assessment on Mozambique's first annual Progress Report was published in June 2003.
2. Unless otherwise indicated, 'PARPA ' refers to the more recent version, PARPA 2001-5.

Republic (AR) has two ordinary sessions per year, starting in February and October, each lasting 45 working days. For historical reasons and due to capacity constraints in Parliament, the Executive tends to dominate the Assembly. Many of the MPs chosen by the political party machine have little or no prior contact with the constituencies they are supposed to represent. The Parliament is, however, slowly but surely improving its capacity to function as a proper legislative body.

Management tends to be of an orthodox top-down type, with limited coordination across ministries. While the individual ministries carry out sector strategic planning, the Ministry of Planning and Finance (MPF) is responsible for integrating sector plans into overall development plans and budgets. The Ministry of Planning and Finance was already responsible for preparing poverty reduction strategies, based on inputs from the sectoral ministries, and the PRSP has not introduced any changes in this respect.

Government at the sub-national level in Mozambique consists of ten provinces, which are divided into 33 independent municipalities (*autarquias*), each with its own budget. There are also 124 districts that come under the central government. While planning and resource allocation is largely done at the centre, the key level in terms of implementation and thus impact is the province. The provinces, however, are facing major human capacity constraints.

Some 80 percent of the population of Mozambique live in rural areas or, in other words, in the districts, where there is little urbanisation. The fact that District Administrators often have little more than primary education and operate with minimal budgets and staff support is a major constraint on national development efforts, and limits the potential for decentralisation. Capacity constraints are aggravated by major communication problems due to large distances between provincial and district capitals and the poor state of the roads.

Beyond financial and organisational limitations, availability of qualified staff poses the most serious challenge to government capacity. It will take time before the education system will be able to supply sufficient number of qualified staff. To service a population of some 17 million, of which 45 percent are under 15 years of age, there are around 7,000 primary schools (grades 1-5), dropping to 554 schools for grades 6 and 7, 94 schools for grades 8 to 10 and just twenty schools for grades 11 and 12.[3]

Civil society

Mozambique has few means and little tradition for sustaining NGOs solely on voluntary contributions. Still, there are some 400 NGOs in Mozambique, roughly half of them located in the capital. Most, however, have a very limited

---

3. Interview with Alcido Eduardo Nguenya, Minister of Education, in *Entrevista*, April 2001.

scale of operations and are heavily dependent on external donor funds. Few have achieved national prominence. Various kinds of NGO umbrella organisations have, however, proven fairly effective when combining their efforts in national campaigns, as shown in the Land Campaign to inform people about their rights under the new Land Law, and an All Against Violence campaign on domestic violence. The Protestant and Catholic churches undertake hands-on development work, in public education and in mobilisation on issues such as AIDS, weapons collection and civic education. The Muslim community is often active on issues that they feel affect them directly.

Businesses/employers have specialist associations and national umbrella organisations. There are two big trade unions, with provincial subdivisions. There is a wide spectrum of communications media, but the written press has limited reach outside Maputo and the provincial capitals. Radio coverage has improved significantly in recent years, but does not yet extend to the whole country. There is considerable press freedom, although the murder in 2000 of the country's most tenacious investigative journalist, Carlos Cardoso, clearly demonstrates the dangers involved in pressing too hard on sensitive issues.

The politics of poverty reduction in Mozambique

The country's economy, and particularly the rural economy, was severely damaged during the war. Socially, the national unity of the immediate post-independence period was undermined by the war, and has suffered further from factors such as an increasing focus on ethnic/language group identities, resentment at uneven development and isolation caused by poor land communications.

Uneven regional development, with the Maputo area seeing the lion's share of the country's GDP growth, has become a source of strong discontent in the centre and north. The relative strength of the Maputo economy leads to a persistent brain drain from the provinces, and the gap in financial and human resources between Maputo and provincial capitals is large. Recent years have also seen rising crime rates, including an increase in violent crime, and growing linkages to regional crime syndicates.

The relationship between the ruling party, Frelimo, and the main opposition party, Renamo, is deeply influenced by their being former contestants in the war. One particular bone of contention is Renamo's demand to appoint the Governors in the provinces where it has a majority of the votes, but this is not called for under the current 'winner takes all' constitution. An accusation often expressed by Renamo in the National Assembly is that Frelimo favours the southern part of the country, where it has most of its supporters, at the expense of the central and northern regions

Renamo refused to accept the results of the elections in 1999, boycotted the first Parliamentary sessions, threatened to make the country 'ungovernable', and organised demonstrations. Strong tension persists which, *inter alia,* negatively affects the working of Parliament. The political tension also affects the economic outlook through its impact on business confidence and the exchange rate. Overall, therefore, the national fabric of Mozambique is fragile, and the government must take great care that its actions in areas such as public sector reform, budgeting processes and public consultations do not contribute to political instability.

The politics of poverty reduction is further complicated by the complex economic and political relationships existing between elites – who are heavily concentrated in the capital – and between them and their various 'clients'. Mozambique is no exception to the African 'economy of affection' phenomenon, whereby people who become more affluent or politically successful are expected to help out relatives, others from the same region and others who provide an important economic, social or political base. And good connections in Mozambique, as elsewhere, mean significant benefits in terms of influence, economic favours, positions, and easier access to social and financial facilities.

On top of these challenges to planning, the government needs to satisfy the multitude of donor priorities, approaches, procedures and requirements. This places a significant burden on the government and makes long-term strategic planning exceedingly difficult.

Corruption is a growing concern, from high-level to petty corruption. Petty corruption directly affects the lives of ordinary people through systems such as under-the-table charges by teachers and health staff, police corruption and abuse, and dubious fees levied on small-scale economic activity. Many of these systems are inevitable given the very low salary levels of government staff.

Limitations of rational planning models

The overriding government concern for political stability and national reconciliation limits the degree to which a purely technocratic approach to planning is feasible in Mozambique. Rational planning models have weaknesses in any context, not least in sub-Saharan Africa. There are severe constraints on what can be achieved in terms of planning, particularly in the short to medium term. However, our initial assumption is that the processes established around the *attempt* to increase the rationality of the policy process are nevertheless likely to have an overall positive effect.

The effects of such initiatives are often not those explicitly intended, but instead emerge in varied and often unpredictable ways. Through meetings, improved analyses, improved statistics, debate and so forth, new opinions about key challenges, greater shared understanding, new goals and improved approaches are created, and these feed back into the various formal and informal systems and contribute to their improvement in various ways. When making an overall assessment of the PRSP process, it is thus not a question of merely comparing the formal aims of the PRSP with the forces working against it, even though these are significant, but rather of making an assessment of the likely total effect of the formal and informal aspects of the PRSP process.

This of course must remain largely a matter of conjecture, especially at this early stage of the process. Moreover, the standards and criteria for making such an assessment are not of an exact nature and are thus difficult to make fully explicit. It should also be noted that our research has not gone into the real-world politics of Mozambique in sufficient depth to make a proper assessment of the 'real' incentives driving the actions of key political actors. The chapter attempts to 'tell a story' in a way that seems reasonable based on the information presented.

External finance

The government is heavily dependent on external support, which currently constitutes about 17 percent of GDP. In recent years, 50 percent of government spending and 75 percent of public investment have been financed by external aid. The authorities' objective of raising significantly the revenue effort over the coming years is a crucial complement to external aid in supporting poverty reduction spending while consolidating the fiscal position.

Dependence on external support leads to competition for these resources among the ministries, and to a desire, and need, to maintain central control of the funds. With provincial taxes providing only a very small income to the provinces, they are highly dependent on transfers from the centre, leaving little room for autonomous sub-national planning and decision making. Donors generally work with the central ministries, which do not necessarily support the decentralisation efforts of the government. This is slightly mitigated by some donors targeting resources to a given province.

The completion of the Enhanced HIPC initiative implies that total debt service relief, including assistance provided under the original initiative, will amount to US$4.3 billion. The annual debt service payments are cut to an average of US$56 million for the period 2002–10, which is almost half that of 1998. The Consultative Group meeting of October 2001 pledged US$722 million in support, compared with the US$600 million asked for by the Mozambican government.

Even though the government has succeeded in obtaining further pledges of foreign resources, government finances have suffered severe damage due to recent scandals around the bad loans contracted by two national banks, their near-collapse and delayed recapitalisation. In addition to the direct costs, there is also a risk that donors in the future will be more hesitant to disburse support if the government does not show a sincere will to recover outstanding debts and prosecute those guilty of the frauds.

Previous poverty plans

The requirement of a PRSP does not involve a radical departure from what was already being done in Mozambique. Government policy has for many years focused on poverty. Even though the PARPA may be the first document with a comprehensive view on policies for fighting poverty, during the last decade several other documents and policies have addressed the issue. The Strategy for Poverty Reduction in Mozambique from 1995 presented the first explicit peace-time poverty reduction strategy. The Five-Year Programme of the Government for 1995 to 1999 incorporated the main objectives of this strategy (GoM, 1999).

The different sector policies that have preceded the PARPA and which now constitute its basis have also had a poverty focus. Limited ownership of the plans at provincial and district level may partly explain the implementation problems that characterise most of these plans.

6.3   The PRSP process in Mozambique

The process leading to the PARPA 2001-5 saw a progressive widening of the concept of 'poverty reduction strategy'. The PARPA is now a broad development plan with a poverty focus, encompassing most of the government's budgetary resources, rather than a strategy focusing narrowly on a few sectors considered of particular importance for poverty reduction.

The PARPA 2000-04 was prepared by several government ministries under the lead of Ministry of Planning and Finance (MPF). To the global objective of reducing poverty incidence from 70 percent to 50 percent in ten years, the PARPA 2000-4 added the intermediate objective of reducing the incidence level to around 60 percent by the year 2004. After the approval of PARPA 2000-4 as Mozambique's iPRSP, the work of preparing the PARPA 2001-5 started. The document went through four different drafts. The first draft, presented in two versions in November 2000, was a rough outline by the MPF that did not include a budget or costings, with the main purpose of initiating discussions about the PRS process. This draft was used for nation-wide consultations in December 2000 and January 2001 and was also commented upon by the IFIs and the bilateral donors.

The second draft, which was completed in February 2001, was not presented to the public. It included the results of the first round of consultations and took into account comments from the IFIs and bilateral donors. This draft was in turn commented upon by the line ministries (education, health, agriculture, etc.) and by the MPF itself. The third draft, which was presented at the end of February 2001, included a budget and an operational matrix and was again commented upon by the IFIs and the bilateral donors.[4] The fourth and final draft was completed in March and presented in April to the Council of Ministers, which approved it with minor corrections. After editing and some postponements, this was presented to the boards of the IFIs as the Mozambican full PRSP.

Stakeholder views on the new conditionality

There seemed to be no perception among key stakeholders that the introduction of the PRSP implied any substantial change in the external requirements that come with aid. However, both the IFI and government representatives pointed to a clear and positive change of emphasis, in basing IFI support on a government-prepared strategy document. Also, the requirement of a PRSP for access to HIPC/IFI resources has given an extra boost at the policy level to the already existing government focus on poverty.

The PRSP does not introduce any significant shifts in government policies or expenditure patterns. It only confirms the present course of the government. For many stakeholders in Mozambique, however, the quality of policies and plans is in any case not the key issue. The key issue is how to secure implementation of existing policies and plans, and whether the PRSP initiative adds a new dimension in this respect.

In terms of macroeconomic targets agreed with the IMF, the government does not consider that the PRSP introduces any major new way of 'doing business'. The main difference is that the government is itself summarising its reform programme and macro-economic targets in an internal strategy document, instead of negotiating this through an externally-led process. This is a significant shift in principle, but not one that can be seen to have any immediate practical consequences.

The government does not see, for example, why the nature of macro-economic benchmarks would change as a result of replacing the Policy Framework Paper with a PRSP. In principle, agreed reform measures should in the future form a subset of the measures spelled out in the PRSP. They may, however, be made more specific in discussions with the IFIs, and other issues not part of the PRSP may also be included in such discussions, if considered necessary.

The PRSP is thus not seen by those interviewed as involving a new form of conditionality, in terms of discussions and agreements on macro-economic and structural reform measures. These must in any case be discussed and agreed on a regular basis in connection with loan arrangements through the IMF or World Bank. For the Bank, agreements on reform measures will continue to be negotiated in the context of individual loans. While these may be drawn from the PRSP, the PRSP will likely not form a sufficient basis for such agreements. As for HIPC and PRGF, an endorsed PRSP is one of several

---

4. The operational matrix was not released until some time after the presentation of the third draft.

requirements, and not a sufficient condition. In the medium term, the PRSP requirement is thus not expected to mean doing away with the 'old system' of lists of requirements to be satisfied for access to external resources.

The PRSP requirement itself, however, places quite heavy *additional* demands on the government compared with the earlier system, in terms of both content and process. These demands are easier to accept than other specific policy and reform requirements, since in the case of PRSP it is clearly the government itself that prepares the document and carries out the consultations. Also, in Mozambique it was possible to base the PRSP on the already developed poverty reduction action programme of the government.

'National ownership' is seen by external partners as the means whereby the PRSP is to be protected from becoming another elaborate planning system driven more by the need to secure external resources than by improving national policy, shifting public expenditure patterns or improving the quality of public service delivery. The nature of institutionalised aid dependency, however, works against ownership in this sense. The PRSP is not exempt from the well-known weaknesses of other aid instruments,[5] while introducing some new ones of its own. Satisfying IFI requirements for HIPC relief and concessional loans – and by implication donor support in general – is still a major motivating force for the government in preparing the new PARPA. Indeed, World Bank/IMF endorsement of the PRSP is paramount to the financial survival of the government.

The relationship between the government and the IFIs in Mozambique is driven by a common interest and with no great divergence in views on key policy issues (with some notable exceptions, especially relating to the cashew and sugar industry). Critics of this relationship, however, have little confidence in the government's freedom to determine national policies that are not in line with the prevailing Washington views.

It therefore came as little surprise to those outside the government interviewed for this study that the key items deemed necessary for IFI endorsement of the PRSP are included in the PARPA, and that the (donor-) required consultations on the overall plan have been carried out. Both the bilateral donors and the World Bank/IMF have been provided with all necessary information and have in return provided extensive comments on consecutive drafts of the plan.[6] This does not in itself imply lack of ownership of the strategy within the government. Nevertheless, the substantial implicit threat to national finances of a possible unfavourable PRSP Joint Staff

---

5. Of which we would mention short time-frames influenced by donor schedules, externally imposed conditions, and insufficient attention by donors to the complexities and constraints of national institutions and political and cultural realities (i.e. the limitations of technocratic-rationalistic planning in developing countries).

6. But notably not the UN organisations (see discussion on the role of the UN in section 6).

Assessment is one likely reason why donors and civil society have received more attention than the elected representatives of the people in the planning process.

There is clearly a danger that donors both implicitly and explicitly will exercise too much influence on the PARPA process, endangering the very ownership that is supposed to be the cornerstone of the PRSP approach. It is not clear how much room for manoeuvre and learning through trial and error the donors will be willing to accord to the government before significant pressure will be applied. The answers to such difficult questions will be the main test of what donors mean by 'national ownership' of the PARPA, not official donor statements.

Approach to participatory process

The government considered consultations carried out under sector planning processes to be an integral and even key element of the PARPA participatory process. Nevertheless, an ambitious overarching participatory strategy was drawn up for the PARPA 2001-5 process. The main activity carried out was a quite extensive series of meetings held with civil society and government officials in Maputo and two of the country's ten provinces (Sofala and Nampula) during December 2000-January 2001.

The primary focus on Maputo, the short notice and the time constraints of this schedule of meetings had the consequence that they offered substantially less than full civil society participation in the process, although they offered opportunities for public discussion. They represented nonetheless a promising start for a new and strengthened government approach to consultations. The meetings seem to have functioned well as arenas for raising general awareness about the PARPA and for voicing views related to government policies and actions in general. According to the government, some of the issues raised in the consultations influenced the final text of the PARPA, such as a greater emphasis on corruption and the issue of decentralisation. It is, however, difficult to determine the degree to which the consultations influenced the final PARPA document.

The PARPA consultations did not function as a fully participatory process in the development of the PARPA, for several reasons:

- The consultation process was rather rushed, without the time or procedures for external stakeholders to be brought gradually into the process, so that they could learn about the draft plan and give thought to their role in providing inputs.

- The purpose, methodology and expected results of the consultation process were not made explicit and discussed with external stakeholders before the consultation process started.

- Draft documents often did not reach stakeholders, or did not reach them in time to prepare them for the consultation meetings.

- Most of the meetings were carried out in Maputo; only two of Mozambique's ten provinces were included in the consultation process.

- The PARPA is so broad in scope that focused discussion on aspects of the plan was not realistic, resulting in rather generalised comments about overall development issues in Mozambique.

- Few of the external stakeholders had the necessary technical skills to provide an overall and in-depth analysis of the plan, particularly as it related to macro-economic issues.

- Some external stakeholders had limited motivation to participate or provide substantial input to the process, as they considered government consultations in general to be of limited value.

These weaknesses are not surprising, given capacity constraints and the fact that this was the first round of broad-based PARPA consultations. The government had also to consider trade-offs and dangers connected with the process. These included occupying the time of senior staff that would otherwise be spent on other important tasks, and the dangers of raising unreasonable expectations and starting processes that could back-fire in political unrest, and of increasing the already existing consultation fatigue.

Overall, it should be said that the government made a determined effort at creating a consultative process around the PARPA, and through this exercise gained important experience that may be used to build a more in-depth process in the future. Good first steps have been taken towards institutionalising a new and strengthened form of participatory process in the country. However, for a consultation process to be successful it is important that the persons consulted feel that their input is being taken seriously. A lesson for the future is that the value of the consultation process lies more in its quality than in the number of consultation occasions.

Political debate and the involvement of parliament

Neither Parliament nor the political parties were brought into the PRSP process. The PARPA was, however, brought to the Council of Ministers for approval. The lack of parliamentary involvement reflects political sensitivities as well as the as yet unclear formal status of the PARPA in relation to other government planning instruments; but it may be considered a significant weakness in the PRSP process so far.

One explanation given for not involving the opposition in the consultation process was the political deadlock that had persisted since December 1999 due to the discord about the election result. The situation deteriorated after the riots in November 2000, with the result that the possibilities for political dialogue during a key period for the PRSP were limited. After that, political interest was focused on the right to appoint provincial Governors, and on the turmoil around the official enquiry into the events of 2000, leaving little time and space for debate on poverty reduction policy.

Civil society participation

Participation by NGOs, the private sector and religious bodies in the PARPA process as such was fairly limited. Generally, awareness among civil society institutions of the content and role of the PARPA is low. At the provincial level, knowledge of the PARPA is particularly weak. For example, a group of representatives from eight national NGOs in Zambezia consulted for this study had not heard of the PARPA at all. In Niassa, there was some knowledge among the NGOs about the PARPA, but only due to information that had been presented in connection with a meeting about debt rescheduling arranged by the Mozambican Debt Group (*Grupo da Divida*) and *Progresso* in December 2000.[7]

This situation reflects the limited scope of the dissemination carried out by the government. But it also testifies to the limited interest in and capacity for involvement in this form of macro planning among NGOs. Overall, the national NGOs seem more interested in sectoral and operational work than in advocacy related to the macro plans of the government. Even some umbrella NGOs at central level had barely heard of the PARPA. With the exception of the Mozambique Debt Group, no NGOs consulted for this study expressed strong opinions about the *content* of the PARPA. With some exceptions, religious bodies also did not seem very active in relation to the PARPA.

This strengthens the government's argument that the participatory process should focus on the sector strategies and on decentralised planning rather than on the PARPA document as a whole. This argument does raise the question, however, about who is to provide substantial inputs on inter-sectoral priorities and linkages in the overall plan, outside of the central Ministry of Planning and Finance. This question is all the more important considering the strong verticality of Mozambican ministries and directorates.

There are processes in place where the private sector meets with the government to discuss key issues relating to the business environment. Of

---

7. The Zambezia NGOs were, on the other hand, invited to participate in the provincial strategy planning efforts recently completed. This is of more direct interest to them than national planning efforts. Both the Niassa and Zambezia NGOs consulted for this study seemed, in general, more focused on various community-based projects and on securing funding for these, than in discussing macro plans and policy advocacy. National and even provincial plans did not seem to be considered strongly relevant to their work.

particular importance are the high-profile Private Sector Conferences, during which lists of priority actions are drawn up and agreed between private sector representatives and the government. Private sector representatives, however, lament the limited ability of the government to carry through with intended reforms. Private sector representatives interviewed for this study were uniformly sceptical about the usefulness of increased consultations with the government, as long as already agreed-upon actions are not better implemented.[8]

The media

There has been limited media focus on the PARPA. This is an indicator of the limitations in the public debate on the PARPA, as well as in the government procedures for disseminating information on the PARPA.

The degree of media focus can be used as an indicator of information availability, of public engagement and of political interest and debate. In 2000-01, the media paid limited attention to both the process of developing the PARPA and the content of the plan. The fact that the PARPA was not brought to Parliament for discussion contributed significantly to this. Like the rest of society, the media focused its attention on the constitutional topics that dominated the Mozambican political scene during that period, along with the consequences of the floods. At the same time, no particular effort seems to have been made by the government to engage the media. In the future, a specific media strategy should probably form part of the overall PARPA consultation system.

Accessibility of the PARPA document

Owing to the complexities and technicality of the PARPA, its content is not fully accessible to a majority of the persons who are consulted. The technical language of the document reduces its accessibility for those who are expected to take part in the consultation process.

Some NGOs have declared that they will start to educate themselves about economics in order to be able to follow the PARPA process. The Women's Forum, for example, plans to arrange seminars in economics in order to enable the members to take part in the consultation process. Even though such courses would serve a purpose by increasing awareness about poverty issues, they probably still would be too rudimentary for the purpose. Even for persons with formal education, a considerable time would have to be put aside to assess the PARPA. Combined with the fact that many consider that the PARPA is not directly relevant to their activities, this may explain why so

---

8   The sentiment of the private sector that the plans of the government are weakly implemented, and that improved planning therefore does not necessarily lead to improved results, is also widespread among other civil society organisations.

few seem to have made the effort to read it.

The MPF seems to agree that the PARPA in its present format is too complicated to be useful in consultations. Thus both those producing the document and the recipients have expressed the opinion that it would be desirable to produce a 'popular' version that would be more easily accessible.

6.4 What difference has the PRSP made?

Government policy and management instruments

The government's overall development framework consists of a number of policy and management instruments that share the overall purpose of reducing poverty. The *Government Five Year Programme* (PDG)[9] is the overarching policy framework, in which the government presents its goals, objectives, targets and actions for the period 2000-04. Although the PDG contains some quantitative targets, it is a generic document describing priority areas of action and activities. The *Economic and Social Plan* (PES) is the government's instrument for programming annual policies and actions. Together with the State Budget (OE), which presents the resource framework in a one-year perspective, the PES is supposed to ensure the immediate functioning of the economy and to give guidance for annual resource allocations. The PES, OE, and PDG have in common that they have to be presented to and approved by Parliament.

In addition, the government also has a set of other instruments which have in common that they do not have to be ratified by the Assembly of the Republic (AR). Besides the PARPA, there is the Medium Term Fiscal Framework (MTFF), which is used for identifying priorities and allocating budgetary resources in the medium term. The MTFF also presents a ten-year resource envelope by source. Finally, the Triennial Public Investment Plan (PTIP) was created in the 1980s as an instrument for keeping track of domestic and foreign investments and thereby functions as a medium-term complement to the annual PES and OE.

Over the last few years the main sectors have seen the development of sector policy and strategy papers, followed by the preparation of medium- to long-term sector plans. The sector plans often have considerable donor input, and are often used as a precursor to discussions on the introduction of SWAP-mechanisms for coordinated assistance. This is the case, for example, in education, health, agriculture and roads. These are all 'first efforts' and of varying quality, with different time-frames and formats. The more recent health document refers specifically to the PARPA, but the earlier education and agriculture documents do not. All take as their point of departure the goal of poverty reduction. All involved broad consultations with stakeholders,

9. Assembly of the Republic Resolution 2/2000 of 22 March.

although mostly with a strong Maputo emphasis.

The provinces have a long tradition of 'provincial plans' which have, however, usually been under central direction. Recently, several provinces have complemented their annual plans and budgets on the basis of provincial multi-year plans and strategies. These have been prepared for fund-raising/ investment promotion conferences to which donors and potential investors are invited. The provincial plans produced so far have projections of provincial growth rates and per capita income (apparently based on their own calculations) and also provide provincial revenue targets. The linkages and coordination with corresponding central estimations, however, seem unclear. The coordination between central and provincial planning is further aggravated by the existence of extra-budgetary donor funds that are not recorded in the central government budget.

It is worth noting that all of the government's relatively new public financial management instruments are characterised by being medium-term and not needing parliamentary approval. Their recent origin helps to explain why they do not have to be subject to parliamentary debate. Still, it must be seen as a matter of concern that the public management instruments most decisive for Mozambique's medium- and long-term development efforts escape constitutional debate.

The PARPA and the MTFF mutually affect each other. In principle, the MTFF sets the medium-term resource envelope for the PARPA and thereby indicates which activities will be financially viable. The PARPA, through prioritisation, provides a basis for the allocation of resources within the MTFF. The PARPA and MTFF coincide to some extent, but PARPA has the wider coverage in the sense that it is not only supposed to prioritise and harmonise between the sector plans but also to provide an overall framework taking into account macroeconomic and fiscal issues. The entire fiscal framework of the MTFF is, however, not included in the PARPA. The explicit poverty focus of the PARPA excludes activities such as military spending, for example.

Adequacy of financial management system

Current budgetary procedures make it difficult to determine whether the commitments of the government as presented in the PARPA will actually be reflected in relevant budget allocations. To begin with, it is still unclear how the linkages between the different management instruments will be carried out in concrete, procedural terms. In theory, the budgetary prioritisation of the PARPA is reflected in the annual budget through the PES. However, a recurrent problem in Mozambican budget procedures has been the low correspondence between the budget and the PES. This incongruity can to a large extent be explained by the fact that coordination within the MPF still suffers from an earlier institutional division of treasury and planning functions.

In 2002, weaknesses in the links between the PES 2002 and PARPA targets were recognised. The PES 2003 targets were to be revised in some areas and presented in the PARPA format. Mismatch between annual plan formats and content with the PARPA remains a major weakness of the PARPA process, however.

Secondly, the financial management system is in serious need of modernisation in order to be able to fulfil the functions outlined in the PARPA. Accounting is based on a manual, single-entry system that dates back to 1901. The classification system is generally considered inadequate with revenues classified in economic terms and expenditures in institutional, functional and economic terms.

Gustafsson and Disch (2001) indicate that as much as three quarters of the resources used in government institutions are off-budget. The main extra-budgetary sources of funds are direct revenues, donor project and programme funds, and donor overseas transactions. With such a large share of total government funds being off-budget, the government's ability to efficiently prioritise, allocate and track resources is substantially reduced.

Since the budget of 2001/02 was the first 'PARPA budget' it is still too early to determine whether the government's intentions will be reflected in actual budget allocations. Whether PARPA will eventually become a key planning instrument for the government is highly dependent on the degree to which it will be able to determine budget priorities. The future importance of the PARPA will greatly depend on what actual impact it will have in terms of budgeting procedures, including the detailed budgeting practicalities at departmental and provincial level. This issue should therefore receive considerable attention as the PARPA is being developed.

Added value of PARPA *in relation to previous poverty plans*

The poverty focus of existing public management instruments in Mozambique has undoubtedly made it easier than it would otherwise have been to integrate the PARPA within the overall development framework. The process of preparing PARPA 2000-4 and making it acceptable as an iPRSP was fast in comparison with experience in other countries. This was because much of the basic work in the sector plans was already done. The existing plans served as inputs to the PARPA, and the PARPA was also able to draw on the experience of participation and consultations gained in the preparation of these plans. The availability of a firm poverty analysis, and the possibility of integrating the plan with public financial management instruments in a macro-economic and fiscal framework provided favourable conditions for the full PARPA.

On the other hand, there have been considerable changes in PARPA 2001-5 compared to the earlier poverty strategies. Based on the Poverty Assessment (1998), the 2000-4 PARPA already represented a considerably more advanced analysis of the causes, context, and remedies for poverty than earlier poverty strategies. PARPA 2001-5 has further deepened, widened and improved these analyses.

Unlike PARPA 2000-4, which was essentially a compilation of sector strategies developed by different line ministries, PARPA 2001-5 integrates the different sector plans within a common fiscal framework, which should contribute to clearer prioritisation between and within sectors. It is to be expected that the full harmonisation of the sector strategies will take time, because of differences in donor priorities, rules and procedures and because the objectives and targets of sector and provincial strategies do not always correspond. Nevertheless, PARPA has the potential to function as a coordinating mechanism with positive effects on the incentives for developing new sector plans and improving existing ones.

There is a continuing need to 'market' the PARPA in the government machinery at all levels and establish procedures to link with decentralised budgeting/planning processes and avoid an overload of poverty reduction and development plans. The possibility of direct duplication is real. Despite the plethora of planning instruments with closely related functions, there is no indication that any of the existing management instruments is considered superfluous on the basis of overlapping functions.

If the PARPA, as intended, becomes an overarching poverty reduction strategy that incorporates the range of existing plans, the risk of overlap will be smaller, even though it implies additional strain on coordination capacity. Even so, judging from the present situation where the PARPA is unknown among many government staff at lower levels, it may be expected that such dissemination of the content and purpose of the PRS strategy will take much time and effort.

What are the key constraints?

Coordination of the poverty reduction strategy process is a major challenge for Mozambique. From the start the Ministry of Planning and Finance was appointed to lead and coordinate a team consisting of ministries and technical units. Within the MPF, the responsibilities for the preparation of the PARPA were shared mainly by the *Direcção Nacional do Plano e Orçamento* (DNPO) and the *Gabinete de Estudos*. However, with the increased emphasis on macro-economic and fiscal issues of PARPA 2001-5 more of the responsibility for the preparatory work has been assumed by the *Gabinete de Estudos*, the unit within the MPF which provides medium and long-term economic projections.

The PARPA will require increased management and monitoring capacity within the government. The much broader approach of the PARPA in comparison with earlier strategies implies that more capacity will be required for planning, budgeting, administration and monitoring than before. Capacity constraints for the execution of these functions can be expected to be a major impediment for the successful implementation of the poverty reduction strategy. Besides involving capacities for the execution of the programme, the nation-wide consultations have involved significant numbers of senior staff from a variety of institutions. This engagement, although basically positive, meant that resources were drawn away from pressing implementation activities.

One problem in creating sufficient capacity is the low salaries offered in the public sector. Key personnel can find more attractive jobs in the private sector, or among donors. For example, the Ministry of Planning and Finance, which has a central function in the continued implementation of the poverty reduction strategy, lost several key persons after the completion of the PARPA 2000-04. The difficulty of attracting and retaining personnel is a threat not only to the poverty reduction strategy process but also to the daily work of the government. Public sector reform issues are therefore crucial to the prospects of the PRSP process.[10]

The fragility of the technical leadership of the PARPA process was highlighted in early 2002. In a cooperation initiated by Harvard University, a group of economists had been stationed in the *Gabinete de Estudos*. At short notice, it was decided that the Harvard group was to be dismantled with respect to the non-Mozambican economists, which left the group with only one senior economist. This change implies that the relative importance of DNPO in the preparation of coming PARPAs has increased.

The PARPA process is highly dependent on a few key people at the central level at the Ministry of Finance and Planning. This dependence is both a risk (vulnerability to loss of staff) and an opportunity (a small but powerful team which can make significant improvements to the overall process and product). Donors should make sure they support critical staff in the Ministry, so that the whole process is not stalled or damaged for the lack of just a few additional staff. They should also try to avoid 'stealing' key staff away from the government to well-paid positions in their own missions.

The PARPA as an on-going consultative process

In Mozambique, there is a history of government consultation with various stakeholders in sectoral and provincial planning, and the consultations for the PARPA were therefore not perceived as something particularly new. However, according to several of those interviewed, the scope and quality of the consultations carried out in the various sectors have often been less than impressive, and PARPA consultations therefore represented an important opportunity for expanding the scope and improving the quality of government consultation processes.

There are several important fora for policy discussions between the government and other stakeholders that are not directly related to the PARPA

---

10. Some steps in this direction have already been taken. Since the middle of the 1990s there have been wage decompression reforms and considerable reductions in the number of the civil service staff. Later wage increases have, however, thwarted much of the wage decompression reform.

document as such. The government was not initially convinced of the need for the extensive additional consultations required for the PARPA to qualify as a PRSP. It must also be recognised that the government faces several challenges in designing and carrying out a consultation process of this nature.

A key concern is political sensitivities. There is a significant degree of 'consultation fatigue', with people demanding action rather than talk, and the government is wary of raising expectations it cannot fulfil. There is also the view that sector strategies offer a more useful focus for public debate. Moreover, as we have said, there are few civil society organisations in Mozambique that have the know-how to provide substantial input on such a complex plan.

The introduction of the added burden of extensive PRSP consultations may have had the advantage that they provided a clear incentive to the government to consolidate and integrate the rather *ad-hoc* and fragmented participatory system that then existed into a more unified system. Government increasingly recognises the need to have guidelines for the process that are agreed with civil society in advance, so that expectations as to their role and degree of involvement are clear and realistic. It also recognises the need for the greater engagement of the political system in the process in the future. This process will probably encompass not only future PARPA consultations, but also sectoral and provincial planning consultations.

It may therefore be expected that the PARPA consultations will be broadened, systematised and institutionalised in the future, and that the consultations during 2000-1 were not just a 'one-off' event to satisfy external requirements related to the PRSP only. It can be expected that, in the future, the quality and usefulness of the consultations will increase, leading to more political debate, a more engaged civil society, a more involved media and, as a result, hopefully improved planning and implementation of poverty reduction activities.

Mozambique illustrates the challenges created by the heavy World Bank/ IMF focus on civil society participation in the PRSP initiative. How strongly should a weak and not necessarily very representative NGO community, heavily dependent on external funding, be allowed to influence government policy? How can one differentiate between major civil society organisations, such as religious groups, and minor NGOs with unclear legitimacy?

During our research, some donors expressed concern that the focus on civil society participation may mean a lesser involvement, and even a possible weakening, of the formal democratic system of the country. Some also argued that securing the involvement of lower levels of government in the planning process is more important than bringing in non-governmental organisations.

The PRSP as a rolling plan

The PRSP, covering the period 2001-5, was envisaged as a rolling document. The frequency of updates was, however, not specified. During our main fieldwork, we got the impression that it would be updated annually. However, it was not updated in 2002, and the government now intends to update it on an 'according to need' basis.

Donors, however, are worried that, without updating, the PARPA will not be able to function as a coordination instrument for donor support, especially budget support. Discrepancies with the annual budget will grow. At the same time, EU and the World Bank as well as other donors are fully committing themselves to providing credit and support based on the PARPA. At the last Joint Donor Review, there were indications that the government now regards the PARPA/PRSP more as a policy declaration than as an operational document. This was expressed in the thought that it is more the spirit of the PARPA/PRSP that is to be preserved than its particular figures. Correspondingly, the efforts of the *Gabinete de Estudos* seem now to be more directed to the MTFF and the budget than to the PARPA/PRSP.

Within the government, moreover, there seems to be disagreement with respect to substantive policy issues as well as about process. For example, different policies have been proposed for the agricultural sector. The ministry of industry reportedly wants to go back to the old type of more centralised policy while the MPF wants to continue to improve the conditions for family agriculture in line with the intentions of the PARPA/PRSP.

6.5   Monitoring the PRSP: a second chance?

Each of the areas identified in the PARPA is supposed to be monitored, and each area is obliged to produce matrices presenting the relevant indicators. A monitoring strategy has been developed, based on three principles: the integration of PARPA monitoring into existing government monitoring mechanisms; differentiation between process and impact indicators; and the use of monitoring for continually revising PARPA targets and plans. According to the document, monitoring will fulfil the functions of tracking the progress of the PRS programme, assessing changes in the level of welfare; and developing a mechanism for the provision and dissemination of information to all PARPA stakeholders (GoM, 2001: 101).

PARPA will use three separate processes for monitoring. The first monitors the sector results, process indicators, and programmed activities; the second monitors budgetary execution, and the third uses national statistical surveys and participatory qualitative evaluations to monitor the effect on households and communities (ibid: 103).

Collection and monitoring of poverty data

The National Statistics Institute (INE) and the MPF are responsible for the collection and monitoring of most poverty data. MPF has the double responsibility of both formulating and monitoring the PRSP, which makes it even more important to involve institutions outside the government in the monitoring task. Capacity constraints are a major challenge to the success of the overall monitoring strategy.

While the PARPA does not directly address the question of monitoring capacity it does state that it is essential to investigate the capacities and activities of the various institutions in order to develop a sustainable monitoring and evaluation system. Furthermore, it is concluded that the monitoring and evaluation of the PRS process requires the participation of both governmental and non-governmental institutions. However, there is no reference to how exactly the mechanisms for participation will be carried out in practice, other than the fact that there 'are already some ideas' (ibid: 106). Some civil society organisations have raised concerns about this, and it may be expected that during the next PARPA an effort will be made to involve civil society organisations more in a dialogue on monitoring and evaluation systems.

INE is the central executive organ of the national statistics system and as such has the main responsibility for collecting data for the poverty indicators. It is estimated that INE, by itself or through the line ministries, will provide 60-70 percent of the statistics related to the PARPA. INE is responsible for and has a supervisory function in the provision of statistics by the Ministries of Health, Education and Agriculture. Complementary statistics used by the PARPA, not covered by INE, are mainly provided by the national bank.

INE needs to strengthen its administrative and technical capacity for managing the country's basic statistics. At present only about 20 per cent of those working in the Department of National Accounts have formal education in statistics or economics. The remaining staff have backgrounds in other areas such as geography or agriculture, and have received on-the-job training at INE. The statistical capacity in the line ministries is even weaker. However, until its domestic capacity is built up, INE expects to be able to perform its task of collecting poverty data with the assistance of promised foreign technical assistance. INE expects this process to take three to four years, although some sources consider this to be overly optimistic.

Responsibility for overall monitoring of the PARPA's progress falls primarily on the Department of Macro-economic Planning and the *Gabinete do Estudos* at MPF. As in the case of data collection, there are human capacity constraints on the monitoring side. Donors have an important role in helping to strengthen the capacity of the data collecting and monitoring institutions. Some contributions have already been made in this area. One example is DFID, which contributes to the administrative and technical capacity of the Department of Macro-economic Planning through technical assistance.

INE has had a four-year twinning arrangement with the Swedish Statistical Bureau (SCB). This arrangement has now finished and has been replaced with support provided jointly by the statistical offices of the Scandinavian countries. The first round was intended to cover four years. It is, however, felt that this period will not be sufficient to ensure the viability and sustainability of INE. The joint Scandinavian project differs from the earlier twinning arrangement in that the funding is significantly larger, includes budget support, and is mainly based on short-term consultancies. A large share of the funding will be directed towards statistical education.

Statistical tools

Annual QUIBB surveys[11] are the major tool that has been adopted for poverty monitoring. Essentially the QUIBB provides qualitative information that is quantified and presented as frequency tables. It includes information about the views of end users on different issues, e.g. the quality of social infrastructure. One advantage of QUIBB is that the method is standardised. QUIBB started in November 2000, with the intention of being repeated once a year. In addition to the core poverty indicators covered in the so-called nuclear questionnaire module, each QUIBB will also cover a special theme. The special theme for 2001 was the impact of the floods and the effects of extended mother/child health care.

The intention is to turn the QUIBB into a thorough household survey every fifth year in order to follow up the results from the 1995/96 National Household Survey. The QUIBB and household surveys will also be complemented by population censuses every tenth year, with the next one planned for 2007.

The PARPA obligations, which in addition to INE's own surveys also include processing statistics from the line ministries and updating the national accounts statistics, have already implied increased delivery requirements with respect to both the quality and quantity of data. These requirements can be expected to increase further as the PARPA process proceeds. Given the limited administrative and technical capacity of INE, an ongoing discussion and analysis of what should be the main responsibilities of INE is therefore desirable, in order to permit an efficient prioritisation between its many different activities.

Indicators of poverty reduction

With a focus on intermediate and final indicators, and an increased focus on impact measurement, PARPA 2001-5 is a considerable improvement over its predecessor. The clear division between intermediate and final indicators in PARPA 2001-5 makes it easier to follow progress in the PRS process. While PARPA 2000-4 seemed to be mostly concerned with inputs, PARPA 2001-5 attempts to follow-up the outcomes of the poverty reduction strategy.

One example of this change can be found in the area of education. PARPA 2000-4 defined indicators based on enrolment rates, admission rates, numbers

---

11. *Questionário dos Indicadores Básicos de Bem-estar* – derived from the Core Welfare Indicators Questionnaire (CWIQ) developed at the World Bank.

of schools, numbers of pupils, percentage of girls, etc. In contrast, PARPA 2001-5 considers the final indicators of illiteracy and illiteracy among rural women and intermediate variables such as repetition rate, dropout rate and pass rate.

Some of the indicators presented in PARPA 2000-04 were criticised for inaccurately reflecting changes in the variable studied. For example, the monitoring of indicators related to the health sector was only based on statistics collected in health centres, such as number of consultations and institutional deliveries, implying that non-official health statistics would not be included in the monitoring. PARPA 2001-5 does not state whether there will be attempts to collect non-institutional health statistics. Some of the indicators chosen, however, such as the number of families with mosquito nets, indicate that this might be the case.

Finally, the PARPA 2000-04 was criticised for having too many indicators. Even though there is no significant change in the numbers of indicators in the PARPA 2001-5, they give an impression of having been more carefully prepared and grouped into better-defined categories.

There are a number of challenges in ensuring that the data and information collected for PARPA monitoring purposes are of sufficiently high quality and that political decision-making processes take these facts seriously into consideration. Reports in 2002 on action taken on various indicators suggest that limited progress has been made on reporting according to the PARPA set of indicators. This may indicate that PARPA is being too ambitious in terms of following up and reporting on indicators. The system is comprehensive, but operationalisation is still lacking, including linkage with the PES and budget cycle.

A positive step is the government's firm intention to establish a Poverty and PARPA Observatory for monitoring, with broad participation. This is not yet operating, however. There are also dangers of overlap with a coordination committee for M&E that has been established. A challenge for the monitoring and evaluation system is to include bottom-up and decentralised approaches, and to ensure that the qualitative reporting and studies that are carried out actually influence policy discussions and decisions, and are not merely quoted in reports.

It seems that limited action has taken place on behalf of non-governmental stakeholders in the PARPA since 2001. The NGO community is probably awaiting a clearer message from the government on its role in monitoring and evaluation. According to a recent report for DANIDA (T&B Consult, 2002), several NGO networks have expressed interest in contributing to PARPA monitoring. Prominent among these are Mozambique Debt Group, Action Aid, and LINK. Action Aid is already working to strengthen district planning processes and participatory approaches in three pilot districts, and sees this as opening spaces and creating capacities for PARPA monitoring at district level.

The weaknesses in PARPA M&E may be expected to persist. The PARPA process nonetheless has already started to contribute to a stronger focus on tangible results and on improved systems for data collection. Overall it is the assessment of the authors that the PARPA process will contribute to improved data quality, as well as to the increased *use* of available data – even if the improvement in many areas may be quite modest in the short term.

Involvement of Parliament in monitoring

A system has been established by law for Parliament to play a role in the monitoring of the PARPA, allowing for discussion and for holding the government accountable, i.e. by giving Parliament the competence to call ministers before it to report on the progress of PARPA. The first presentation and discussion in Parliament was held in March 2002, and it is planned that such events will take place regularly.

This is progress since 2001, when Parliament had very little involvement in the process. It may provide an example of PRSP monitoring offering a 'second chance', an opportunity to remedy deficiencies in the initial process. However, such a conclusion may be premature, because at the same time the political profile of the PARPA has been reduced. More attention is now being given to the annual plan (PES) and the budget, which are being seen as of more concrete and immediate financial interest. In the view of one donor representative, because the PARPA's linkages to the budget have not been made clear or firm, the annual budget is likely to remain the main political focus. Indeed, some donors are sceptical of the seriousness of the government in making real use of the PARPA.

6.6   Towards a new aid relationship

The World Bank and IMF

The relationship between the government and the World Bank/IMF with respect to the PARPA has been seen as constructive by both sides. The government seems to have been strongly in the driving seat during the process, while the World Bank and IMF have provided support and advice as and when requested. The latter did not push for early completion of the PARPA. Rather, it was the government that kept to the rather tight schedule aimed at completion in March/April 2001. This was no doubt influenced by the desire to achieve early completion point for HIPC debt relief, although a postponement would not have had any substantial consequences for the volume of debt relief.

Overall, it seems that the IMF and the World Bank are collaborating well on the PARPA process in Mozambique, and that there are no major differences in views on key policy issues between the institutions. A new World Bank Country Assistance Strategy (CAS) was prepared simultaneously with the first PARPA, and involved a major analysis phase and extensive consultations. No major changes in World Bank operations around the CAS were noticeable as a result of the introduction of the PRSP requirement. In the future, one would expect that the CAS should become simpler, be built on the PARPA, and not require such broad consultations, since these would be covered by the PARPA consultations.

As of 2002, the World Bank was reported to be changing its loan programme significantly as a result of the PRSP, and moving towards credits linked to it. There will be no more of the traditional structural adjustment credits. IMF conditioned the fourth PRGF on the government trying to find a solution to the banking crisis. Preliminary results from its Article 4 consultations indicated that Mozambique is considered to be on-track with respect to macro-economic variables.

Even if the World Bank and IMF 'step back' and avoid undue interference in the PARPA process, there is still a danger that, by nature of the support and advice they are able to provide and the close relationship they have with the Ministry of Planning and Finance, they will become the dominant influence on both process and content. The importance of their endorsement of the PARPA also works in this direction. This makes broad-based national consultations even more important, as they provide an important counterweight to donor influence in general and to World Bank/IMF influence in particular.

The UN

The UN has played a significant role in sector strategic planning in Mozambique, but has had little involvement with the PARPA document as such. The UN has a strong presence and provides a significant volume of support to Mozambique. Progress has been made in coordinating the work of the UN since the mid-90s. A comprehensive *Common Country Assessment 2000* (CCA) has been prepared, providing the UN's view of the country's development challenges and opportunities. The *UNDAF 2002-2006*, with a total resource framework in excess of US$300 million, sets out the goals, roles and responsibilities of the UN, based largely on the analysis of the CCA.

The UN has been involved in the PARPA only indirectly, through its support to sector strategy development. It was minimally involved in the PARPA process itself, and did not provide formal comments on PARPA drafts. Nor does the government seem to have made much effort to involve the UN agencies in the PARPA process. Several UN agencies noted that they received drafts of the PARPA, if at all, through the World Bank and not directly from the government. Generally it is the perception of the UN agencies that the PARPA process is very much a government-World Bank/IMF initiative. A somewhat critical view is taken of the fact that the PRSP has to be endorsed by the IMF/World Bank Boards.

In important ways it seems that the Common Country Assessment and the PARPA are similar and overlapping exercises. While the CCA is a quality document with a distinct role as a basis for programming UN support, to a significant degree it represents a duplication of efforts to that of the PARPA process. The UN expends very considerable effort in preparing, and securing, government involvement in the CCA and the UNDAF, while the government's own planning system is focused around sectoral strategic planning and the PARPA. The UN approach thus in many ways seems to be parallel rather than complementary to the PARPA process, with unclear synergies between the processes.[12]

Clearly the UN agencies, other external partners and, in particular, the government would benefit from a stronger linkage or even a merging of these UN-driven processes with the national planning system. This may become the case as the PARPA is established as *the* government planning instrument for poverty reduction.

On the other hand, the UN represents an important alternative and/or additional conceptual approach to one based largely on economic justifications. The CCA/UNDAF in Mozambique is a good illustration of this. The UN in Mozambique is now using human rights as a conceptual framework for development and poverty reduction.[13] This contrasts with the conceptual framework promoted by the IMF and the World Bank, which is influenced by the fact that according to their mandates these institutions must deal only with economic issues.

It is not always acknowledged that the World Bank/IMF *must* interpret the world in these terms due to its economic mandate, and that, therefore, it is only *outside* the World Bank/IMF – which in global terms primarily means the UN – that alternative analytic frameworks can be promoted. Over the last decade, the World Bank has developed a conceptual framework to justify and facilitate its major expansion into areas previously considered 'non-economic', such as health, education, governance, HIV/AIDS, corruption, human rights and civil society partnerships. However, a neglected consequence of this effort is that it has become increasingly acceptable to define and/or interpret all aspects of human life in terms of their impact on the economy. This is illustrated by the recently increased popularity of terms such as 'human capital' and 'social capital' to describe basic human and social capacities.[14]

---

12. The linkage of the CCA with the PARPA is further weakened by the fact that the main counterpart for the CCA planning is the Ministry of Foreign Affairs, not the Ministry of Planning and Finance.

13. Four categories are used: 1) the right to personal security, 2) the right to knowledge and a long and healthy life, 3) the right to sustainable livelihoods, and 4) the right to equity and participation.

14. It should be noted that the recent World Bank emphasis on 'voice ' and 'security' in addition to 'opportunity ' also needs to be interpreted/justified in economic terms, and that this necessarily influences the way these concepts are used and

While the relationship between the World Bank and the UN in general seems good in Mozambique, key UN representatives in Mozambique are very critical of the way the PRSP has been used to extend the influence of the World Bank and IMF into areas in which the UN considers itself to have far more experience and a stronger mandate. The new UNDAF in Mozambique includes a description of what are seen as the appropriate respective roles and responsibilities of the different UN organisations as well as the World Bank and IMF. The rather marginal involvement of the UN organisations in the PRSP exercise must be seen in light of these considerations.

Bilateral donors

Bilateral partners have gradually become more involved in the PARPA process. Donor coordination, including joint donor budget support, has started to benefit from the shared focus that the PARPA offers. It is, however, still too early to judge whether bilateral donors will use the PARPA as an opportunity for major change in their approaches.

While bilateral donor involvement in the first PARPA formulation was minimal, a group of donors that meets regularly to discuss PARPA and other issues prepared joint comments on the third draft PARPA 2001-5. The danger of the PRSP's contributing to donors' 'ganging up' to push the government into accepting unwanted policy choices seems at present to be limited in Mozambique, since there are no great divergences between government and donor views on appropriate poverty reduction strategies. Overall, the PARPA process seems to benefit donor collaboration, and provides a strong point of reference for shared dialogue with the government.

Several interviewees expressed the hope that all donor agencies would coordinate their efforts in supporting the PARPA process and simplify their own strategy and programming procedures, thus reducing transaction costs both for the government and for donors. The potential is clearly there.

It is too early to judge how far the PARPA will influence donor collaboration and simplification of the aid relationship. It should be noted, however, that a group of external partners to Mozambique have already made significant progress in collaborating on budget support to the government. The Joint Programme of Macro-Financial Support to Mozambique supports economic reforms and poverty reduction in Mozambique by combining an efficient transfer mechanism for budgetary resources with a structured dialogue between government and donors, enabling more flexibility for the government in the use of external support.

This Joint Donor Group has already embraced the PARPA as the key platform for their programme support. The participating donors are: Belgium,

---

understood. The UN itself is, however, also influenced by the prevailing understanding, and does not *necessarily* or by default represent alternative perspectives to those promoted by the World Bank.

Denmark, the European Commission, Ireland, Netherlands, Norway, Sweden, Switzerland and the United Kingdom. Terms and procedures are defined in a common framework agreement. Individual bilateral agreements defining support volumes and in some cases complementary technical assistance have been signed with Denmark, the European Commission, the Netherlands, Norway, Switzerland and UK. This form of cooperation could function as an example for development partners wishing to pursue the same approach in other countries.

However, the new understandings are fragile. The bank scandals of the last years have seriously affected donor commitment. Mozambique had been promised US$300 million in budget and programme support for 2001, but by the beginning of the year had only received US$212 million. This was explained to some degree by bureaucratic procedures in the donor countries. However, another part of the explanation is that the bilateral donors were dissatisfied by the government's handling of the bank scandal and therefore postponed payments due in May 2001 until the IMF and World Bank gave their official declaration of satisfaction in September. As a result of the late disbursements, the government was forced to borrow on the domestic market, which contributed to an increase in the money supply and inflation.

6.7   Conclusions

This chapter has sought to assess the extent to which the PARPA/PRSP process in Mozambique is leading to (or is likely to lead to) institutionalised changes that could increase the success of national poverty reduction efforts. Our assessment is broadly positive. National ownership of the PARPA/PRSP process in Mozambique must be considered quite strong, and it seems likely that the process will continue after HIPC completion. It is also our assessment that the PARPA is likely to contribute positively to the poverty reduction efforts of Mozambique, and to facilitate more efficient and effective relationships between internal and external partners.

A premise behind the PRSP approach is that national ownership of development plans and initiatives is a precondition for successful poverty reduction efforts. Therefore, one of the main issues to be assessed is the degree of national ownership of the PARPA/PRSP. This is not a simple question, since we can distinguish between at least four different dimensions of 'ownership'.[15] These are: 1) ownership in the sense of who it is who initiates the plans/programmes – i.e. the government or external partners, 2) the degree of intellectual conviction of key policy-makers or ministries (the technocratic dimension), 3) the degree of top leadership conviction, reflected in specific and clear actions (the political dimension), and 4) the breadth of support for the plans/programme, within and outside government institutions.

---

15. Based on Killick (1998: 86-87).

A further and more fundamental criterion of ownership is the degree to which policies have 'consolidated'; that is, have been institutionalised within the policy system.[16] This involves stabilising expectations around a new set of incentives and convincing economic agents that they cannot easily be reversed. Ownership in this sense can emerge even if there initially was little ownership in one or more of the four dimensions identified above.

When judged against these criteria, our findings on PARPA ownership point in the following direction:

Ownership as initiation: Ownership in this sense must be considered strong in Mozambique – even if, both directly and indirectly, external partners certainly have an influence over the content of policy documents.

Technocratic ownership: There seems to be a very strong ownership in Mozambique in this dimension, particularly in the Ministry of Planning and Finance. However, ownership in this sense drops significantly as one goes to the provincial level or to levels below top or mid-level management in central ministries.

Political ownership: Ownership in this dimension is less clear. Certainly, there is no *broad* political ownership, in the sense of also encompassing the opposition. Lack of parliamentary discussion of the PARPA, and the limited interest in and/or awareness of the PARPA among the mass media, also point in the direction of limitations to political ownership of the PARPA as such, even if there is a significant political ownership of poverty reduction efforts in general.

Ownership as broad-based support: Ownership of the PARPA in this sense cannot be considered very strong in Mozambique. Here the problem, however, is less one of *disagreement* with PARPA policies (although there is some), as with *lack of knowledge* of the PARPA policies among many stakeholders. A good start has been made in creating ownership in this sense.

Ownership as consolidated change: This is the 'proof of the pudding', the real test of ownership which determines whether positive change actually takes place or not – irrespective of the quality of plans and planning processes. This form of ownership, however, can only be expected to develop over the course of several years. At this early stage in the PARPA/PRSP process, only tentative suggestions can be made concerning ownership in this sense.

It should be emphasised in this connection that ownership of plans does not seem to be the critical issue in Mozambique. It is action on the ground that is called for – which is the dimension captured by ownership in the sense of consolidated change. There is a large perceived gap between the government's ability to prepare comprehensive plans, and its capability to implement those plans.

A further key positive value of the PARPA should be highlighted. This is the way the PARPA facilitates dialogue among all stakeholders involved in poverty reduction efforts in Mozambique. Through the PARPA, weaknesses

16. Ibid, drawing on Haggard and Kaufman (1992).

in data collection, poverty analysis and policy choices have been exposed and debated. The PARPA is a statement of the government's understanding of the poverty situation and key development challenges and options. There is now, therefore, a common document around which a focused intellectual and political debate and dialogue can be held. In a complex development environment such as that of Mozambique, where a large number of internal and external partners come with a multitude of viewpoints and preferences pulling in all directions, this may prove to be one of the most valuable benefits provided by the PRSP process.

It follows from the analysis in this chapter that the government should follow through with its current intentions, in two areas in particular. It should complete the task of making PARPA a rolling plan strongly linked to the budget, and it should broaden its support base through a deeper participatory process. Mozambique's external partners, for their part, should support the government in developing the PARPA; base their support on the PARPA; and use it as an opportunity for better coordination and simplification of procedures.

References

Government of Mozambique (2000a) *The Interim Poverty Reduction Strategy Paper.* Maputo: Ministry of Planning and Finance.

Government of Mozambique (2000b) *The National Action Plan for the Reduction of Absolute Poverty 2000-2004* (PARPA). Maputo: Ministry of Planning and Finance.

Government of Mozambique (2001) *Action Plan for the Reduction of Absolute Poverty (2001-5) (PARPA): Strategy Document for the Reduction of Poverty and the Promotion of Economic Growth.* Maputo: Ministry of Planning and Finance.

Gustafsson, A. and Disch, A. (2001) *Joint Macro-Financial Aid Programme to Mozambique – Background Study for Joint Programme Review 2001.* Report commissioned by the European Commission delegation in Maputo from Stanteam, Oslo/SPM Consultants, Stockholm.

Haggard, Stephan and Kaufman, Robert R. (eds.) (1992) *The Politics of Economic Adjustment: International Constraints, Distributive Conflicts, and the State.* Princeton, NJ: Princeton University Press.

Killick, Tony with Gunatilaka, Ramani and Marr, Ana (1998) *Aid and the Political Economy of Policy Change.* London: Routledge for the Overseas Development Institute.

T&B Consult (2002) 'Monitoring and Evaluation of the ARPA', Maputo, April.

Chapter 7: Rwanda

by Frederick Golooba Mutebi, Simon Stone and Neil Thin[*]

The PRSP process has been given a prominent place in government business in Rwanda. Poverty increased dramatically in the years leading up to and following the 1994 genocide, so reducing poverty is seen as critical to establishing the credentials of the government. This chapter argues that a degree of optimism is justified regarding the prospects for the institutionalisation of the PRSP approach in Rwanda. However, realising this promise will require further progress towards peace, stability, reconciliation, decentralisation and democratic governance. External financing agencies should consider altering the way they interact with government agencies. And continued improvements will be needed in budgetary control, forecasting and prioritisation, involving closer linkage of the PRSP and MTEF processes.

7.1 Introduction

Rwanda is a country in dire need of the kind of poverty reduction strategy and process that the PRSP initiative promotes. It is extremely poor, recovering from the 1994 genocide and its subsequent instabilities, and highly aid-dependent but needing better aid coordination. It is also undertaking critically important national reconstruction processes whose success is mutually interdependent with poverty reduction – namely, national reconciliation, decentralisation, and the application of a Constitution as the basis for democratic governance.

As the full PRSP (June 2002) puts it, 'Broad consultation is particularly necessary in a country emerging from conflict, and cooperation on local questions can help direct attention away from the divisive national politics of the past'. Participatory consultation, planning, and learning are vital but difficult in a country whose governance has for many years been authoritarian and non-participatory, and whose citizenry is therefore often described as obedient and lacking in policy-oriented civil society organisations.

When the initial country reports for the present study were compared, our Rwanda report emerged as the one most optimistic about prospects of the PRS process offering important and beneficial new opportunities for coordinated poverty reduction. During our second visit (March-April 2001) and follow-up correspondence during 2001-2002 we therefore concentrated on checking whether our optimism seemed justified, if so why, and whether

---

* Associates of Oxford Policy Management, Oxford, UK.

there were dissenting voices or signs of major impediments to effective institutionalisation of the process across the full range of development agencies in Rwanda.

This chapter summarises our conclusions. The next section describes the rather singular features of the country context. Section 3 describes the PRSP process in Rwanda, while section 4 analyses its longer-term implications. Two further sections consider the challenges of monitoring and evaluation in the context of Rwanda's PRSP, and the ways donors may be expected to respond to the process.

7.2   Poverty reduction and the policy context

Key institutional issues

Prior to the 1994 genocide, Rwanda experienced rising poverty and inequality. Governance was hierarchical and authoritarian, racist, biased towards certain regions, and elitist.[1] The genocide and civil war of 1994 and the emergency situation that followed caused massive population movements, with further social and political instability, and disrupted social relations and organisations. Child and adult mortality rose steeply and poverty broadened and deepened. It has also been argued that the late and hasty introduction of structural adjustment measures in the early 1990s contributed to the governance problems that preceded the genocide (Uvin, 1998; Storey, 1999).

Regional insecurity continues to delay resolution of the problems facing displaced people, and also absorbs domestic resources that could otherwise be devoted to poverty reduction.[2] Rwanda's role in the conflict in the Great Lakes region is linked to its need to establish security and protect itself from external threat. Various foreign governments, donors, international NGOs, and the UN's Panel of Experts have criticised Rwanda's role and intentions particularly with respect to its presence in the Democratic Republic of Congo (DRC). Developments in the DRC will influence Rwanda's ability to move out of the post-genocide emergency phase into one of sustainable development: peace is a pre-requisite for sustainable poverty reduction. This applies equally to social relations within Rwanda. The work of the National Unity and

---

1. It is normal for public speeches and documents to avoid all reference to Hutu/ Tutsi distinction, as part of a conscious strategy to promote national reconciliation. For a compelling account of this context and of the role of aid in perpetuating inequality and racist hatred, see Uvin (1998).
2. The government has reduced defence expenditure slightly since 1999, which, combined with HIPC debt relief, is expected to allow an increase in recurrent 'social/anti-poverty spending' from 3.9 percent in 1999 to about 6.9 percent by 2004. The Victims of Genocide Fund automatically receives 5 percent of domestic revenues.

Reconciliation Commission will influence how lasting poverty reduction can be promoted through participatory processes.

The government is still preparing to clear the bulk of the cases of genocide suspects using *gacaca* – community-level councils adjudicating cases and allowing the guilty to serve most of the balance of their sentences through community services. There are more than 100 thousand people held in prison on genocide-related charges. *Gacaca* processes entered the first major implementation phase in June 2002 following the election of 200,000 judges and establishment of 11,000 *gacaca* jurisdictions during 2001.

Another major challenge with implications for security, poverty, and rights, is to improve the *imidugudu* process in which displaced people are moved into new sites which are meant to be organised in such a way as to foster social cohesion, promote security, facilitate service delivery, and encourage the development of off-farm activities and the commercialisation of agriculture. Many NGOs, especially human rights agencies, have been strongly critical of various aspects of this process, referring not only to technical flaws such as poor infrastructure and planning, but also to political issues such as coercive resettlement, authoritarian and non-consultative planning, violation of property rights without compension, violation of the right to freedom of movement and choice of residence (Human Rights Watch, 2001). The PRSP acknowledges that overcoming technical difficulties of *imidugudu* must be a priority.

At the time of our study, Rwanda had no elected parliament but a National Transitory Assembly with 70 appointed members. Parliamentary and presidential elections were held under a new constitution in mid-2003. President Kagame was returned with 95 percent of the vote in a process described by some external observers as fair, although the European Union observers said it was 'not entirely' free and fair. Over a number of years, the government has been democratising and decentralising government structures to promote stability, peace and unity and reconciliation. Following the 1999 elections at local sector and cell levels, elections at Commune level were held in March 2001, and Communes were replaced by Districts. These were a success in terms of the 90 percent voter turnout, but it was also widely noted that voters had little effective choice. Mayors (replacing the old *Bourgmestres*) were elected indirectly through an electoral college: 87 percent of the new Mayors were re-elected from their old *Bourgmestre* positions. There are some doubts about how de-centralisation will develop – for example, how the *Préfets*' roles will change as local officials become more empowered.

There is a general problem of weak capacity in government. Many of the key agencies of government are staffed predominantly by people who either lack the skills to operate the systems that exist or who have limited skills and experience in designing and managing the implementation of institutional change.

In November 2001, the Government held a National Workshop for Evaluation and Planning to Strengthen Good Governance for Poverty

Reduction in Rwanda, and produced a Strategic Framework Paper on Strengthening Good Government for Poverty Reduction, which from the first sentence emphasised close linkage with the PRSP (Republic of Rwanda, 2001). Weak governance includes deficient capacity for policy dialogue between and among state and civil society organisations, and it is noteworthy that while foreign donors were invited to the Workshop, civil society and private sector representatives were not. Nonetheless, the Strategic Framework paper made numerous references to the importance of civil society and the private sector, and a major section was dedicated to these, proposing a database on CSOs, a new Forum for coordination of government with CSOs and government support for CSO capacity-building and revenue-raising, plus improvements in the 'enabling environment' for private sector development. Governance issues became more prominent in the revised PRSP following a complaint by the World Bank in March 2002.

Economic background and the poverty situation

Rwanda is now in transition from post-emergency recovery to building the future for sustainable development. Progress is steady but there remain structural problems that cause the high incidence and depth of poverty. These structural problems include: high population density and growth; low human resource development; low agricultural productivity; cyclical droughts and recurrent localised famines; environmental degradation; high transport costs; and limited employment opportunities. At the meso and macro levels there are the linked problems of high trade vulnerability due to reliance on exports of coffee and tea; a structural trade deficit; a structural imbalance between government revenues and expenditures; negative savings; and a low level of private investment.

Over 90 percent of the population work in smallholder agriculture, whose productivity and sustainability is constrained by uncertainty of land rights and by inadequate levels of inputs such as fertiliser and soil protection. The large proportion of households are labour constrained, often headed by a child, a widow, or a prisoner's wife. Land scarcity and environmental degradation are crucial constraints: while 85 percent of rural households own land, the average holding is just 0.71ha and 95 percent of farmers farm 2ha or less; few use inorganic fertilisers and there have been steep declines in the use of organic inputs.

A wealth of survey data became available during 2001, just in time to inform the PRSP, whereas until then most information on poverty had been old and/or of dubious quality. In 2000, Rwanda's population was 7.97 million and growing at 2.5 percent per year. 60 percent were below the poverty line, up from the 1985 estimate of 46 percent, but down from the 1994 post-genocide estimate of 78 percent.

Life expectancy at birth is now 49 years, infant mortality is 107 per thousand, child mortality (deaths before 5th birthday) 198 per thousand,

and maternal mortality 810 per hundred thousand births. HIV prevalence is 11.2 percent. Adult literacy (>15 years) is 52.36 percent and the net primary and secondary school enrolments are 73.3 percent and 6 percent. Access to safe water is given as 44 percent.

High rural-urban inequality is confirmed by the estimate that 75 percent of the urban Kigali population are in the top expenditure quintile for the country, and 96 percent of the food-poor live in rural areas. On some indicators, such as housing and consumption poverty, there are big differences between provinces. The overwhelming majority of the population are unwaged and have no cash savings or contact with formal financial institutions.

After a collapse in 1994, GDP recovered at a rapid and then decelerating rate from 1995 to reach its pre-1994 level by 1999. GDP is about US$1.8 billion and average per capita incomes US$222. For the future, the government has developed a macroeconomic programme aimed at achieving annual average growth in real GDP of at least 6 percent per year, keeping inflation below 5 percent per year and gradually reducing the current account deficit (excluding official transfers) from 16.8 percent in 2000 to 10.8 percent by 2004. The programme also includes a goal of increasing the ratio of domestic revenue to GDP by one half of one percentage point per year.

Aid dependence

As a reaction to the emergency, there were massive inflows of donor funds, but most of this did not go through government and was not coordinated or strategic. The debt burden rose sharply. At the end of 1999, total external public debt outstanding amounted to about US$1.3 billion, representing close to 65 percent of GDP or, in Net Present Value terms, over five times export earnings.

Rwanda reached the Decision Point under the HIPC2 Initiative in December 2000, following completion of its PRGF review and Interim PRSP (iPRSP). In November 2001 the IMF completed the final review of Rwanda's PRGF loan, releasing a further US$12 million, and commending the country's strong performances in economic growth, low inflation, and build-up of foreign exchange reserves with a stable exchange rate. It was expected to approve a new PRGF arrangement in mid-July 2002. HIPC Completion Point was scheduled for July 2003.

Despite the consistently improving external current account performance envisaged in the macroeconomic framework, the desired debt sustainability will still only come about (and the NPV of debt to exports ratio will be held to sustainable levels) if donor grants – as opposed to loans – are substantially higher than the historical trend, at least for a number of years. The importance of continued donor grants in the short and medium term after the Decision Point cannot be over-emphasised, as even after full application of enhanced HIPC assistance, and assuming new financing consisting of at least 75 percent official transfers, Rwanda's debt ratios would otherwise stay above the debt sustainability target.

Previous poverty plans

In 1994, the new government issued a Declaration of Principles setting out medium-term principles for social, political, and economic development, emphasising reduced state roles and liberalising the market. A further Framework of Economic Policies, agreed with the World Bank and IMF, set out strategies for making the transition from emergency to development from 1998 to 2000. In 1999, a three-year plan of action was prepared to manage the introduction and development of a Medium-Term Expenditure Framework (MTEF) from 2000 to 2002. In 1999, the Policy Framework Paper agreed between the government and the IMF set macro-economic and structural priorities for 1999-2002, and the government's Vision for the Future, published in 1999, announced long-term objectives for the reduction in poverty through increasing agricultural productivity, generating higher rural skills and incomes, and off-farm employment (among other objectives for governance, grassroots participation in development and decision making, an all-inclusive economic system, macroeconomic stability, and human resource development).

The term 'transition', referring both to a graduation towards increased stability and to a change from short-term 'emergency' and 'reconstruction' efforts towards medium-term development planning, is frequently referred to in discussions and documents relating to Rwanda's current strategic opportunities and aid flows. In terms of planning, 'transition' refers to a desire for more explicit and coherent inter-agency and inter-sectoral policies and strategies with longer time horizons and increased transparency and rationality. In terms of financial flows, the hope is that transition will bring greater domestic capabilities for raising and predicting revenues, and that foreign donors and IFIs will increasingly bring their contributions into a comprehensive national planning framework, and agree to finance 'developmental' rather than 'welfare' programmes. Transition is also intended to bring better accounting, reporting and monitoring arrangements within government that can serve the needs of the IFIs as well as the government.

Until 2001, key reviews of poverty (e.g. UNDP, 1999; World Bank, 1994, 1998) and key documents on anti-poverty strategies had been drafted by donors and foreign consultants. The Ministry of Economy and Finance (MINECOFIN) has used a number of short-term expatriates in advisory roles and has to a large extent relied on them in its interaction with the IFIs. Many senior positions in the government are held by Rwandan people who first came to Rwanda in 1994 or later. The demand for 'national ownership' of anti-poverty strategies needs to be understood in this context. On the one hand demand for national ownership is being directly boosted through aid-funded national consultation and planning, while on the other hand it is inhibited by the need for foreign expertise in drafting, implementing, and monitoring these strategies. Some Rwandans expressed to us concern that donors are holding back too much for fear of intruding on national strategic planning, and suggested that stronger donor involvement remains essential.

7.3   The PRSP process in Rwanda

The PRS process was officially started in Rwanda in June 2000 with the production of a 'zero draft' and announcement of the process by the President in Parliament. Following a consultation process among various Ministries, donor agencies and CSOs mainly at national level, plus some provincial-level meetings, the iPRSP was finalised in November 2000 and endorsed as a suitable document by the World Bank/IMF Joint Staff Assessment (JSA) in December.

The National Poverty Reduction Programme (NPRP) was the unit within MINECOFIN charged with leading the coordination and implementation of the PRS process. During 2001-2, it planned and implemented a major set of consultations at all levels. Financing of the consultation process and of the NPRP unit has come mainly from the UK Department for International Development (DFID), which along with the UNDP has been closely involved in providing technical assistance and regular advice. At national level, there were several well-attended meetings to discuss the general content of the PRSP and the closely-related National Five-Year Plan of Action. At sub-national levels the key activity was the National Poverty Assessment (NPA), which was conducted mainly from May to December 2001. There was also a more intensive pilot exercise in Community Action Planning at *cellule* level in Butare, led by ActionAid, and a Policy Relevance Test (PRT).

On the basis of the Butare experience, a discussion document was produced by the NPRP together with the Ministry of Local Government and Social Affairs (MINALOC) in August 2001. Entitled *Ubudehe to Fight Poverty*, this argued for the relevance of the traditional concept and associated practices of *ubudehe mu kurwanya ubukene* – working together to solve problems. The emphasis is on the importance of collective, inclusive, and participatory planning and action at 'community' level. As is the case with *gacaca*, the term *ubudehe* has quickly become a standard part of the national discourse in which contemporary development and reconciliation efforts are rooted in tradition. The Butare pilot was replicated nationwide during 2002 as part of the process of devolving planning and budgetary responsibilities to local levels, particularly through the new Common Development Funds.

The PRT was commissioned by the NPRP (with DFID funding) and was conducted between April and July 2001 by the National University of Rwanda, covering 38 of the 100 Districts in groups of twenty-five people, selected on the basis of a series of criteria to cover different social and economic groups. This study, implemented by a team of 18 social scientists from the

Rwanda chapter of the Organisation for Social Science Research in Eastern and Southern Africa (OSSREA), informed the NPRP about the knowledge and attitudes of all relevant stakeholder categories at all levels concerning the PRS process, and about relevant policies which need to be linked with the PRS. It was also expected to contribute to the process of strengthening the sense of co-responsibility for the PRS process among all of these stakeholders.

The NPRP staff soon became aware of the need for persistent efforts on their part to elicit active participation from stakeholders outside MINECOFIN. Already in September 2000, they were noticing that simply sending the draft iPRSP and inviting people to consultation meetings was not in itself enough to make people feel part of the process. Even key staff in key Ministries such as the Ministry of Gender (MIGEPROF) and the Ministry of Agriculture (MINAGRI) appeared still to be waiting to be more actively wooed by the NPRP, rather than taking their own initiative in responding to the document.

The iPRSP was finalised on schedule in mid-November 2000, and was formally adopted by the National Assembly after a one-day meeting by the cabinet to discuss the final draft. IMF staff visited MPs in Parliament in January 2001 to discuss the process of producing the full PRSP. In early September 2001, a draft outline of the PRSP was sent out to most key stakeholders for comment before production of the 'zero draft PRSP' later in September, translated from English to French.

The zero draft of the full PRSP was discussed in October 2001 by a national validation workshop with representatives of major stakeholder categories in public, private, and civil-society sectors. There followed considerable debate over several months, particularly with the IMF, concerning mainly the macro-economic framework and the deployment of three public expenditure scenarios. The World Bank also had concerns about some of the sectoral substance, about the need for more prominent attention to governance as a set of cross-cutting issues and more minor matters of presentation; in March 2002 the Bank insisted that the PRSP be revised before it could be submitted for approval. This intervention was seen by the NPRP and some donors as unreasonable and late interference.

The PRSP became available on the web in English by August 2002, having been circulated by email (mainly to foreign donors and government departments) in June. A French version was circulated by email in November 2002, and a Kinyarwanda translation was expected to follow shortly and to be widely disseminated. It is a lengthy document – over 85,000 words –[3] offering a richness of information and analysis that is rare in PRSP documents. It was well received by the IMF/World Bank JSA.

---

3. Cf Uganda's PRSP 12,000 words; Tanzania's PRSP 21,000. Even Rwanda's 34-page (13,000-word) summary version is longer than Uganda's full PRSP.

Questions of ownership and conditionality

In our initial research, we addressed the issue of 'ownership' mainly indirectly, by asking people what they understood about the new PRS process, whether they had read, responded to, and discussed the iPRSP, and what role they expected to play in its formulation, implementation and monitoring. The overwhelming impression we gained from all parties outside MINECOFIN was that, while most knew something about the iPRSP and provisionally could see that they had contributions to make to the PRSP and to its implementation and monitoring, they had yet to develop a sense of co-responsibility for it or a sense of close partnership with MINECOFIN. In more pragmatic terms, the critical ingredients missing were the allocation of specific responsibilities within Ministries and other development agencies for liaising with specific MINECOFIN staff on specific issues. Key exceptions were DFID and UNDP, both of which were contributing substantial resources in the form of both finance and technical support through consultancies, advice and secondments.

These inevitable shortcomings aside, the PRS process is widely seen as providing opportunities for a substantially Rwandan-owned process and not just an IFI imposition. Nevertheless, several staff in MINECOFIN and among major bilateral donors mentioned to us that IFI staff in Rwanda and visiting missions have yet to adapt their own practices to bring them into line with the principles of PRS theory. The above-mentioned requirements for alteration to form and content of the PRSP delayed by several months the production of the final version, yet previously the World Bank was trying to hurry the consultation process through to produce a PRSP by July 2001 when its Country Assistance Strategy (CAS) was due for a three-year renewal.

For this study, four Bank staff were sent twice each a short email questionnaire on donor responses to the PRSP, together with a specific request for views on 'how the Bank's CAS for Rwanda will reflect the PRSP, both in terms of content and in terms of timing and the process by which the CAS is adapted and assessed'. Only one responded, but his helpful overview of the Rwanda situation and donor responses in general made no reference to the CAS or to any specific Bank responses. In other words, it was not only Rwandan stakeholders who were at this point unsure as to what extent they would participate in the PRS process.

The IMF's role and credibility in the PRS process remains somewhat ambiguous. From our field visits in 2000 and 2001 we concluded that the IMF were being short-termist and over-directive in setting unrealistic revenue forecasts for the MTEF. We felt that this was setting unrealistic conditions for PRGF loans and was not consistent with the spirit of a longer-term approach to sustainable economic management. As it turned out, the IMF's revenue forecasts were not over-optimistic, and 2001 revenue performance exceeded the IMF and government targets, due mainly to performance of VAT introduced in January 2001.

Government plans, approach, and capabilities

In comparison to the drafting of other policy documents such as the national strategies on agriculture, environment, and gender, the approach to drafting the PRSP appears to have been considerably more participatory and inclusive. The National Gender Policy, for example, appears to have been drafted by a short-term consultant from Tanzania assisted by two local consultants, with minimal consultation and minimal cross-referencing with other policy documents and processes including the iPRSP and at least three other gender policy/strategy documents.

The PRSP has prompted discussion within government of the role of planning. Vision 2020 represents a long-term strategic perspective on Rwanda's development prospects and intentions. Whatever critics of this form of planning say, it has supporters in Rwanda. This would seem to reflect a tradition of planning in the country, but also a desire to show how the country can develop in the future and put the 1990s behind it.

Planning for many (mostly critics) means centralised, quantitative planning supported by a dominant role for the state in the economy. For others it is simply a process (and a document) that defines intended activities in a consistent way within the sphere of operation of the institution that is planning. It does not automatically mean an extension of the sphere of operation. Planning is used in a number of contexts in Rwanda. The Poverty Reduction Strategy was for several months in 2001 referred to as the Poverty Reduction Action Plan, echoing the use of the term 'Plan' in the PRSP of neighbouring Uganda.

Though the term PRSP returned, the document retained a stronger emphasis on pragmatism than is expected in most PRSPs, its length and detail allowing it to be more specific about actions than the term 'strategy' implies. It is also 'strategic' in the sense that it is based on a costing exercise that explicitly asked sectoral Ministries to produce budgetary scenarios according to needs rather than anticipated constraints. The hope is that a good PRSP may attract more foreign funds.

Central government response

The government has responded positively and in a high-profile way to the PRSP initiative. The Council of Ministers set up an Inter-Ministerial Committee on Poverty (IMCP) chaired by the prime minister and with representation of the National Assembly through the Deputy Speaker. The full PRSP was promoted in speeches by the President, the Finance Minister and several other Cabinet members during 2002.

There is a Steering Committee charged with monitoring the PRS process, with senior representatives from all key ministries (mainly Secretaries-General), plus representatives from civil society organisations, donors, and the private sector. This is supported by a Technical Committee, which organised the consultations, worked with sectoral ministries to review action plans and costings, has undertaken expenditure outcome and tracking studies, and oversaw the drafting of the PRSP.

The NPRP did not emphasise the potential HIPC2 benefits or related conditionalities to participants, preferring to focus on the need for a coherent and feasible national strategy and the opportunities for participation to release community-level (non-financial) resources and capacities. The PRSP mentions HIPC only briefly in footnotes near the end of the document. None of the interlocutors (outside central government) in Phase 1 of this study referred unprompted to HIPC and none commented on either conditionalities or benefits.

The PRSP emphasises that it is not a 'final' document (in contrast with the Constitution, which was being drafted concurrently).[4] It is rather the first of many expected two-yearly outputs from the ongoing PRS process. Concerns were being expressed about financing the PRS. These concerns related to the realism of its three-year forecasts of domestic revenue and the impact of the cash budget. While there was strong agreement on the need to define a poverty focus, there were concerns that existing programmes might simply be relabelled as 'poverty' programmes, given the short time available and the lack of capacity in many sector ministries for substantial strategic change. It remained to be seen whether all sector ministries would, in the preparation of the 2002-04 MTEF, be able to restructure and develop priority rankings of their activities and expenditure programmes to define avenues towards poverty reduction that are explicit, plausible, and monitorable.

Local government response

Local government is crucial to the PRS process, as local-level consultations and future implementation of anti-poverty programmes can best be carried out through its structures. The centrality of local authorities to the consultation and implementation process has rendered close cooperation between the NPRP and Ministry of Local Government and Social Affairs (MINALOC) essential. And, through MINALOC, links have been established with local authorities, particularly the prefectures.

The response of *Préfectures* to the PRS initiative has been positive to the extent that it is seen as supporting the process of decentralisation. There are some incipient signs of consultation fatigue, and one *Préfet* said he felt that most of the development issues at the *Préfecture* level had already been discussed and agreed with central ministries and that it was time to 'get on with it'. It is unlikely, however, that this view takes adequate account of the need for consultation at more local levels. The switch to a poverty reduction

---

4. The Constitution is like the PRSP meant to be based 'based on the views of the people', according to the Government of Rwanda website www.rwanda1.com/government/

rather than sectoral approach was recognised by some as new and useful. Yet, at least in the North-West (Gisenyi and Ruhengeri), there was a feeling that regional security issues dictate a need for resolution of emergency issues (regional insecurity and population displacement) before attempts to reduce poverty can begin to be successful.

Non-governmental organisations

The NPRP copied the draft iPRSP in September 2000 to representatives of several national-level NGOs, mainly international NGOs but also major indigenous NGOs and NGO federations such as CCOAIB and Pro-Femmes. It also held a one-day meeting with them. Few NGOs responded. The main constraint seems to have been the fact that the iPRSP was drafted only in English and was not made available in French and Kinyarwanda until the end of March 2001. Secondly, NGOs and NGO networks were ill-prepared for this opportunity. Several read the document and some sent in comments, but they were unable to provide individual or collective responses on substantive issues. Like the Ministries, they have so far waited for more direct soliciting of views on specific issues from NPRP staff.

International NGOs were expecting in September 2000 to prepare a set of collective responses through their own INGO forum, but this dwindled into inactivity due to lack of leadership. Christian Aid and Trocaire convened local NGOs to discuss the PRSP in November 2000 and found that only two of thirty representatives had even heard of the PRSP before being invited to the meeting. NGOs and other civil society organisations have been inhibited from policy dialogue and advocacy roles by their focus on service delivery. A multi-country study of PRS processes by ActionAid portrayed Rwanda as one of the best examples of participatory PRS processes and a PRSP which responds to findings from the PPA, although it points to complaints of consultation fatigue as well as limited 'country-ownership' (Zaman, 2002).

A report by Christian Aid (Painter, 2002) argues that the civil society response has mainly been to collaborate with government in collecting better information about poverty and responding to draft documents, rather than engaging in policy dialogue or joint decision-making. Nevertheless, this three-country synthesis report (Rwanda, Malawi, and Bolivia) says that the participatory process was much better and more substantial in Rwanda than in the other two countries, and commends the government's efforts in opening up a space for participation despite the lack of experience and capacity for this on the parts of both government and civil society. The report is not uncritical of the Rwandan PRS process. The Rwanda case-study (Bugingo, 2002) argues that the lack of a 'conceptual framework' for participation and consequent inadequate planning of participation (stakeholder mapping, agendas, documentation, timing, output definition) weakened the process. It also points out the limited involvement of the mass media, religious organisations, and the private sector and especially the informal sector.

More serious than the criticisms embedded in these studies is one accusation of deliberate prevention of civil society involvement in policy dialogue. According to the 2002 Human Rights Watch Annual Report on Rwanda, 'Security agents detained and interrogated representatives of the Rwanda Debt Relief Network in September after they made critical statements about poverty in Rwanda. Authorities accused these civil society actors of representing political parties and of inciting ethnic divisions.' We have not been able to explore this further.

Other civil society responses

The NPRP used various forms of media to make itself known to the public and explain its approach. However, journalists (from the three main English language newspapers, *The Rwanda Herald*, *The New Times*, and *Newsline)* told us that they did not see it as particularly newsworthy. They did not see their job as promoting or engaging in a strategy/policy debate. Politics is the major interest of their mostly urban-dwelling, mostly Kigali-based readership, but this is inhibited by self-censorship 'as a survival mechanism', according to one Editor-in-Chief. Apparently both the government and the public are intolerant towards 'excessive criticism' of the government during what is regarded as a period of national healing.

Media coverage of the PRS process was very limited. The main weekly paper *Rwanda Newsline* did give it a front-page coverage in its edition of November 13-19, 2000, but the main story line was the link with donor responses to the war in Congo rather than the PRS itself. In many cases the PRS was mentioned within articles covering subjects related to poverty, Rwanda's involvement in the Congo, and foreign assistance, under headlines such as 'Government defines poverty indicators';[5] and 'EU committed to poverty reduction'.[6] Notably, several articles on development issues, poverty and foreign assistance[7] failed to mention the PRS process.

Involvement of civil society other than international NGOs was limited. The PRS Unit's meeting with civil society organisations in September 2000 was attended by the Rectors of the two Universities, and some trade union and church representatives. A surprising absence in early PRSP discussions was the private sector. During our meetings in September 2000 and April 2001 with the head of the *Fédération Rwandaise du Secteur Privé*, we were told that the *Fédération* had not been involved and did not see a role for itself in the forthcoming discussions. Subsequently, however, it attended meetings on the PRSP and looked likely to become more involved. The full June 2002 PRSP emphasises that it is vital for the private sector to be 'fully

---

5. *The New Times*, Sept 11-17, 2000.
6. *The New Times*, January 15-18, 2001.
7. See 'Focus on poverty alleviation', *The New Times*, Sept. 11-17, 2000; also 'Rwanda meets development partners', *The New Times*, November 13 -15, 2000.

involved in the formulation of policy'.

The churches are also potentially important facilitators of consultation, but a widespread view is that, although church structures are important, they remain severely inhibited from overt participation in political and social discussions due to shame about the Catholic Church's mixed but often collaborative role in the genocide. The full PRSP mentions the integration of religious organisations within the public health system as an example of close state-civil society collaboration, along with a general reference to the importance of civil society organisations as 'interlocutors between people and the state'.

There has been limited involvement of academics except for the 18 members of the OSSREA research group in the National University of Rwanda, who conducted the Policy Relevance Test study from April to July 2001. In general, Rwandan academics have little research capability, and are not involved in policy or planning processes (having concentrated their efforts in the Emergency Phase on teaching activities).

Donors and IFIs

Relations between the government and donors have been central to political debates since the genocide, given the very high aid-dependency and limited national capacity to work effectively with a largely uncoordinated donor community. Over recent years, the Kagame regime has frequently made public pleas for donors to provide programme and budgetary support for long-term development, rather than continuing with the fragmentary approach that has emphasised post-conflict reconstruction and rehabilitation projects outside the budgetary system.

Donors and of course the IFIs are in principle united in their agreement on the importance and value of the PRS process. As emphasised throughout this chapter, donors in many ways hold the key to the success of the PRS process. Yet partly because of the inhibitions arising from the concept of a 'country-owned' strategy, and partly due to inertia and lack of incentive for change, most donors have yet to respond effectively to the new opportunities afforded by the PRSP.

Only DFID, the World Bank, and the UNDP have been providing substantial amounts of budgetary rather than projectised or sectoral support. It is no coincidence that it is DFID and UNDP that have been most closely involved with the establishment and strengthening of the NPRP. Earlier models for budgetary and flexible support to Rwanda are the UNDP Trust Fund for Rwanda (mainly 1996-98), and the multi-donor Multilateral Debt Trust Fund for Rwanda. It has yet to be seen whether these emergency-related structures will be replicated in support of the PRS. The European Commission was expected to embark on budgetary support for Rwanda in the near future.

In general, donors are also supportive of the strategies outlined in the PRSP. We did not hear any suggestion that donors may differ substantially from the PRSP in what they see as the priorities for Rwanda.[8]

The Joint Staff Assessment of the iPRSP by the IFIs was generally favourable, as already noted. The staffs commended its comprehensive coverage and its confirmation of the Vision 2020 linkage between poverty and national reconciliation. They also argued that the consultative process was good because Rwanda is 'a country with a tradition of consultation' – a somewhat contentious claim given the evidently authoritarian traditions of the Rwandan state. The strongest JSA criticisms of the iPRSP were with reference to trade liberalisation, private investments and credit, warning the Government against protectionism and state intervention in the market. They also advised the Government against adopting a Poverty Action Fund, on the Ugandan model, as this 'might delay the ongoing budget reform program, create duplication and governance problems'.

In their comments on approving Rwanda's HIPC Decision Point in January 2001, the IMF Directors 'welcomed the large increase and improved composition of antipoverty expenditures envisaged for 2001, which in part is to be achieved through reallocation of resources from defence expenditure'. However, they also 'expressed concern over the extra-budgetary expenditures, especially those relating to military spending, and welcomed the authorities' intention to bring them into the 2002 budget'.

The JSA comments on the final PRSP commend among other things its strong linkage with traditional decision-making systems, reiterating the earlier statement about consultative traditions. They point out that it could have offered better analysis of the impacts of recent government policies on poverty, of conflict and past policies of exclusion, and of the trend towards increasing inequality.

7.4 What difference has the PRSP made?

The prospects for the PRS process in Rwanda to institutionalise poverty reduction policies, programmes, practices and monitoring systems are inextricably interlinked with the national unity and reconciliation process and the decentralisation process. Success in any one will depend on institutionalisation of the others. These in turn depend on the success of participation by stakeholders in the PRS process and how this will translate into lasting institutional arrangements. In Rwanda these prospects need to

---

8. By contrast, the OECD DAC report of the Informal Task Force On Conflict, Peace and Development Co-operation offered the key recommendation that donors should 'realise the inevitability of initial donor-driven support in key sectors such as justice and security framework reform. If donors are convinced that certain actions are important and the government does not prioritise these actions, but does also not oppose donor investment in them, donors must be willing to pay for them' (Baaré et al., 1999: 6).

be set in the context of the political traditions of the country and how these are intended to change in the future and bring about a new democratic system of governance. Beyond that, institutionalisation of the PRS will depend on how it interacts with public expenditure management both within government and in terms of donor and IFI responses.

Stakeholder participation and political traditions

In late 2000, the former Minister for Foreign Affairs was appointed as Minister for Civil Society, indicating a new interest in formalising and upgrading the importance of relations between government and civil society. Shortly afterwards, this new Ministry became a Department within the President's Office. In addition, MINALOC has a Department for NGO Liaison. So far, this has concerned itself mainly with the bureaucratic functions of checking up on what NGOs are doing, rather than with policy dialogue on matters relating to NGO roles.

Both Rwandans and foreigners in Rwanda frequently refer to the 'culture of obedience/passivity', meaning that most people generally expect to carry out the instructions of those in power, and have minimal interest in participatory politics and policy-making. Whether or not this is a safe generalisation, it clearly casts doubt on the short-term prospects for developing participatory processes. At the national level, consensus politics remains the order of the day, the absence of official political parties being matched by a striking lack of policy debates.

The National Poverty Assessment and scaling-up of the Butare pilot Community Action Planning are seen as keys to the longer-term process of local-level planning for anti-poverty actions drawing on the budgets that are being devolved to local administrations. At the time of our study, local staff were being trained in participatory methods. They were mainly being drawn from the ranks of elected local administrators, plus some teachers and local NGO staff. MINALOC and the Unity and Reconciliation Commission had both seconded personnel to be members of the training team for the PPA. MINALOC was planning to build on this process over the next year, conducting a national version of the Butare pilot, with support from the NPRP before taking over the process as a regular part of its activities.

Another important spin-off from the PRSP process is the proposal to introduce Citizens' Report Cards in Rwanda. This is an innovative approach to generating information and discussion to help public service providers learn about users' perceptions of their services. The current plan is for members of MINECOFIN to be trained by the Centre for Public Accountability in Bangalore (the originator of the Report Card innovation).

National unity and reconciliation

A major national priority is to promote stability through 'reconciliation'.

Although not directly related to poverty reduction objectives, this is clearly relevant since reconciliation and poverty reduction are mutually interdependent. Poverty reduction may, in the longer term, help heal the social and psychological damage of the genocide; promotion of equity should help avoid a repetition of the violence; and the gradual building up of mutual trust and cooperation through associational life and networks should strengthen the economy and help reduce poverty.

Undoubtedly, Rwanda's long-term stability will depend on the government's ability to reduce inequality and bring about tangible improvements to people's day-to-day lives. Ultimately the task of winning the confidence of all its citizens will be rendered much easier by success in convincing them that improvement in their material circumstances is as much a priority as any other. As one official pointed out, 'a hungry man is an angry man; you cannot reconcile two hungry people'.

Decentralisation

The poverty reduction strategy is intimately connected with the active steps being taken towards financial and political decentralisation. Following the 1999 and 2001 elections of local government officials at Sector and District levels, MINALOC embarked on a programme of decentralisation to the *préfecture* and *commune* (now district) levels. The *secteur* will be the basic level for development planning and the *cellule* will be the fundamental unit for information generation and monitoring. The overall objective is to ensure political, economic, social, managerial/administrative and technical empowerment of local populations to fight poverty by participating in the planning and management of their development processes (Republic of Rwanda/MINALOC, 2000: 7-8). This process will be supported by new Common Development Funds (for which there are international donor commitments).

At the time of the study, all the Prefectures were expected to renew their three-year Provincial Action Plans complete with costings for 2001-04, although it would be the District Councils, not the Prefectures, that controlled the budgets. UNDP were intending to provide technical training for the management of Community Action Funds. It remained unclear how these would fit in with the budgeting of the MTEF and the PRSP.

Understanding of the existing and future structures and roles of local government organisation is loose and variable in Rwanda. This seems to reflect the novelty of using governance hierarchies to encourage and incorporate grassroots opinions and encourage accountability. It also reflects the rapid pace of change in structures and their roles. Yet the hope is that by encouraging people to work together in pursuit of common objectives, such as improvement in service delivery, decentralisation will promote unity and reconciliation.

Public expenditure management and institutional change

Institutionalisation of the PRS will require improvements in public financial management and the development of the MTEF – the translation of policies into costed public expenditure programmes designed to contribute to policy outcomes. Within these programmes, the provision of public goods and services will need to be oriented to the delivery of monitorable outputs. The costs of these programmes must be assessed for their long-term sustainability with reference to realistic assessments of the resources likely to be available. Improvements will be needed in financial accounting and reporting to promote fiscal transparency and to support monitoring of output performance.

The time and effort necessary to improve public financial management and develop an MTEF should not be underestimated. Rwanda has gone a long way in preparing for this process, but a great deal remains to be done. The development of an effective MTEF will require sustained and coordinated activity between the Parliament, the cabinet, MINECOFIN, the sector ministries, the various tiers of local government, and supporting institutions such as the Rwanda Revenue Authority, the Auditor General, and accounting and treasury functions in government and the financial sector. Donors and IFIs will also need to engage positively, with a long-term commitment. Expectations of the timing of future progress are being revised in the light of emerging constraints to more effective public financial management.

Reforms to public financial management are under way, but existing expenditure management systems at the centre are weak. The accounting, commitment control and cash management systems have not been able to prevent the build-up of arrears. Audited government accounts have not been produced since the early 1990s. The government's response to these expenditure management problems, and particularly to the shortfalls of revenue collections from revenue forecasts in 2000, has been to introduce a cash budget with strict cash release rules. The wider governance problem of accountability is being addressed but an effective system that includes independent audit has yet to be implemented.

Following repeated complaints about weakness in the budgetary system at cabinet and parliamentary levels, a joint government and World Bank Public Expenditure Review in 1997/98 recommended a gradual shift towards an MTEF system. This continued in 1998 and 1999, with changes in the budget law being introduced to permit decentralisation of budgetary authority to sector ministries. Sector expenditure reviews were undertaken in education, health and water.[9]

In 1999, GoR drew up a three-year Plan of Action for MTEF development

---

9. During the course of 1999, a second round of Sector Expenditure Reviews was completed in the Health and Education ministries. The Sector Expenditure Review for the water sector was updated and a first review of public expenditures in the Justice sector was completed in 2000

and implementation over the period 2000 to 2002. Progress so far has been mixed. During 2000, the first critical step in the MTEF was delayed, namely the resource forecast and the setting of expenditure ceilings. The formalisation of a cash budget system has led to concerns in sector ministries about the relevance of planning and forward budgeting without predictable resource flows. The 2001 Budget included mission statements, programmes, objectives and outputs for each ministry, but these were loosely defined, with no information on expenditures or budgets before or after the current budget year.

There remains the challenge of strengthening the links between the output indicators of the MTEF/budget and the poverty monitoring processes established under the PRS. The 2002 budget had an extended format, including sub-programmes that were intended to have a clearer definition of outputs. It appears that until now policy has been too loosely articulated to permit definition of clear objectives and supporting programmes with consequences for output and indicator definitions. It also appears that the senior management of many ministries do not engage in the detail of the process of translating policy into objectives, expenditure programmes and expected outputs at an early enough stage. Budget Committees have been created, but these do not yet seem to have engaged in a practical way with the MTEF process; many sanctioned the presentation of budget estimates for 2001 far in excess of the ceilings indicated by MINECOFIN.

Despite the enthusiastic response from sector ministries to the principle of the MTEF, there is a marked absence of any real commitment to plan and budget within expenditure ceilings. This suggests that the practical implementation of the MTEF will take more time. A key constraint is the limited understanding of what 'prioritising' entails. 'Priority' tends to be used to mean simply 'important', ignoring the need for distinguishing among higher and lower priorities and ultimately to favour some over others.

Donors (especially those providing budget support) likewise need to become more closely engaged in understanding the outputs that the government intends to deliver from its public expenditure, as well as the priority ranking of those outputs, so as to ensure that they provide appropriate technical assistance and advisory support. So far, donors are inhibited from such close engagement by their worries about the quality, comprehensiveness, and transparency of government accounting and reporting systems. This lack of trust perpetuates the project approach, with separate project implementation units, bank accounts and accounting systems – all of which drains qualified staff from the government and weakens its capacity to address the accounting and reporting problem that causes donors' lack of trust in the first place.

In 2001, the government instituted a cash budget system in a classic response to mismanagement of public finances. The cash budget sets up rules for the allocation of cash resources released each month. MINECOFIN has set up a priority ranking for the items and activities that are to be funded. Its purpose is to stop expenditures being made in advance of receipts and thus to avoid domestic borrowing and the further accumulation of arrears. As a means of securing fiscal stability, a cash budget can be effective. It undermines, however, the idea of creating predictability in the MTEF. Cash budgets treat symptoms and not causes. What is needed to treat the cause is a process of re-instituting proper control of expenditure commitments to avoid the build up of arrears and a system where budgets are made and controlled within predictable resource envelopes, i.e., an effective MTEF process. At a minimum MINECOFIN must develop proper cash forecasting systems. This was being addressed, belatedly, in 2002.

Progress with the creation of a comprehensive database of public sector activities financed off-budget and through donor flows in the development budget appears to be slow for capacity reasons. Links between the PRS and MTEF processes are being built. Formerly, the Strategic Planning Department of MINECOFIN had responsibility for inter-ministry coordination in the development of sector plans, but it had weak capacity and was unable to establish strong links between policies and resources, or to link poverty monitoring requirements with sector programme definitions, outputs and indicators. In 2002, the NPRP was merged with the Poverty Observatory and the Strategic Planning Department of MINECOFIN to form a new Strategic Planning and Poverty Monitoring Department (SPPMD).

This realignment may help. However, it will be important to avoid raising unrealistic expectations through the new MTEF and PRS processes. This applies to the 'contract' between MINECOFIN and the sector ministries and will apply to the more complicated and indirect 'contract' systems between central fiscal managers and the various decentralised structures of government on which effective participative implementation of a PRS will rely.[10] The chances of institutionalising the MTEF and PRS processes will be undermined by disillusionment, if the contract cannot be honoured because resources do not flow in a predictable way to support the implementation of the strategy. A critical first step is the timely setting of expenditure ceilings by the cabinet, on which both the MTEF and the implementation of a PRS will depend.

The politics of poverty reduction in Rwanda

The PRS process has been fairly high-profile within government (though less so in the ill-developed media which, as we have explained, tend to focus on more sensational news). Since poverty increased dramatically in the years leading up to and following the 1994 genocide, reducing poverty is seen as critical to establishing the credentials of the government and the basis for national security, reconciliation and long-term development. The establishment of a national Constitution by 2003 is to a lesser extent also

---

10. The essence of the contract is that MINECOFIN will endorse and guarantee allocations to programmes on the basis of good quality planning, implementation and monitoring of poverty focused service delivery.

linked with the PRS process in that progress in poverty reduction is seen as vital to the establishment of the legitimacy of the government.

The key challenge for the new SPPMD is to try to bring about or influence changes in the incentives which shape the planning of line ministries and donor agencies, such that all recognise not just shared responsibility for the PRSP but that it is in their interest to integrate their activities within it. Several donors mentioned to us that so far there is no real incentive to change, although peer pressure exerted particularly by DFID, UNDP and the World Bank may be generating momentum for a shift towards budget support.

Participatory and integrated planning

Perhaps the most important outcome so far from the PRS process has been the rapid development of national capabilities and activities in participatory planning and assessment under the Participatory Poverty Assessment (PPA) rubric. The test will be whether the PPA processes, and subsequent findings and recommendations, actually lead to changes in the policies and practices of local and national development agencies.

An important step will be to ensure that the PPA process and outputs are recognised as legitimate and important at national level. UNDP staff are reported to have recommended that PPA findings should be reported directly to cabinet as they are produced. SPPMD staff appeared to favour this idea, but had yet to work out how frequently it would be realistic to expect to report to cabinet, and in what kind of form PPA reports could be produced. Another task will be to persuade individual line ministries that the PPA is relevant to their work and to their priority setting. The Unity and Reconciliation Commission is an encouraging example of a key agency that has shown strong interest in working with SPPMD to assist with and use the findings of the PPA. By contrast, the view from the Ministry of Agriculture was that there is no prospect of the PPA resulting in any modification of the National Agricultural Strategy, since this is already seen as being entirely geared towards reducing poverty, as well as being based on sound participatory consultation.

7.5 Monitoring the PRSP: a second chance?

Generating information and managing understanding for pro-poor policy-making

Formal national-level management of understanding[11] about poverty and

---

11. Knowledge-management is of course the more familiar term; but for contexts and subject matters characterised by high degrees of uncertainty, softer and more processual terms such as 'understanding' and 'learning' seem more suitable.

about the efficacy of anti-poverty strategies is minimal in Rwanda. There is an important distinction to be made here between the *generation of information* (capture and collation) on the one hand, and the *management of knowledge* on the other – the latter including sharing and analysis of information, and the generation, sharing, and application of knowledge to policy and practice.

There is a wealth of information on various dimensions of poverty held by a variety of organisations and in general unused. MINECOFIN staff members emphasised that the main challenge is not to generate new statistical data but to make good use of the data that are already available but are unused and un-collated. For example, a great deal of information on poverty has been generated by the National Unity and Reconciliation Commission through its country-wide consultations and solidarity camps focusing on the causes of conflict and disunity and how to address them. This information proved hard for the NPRP to make use of in developing the PRSP, because of its diversity, difficulty of access, and lack of a formal link with the PRS process.

To take another example, as long ago as 1997 the government conducted a Participatory Poverty Assessment (PPA) in ten rural and two urban communes, which resulted in an excellent and comprehensive report on the multiple dimensions of poverty, complete with numerous sound recommendations on strategic priorities for anti-poverty action. There is little sign that the information or recommendations were ever applied. There was no explicit channel for translating understandings from the PPA into policies and actions – although some who participated in the PPA, including the head of the new SPPMD, have applied informally the lessons and experience gained from it.

Another type of difficulty concerns figures from different sources that often contradict each other. For example, three different figures have been given for nation-wide access to safe water: 44, 70, and 80 percent. Sometimes contradictions arise from different indicators or different interpretation of indicators: the figure for 'access to health facilities' is 81 percent, for example, but it has been estimated that only 27 percent of people actually use health facilities, suggesting that some quite complex interpretation and further qualitative research are needed to establish how many of the remaining 73 percent feel they have inadequate access to health facilities. The key challenge, then, is to develop an effective system for coordinating and analysing the available information, and for disseminating and ensuring the application of the new understandings that are generated.

Until 2000-01, scarcity of information on the extent and diversity of poverty in Rwanda (due to the destruction of information during the genocide, and to the fact that information has received low priority during the post-emergency reconstruction phase) was widely seen as a key constraint on managing understanding about poverty and development. However, as we have seen, several major information-gathering exercises were completed before the PRSP was finalised, and a full national population census is scheduled for 2003.

Learning strategies for the PRS

The PRSP identifies the Poverty Observatory (now part of the SPPMD) as the main agency responsible for coordinating and disseminating understanding about poverty and anti-poverty strategies. This was established as the main national poverty monitoring office in February 2000 following a Prime Minister's Decree in November 1999 (i.e., well before the PRSP process was formally launched in June 2000). It is staffed by a Coordinator and an economist assistant, plus an ODI Fellow economist and a statistician. It has also been assisted by several short-term DFID-financed consultancies.

There has been considerable debate about how extensive the Poverty Observatory's mandate should be, given its limited capacity and the information management structures and systems that already exist. Crucially, the PRS process has brought about much clearer partnerships and divisions of responsibility (spelled out in the PRSP) among the Statistics Department, the Poverty Observatory, the Budget Department/CEPEX (responsible especially for monitoring inputs and linking PRS and MTEF input/output monitoring), line ministries, and local administrative structures. Notably, however, no roles in the learning strategy are assigned to civil society or the private sector.

The Department of Statistics (in MINECOFIN) completed a major national household living standards survey in 2001. The Ministry of Health has its own health management information system, and the Ministry of Education is being assisted by DFID to strengthen its planning system, which could ultimately lead to an education Management Information System. It is expected that through the Poverty Observatory these will be closely integrated with the overall learning strategy associated with the PRSP.

The PRSP's section on 'monitoring and evaluation' charts out some steps towards better management of information. It provides a draft set of indicators, identifies responsibilities and timings for information gathering, and proposes development of a master plan of studies and surveys. What it does not do is articulate an overall approach to learning or a system for managing and applying knowledge about poverty. The emphasis is on basic information needs rather than on strategic management of a learning process. However, SPPMD's agreement for DFID's support specifies that it will draw up a Poverty Monitoring Plan (to capture information from both governmental and non-governmental sources) and a Poverty Information Plan (for publicising information about poverty).

Rwanda's PRSP, like most others, lacks systematic identification of new departures from previous policies and expenditure patterns. With the iPRSP this was not surprising, as it needed to build on previous policies and develop a policy dialogue to feed into the PRSP. But the PRSP still lacks a clear rationale, or statements of 'theories'[12] about how changes in policies and expenditures might lead to specific kinds of poverty-reducing outcomes. Without such hypotheses, rational planning of investment in knowledge is impossible.

The SPPMD has a long way to go before it will develop a clear understanding of what it wants to learn about poverty reduction and how it wants to learn it. It is encouraging, however, that the Poverty Observatory is explicitly being seen as an analytical and advisory rather than an information-gathering unit. If it continues to focus on knowledge and understanding rather than on the generation of new data sets it should in the longer term help the people of Rwanda develop an understanding of the links between policies, practices, and poverty.

Indicators for monitoring/tracking PRSPs

The PRSP focuses its performance tracking on two long-term targets adapted from the Millennium Development Goals (MDGs):

- to reduce by half the proportion of the population living below the poverty line by 2015 (from 60 percent to under 30 percent); and
- to reduce by three quarters the infant and maternal mortality rates by 2015 (from 107 to 35 per thousand and from 810 to 202 per hundred thousand respectively).

Observatory staff have worked with international development advisers to identify indicators by which progress of the PRS can be monitored. The proposed system will track both expenditure and the delivery of social services. However, two important aspects of this system are as yet unclear: how complementarity with the monitoring system of the MTEF will be ensured, and how information on developmental outcomes will be tracked. It is hoped that the situation will be clarified by further meetings between the Observatory and those MINECOFIN staff dedicated to the MTEF.

The PRSP emphasises the distinction between two levels of indicator: changes in living conditions (i.e. ultimate benefits) and indicators of sector strategy contributions (actually several levels here – inputs, outputs, and quality of service delivery and outcomes). There is a further distinction worth making which could be useful, namely between the above core set of indicators (by which the whole PRS will be judged, and which may eventually be used to inform decisions by donors and IFIs) and a much broader set of indicators and analytical questions which will offer a menu of issues for participatory monitoring, surveys, and research projects to assess.

---

12. This term is not intended here in the abstract sense of academic grand narratives. All policy is based on explicit or more often implicit understandings about how specific changes of action might result in specific kinds of outcome.

Evaluation of policies, programmes and projects

The above point about the lack of a learning strategy in the PRSP is confirmed by the fact that in the M&E section there is only one brief mention of 'evaluation'. Tellingly, this is equated with 'impact assessment', missing the point that evaluation needs to develop stories about how decisions and actions lead to particular kinds of change. The rest of the text makes little attempt to present the PRS as if it were based on lessons learned from past experience. In post-genocide Rwanda there has been minimal evaluation of the effectiveness of development policies, programmes or projects.

The apparent lack of interest in evaluation is particularly striking given that Rwanda was the focus of one of the world's most ambitious evaluation studies ever conducted, namely the 1995 multi-agency study of international roles before and after the genocide. It is, however, reasonable to regard the basic management of information on poverty and on anti-poverty policies and processes as a prior requirement before trying to conduct evaluation of the effectiveness and impacts of policies, programmes, and projects.

Donors' information requirements

There is as yet no clear sign of the PRS process leading towards coordination of donor information requirements. Apart from DFID, the World Bank, UNDP and the IMF, most donors are still emphasising discrete projects and requiring separate assessment and reporting in relation to project-specific activities and outcomes, rather than being prepared to accept monitoring and assessment of national processes as legitimate forms of accountability and learning. Staff at MINECOFIN say that many donors simply lack the capacity to participate effectively in national planning and learning, and that this is why they continue to focus exclusively on their 'own' projects.

International NGOs, and Rwandan NGOs with international funding, constitute a major potential source of basic information on poverty indicators and trends, particularly at grassroots level. There is, however, a long way to go before they will share such information effectively amongst one another let alone with government. Only a few NGOs – for example, World Vision, Oxfam, SCF and Human Rights Watch – have made serious attempts to disseminate information based on their grassroots experience in Rwanda. Understandably, in the post-emergency phase they have concentrated mainly on activities rather than on learning about the processes that influence poverty and well-being. In principle, NGOs appear to accept the need to collaborate and coordinate with government and share information with all relevant stakeholders, but there is as yet no sign of any serious drive to incorporate mutual learning into their plans.

Between our first and second visits, we noticed an increased recognition of the importance of international donors as both users and producers of information on poverty and anti-poverty strategies. An important qualification to the concept of a 'country-driven' PRS and associated poverty monitoring is that international donors (including NGOs) will for many years to come be needed as funders, technical advisers, and users of poverty information.

The immediate priority must be for the PRSP to identify the critical information needs for planning and learning, the indicators that both reflect key anti-poverty priorities and can be assessed cost-efficiently, and the means for assessing these. However, there would be little point in addressing the supply side in information management without a clearer view on where the demands for information are coming from. Without clearly articulated information demands, resources invested in M&E could well be wasted, and findings not incorporated into plans. An important step would be for the Observatory to conduct a survey of potential user demands for particular kinds of poverty-related information.

7.6   Towards a new aid relationship

Foreign donors and financing agencies influence Rwanda's PRS process in the following ways:

- providing financial and technical support to PRS-related consultation, monitoring, and capacity-building;
- financing and supporting specific anti-poverty initiatives which are being explicitly incorporated within the PRS;
- providing general budgetary and technical support to the government;
- indirectly influencing the PRS process by continuing to finance projects or develop strategies without serious attempts to coordinate these within the PRS and MTEF processes; and
- combining with other external political and economic influences to link aid to political processes such as conflicts in the DRC, the constitutional process, and human rights monitoring.

The Government of Rwanda is particularly concerned about the need for stronger coordination of the developmental activities of both government agencies and foreign donors. A 'Poverty Note' of 2000 on the Government of Rwanda's website refers to the 'disjointed poverty initiatives of both government and donors' and to the 'poor statistical base'. It further argues that 'the definition and coverage of priority program areas for poverty reduction needs to be expanded beyond the social sector spending on health and education to include other key economic sectors like agriculture and road infrastructure and settlements'.[13]

Consultations with donor agencies on the PRS process began with an Aid Coordination meeting on 22 February 2000 (several months before the June

---

13. www.rwanda1.com/government/poverty.

launch of the PRS process) at which the government presented to donors a document elaborating the approach to poverty reduction and sustainable growth. UNDP developed during 2001 a three-year programme of assistance to the NPRP, emphasising its pivotal role in helping CEPEX, the MINECOFIN section in charge of projects and investment, to coordinate donor support based on the PRSP. However, much else remained to be done. Donors could at least ensure coordination among the various national strategies that they are supporting. This cannot be said to be happening at present.

Rwanda is capacity constrained, is committed to working with its development partners and expects technical and advisory support from that partnership. Many, but not all, of the policy issues that government is developing are similar to those in other countries. There is thus much that the donors and IFIs can offer in terms of bringing experience from elsewhere to support Rwanda. Yet there is concern that some of the donors do not have the capacity to engage at a sufficiently senior level in the detail of the process of change that is going on. Part of the problem here lies in the duplication of donors' efforts. Bilateral donors admit that they do not coordinate their efforts.

Technical and advisory support to the MTEF

MINECOFIN has established an MTEF Unit to manage the implementation of the plan. This includes one permanent MINECOFIN staff member, a temporary employee, an ODI Fellow and a DFID-funded co-ordinator. The unit co-operates closely with the Budget Division. The DFID funding includes a pool for drawing down additional short-term technical inputs. The process of MTEF preparation workshops for line Ministries was facilitated by a short-term advisor funded by the World Bank. Coordination and cooperation with other departments within MINECOFIN and with the Minister's *cabinet* of external advisers is being built up slowly through the MTEF preparation process.

DFID provided short-term inputs to assist in the costing of the PRS, with key Ministries being asked to estimate costs strategically on the basis of needs rather than expected availability of funds. This was a novel exercise, and there were some difficulties, for example arising from inconsistent classifications of the development and recurrent budgets. This process resulted in three expenditure scenarios: a base scenario with total PRSP public expenditures of 15.2-15.7 percent of GDP from 2002 to 2004; a 'constrained scenario' with expenditures between 18.0 and 19.2 percent of GDP; and an 'unconstrained scenario' based on estimates of needs, with expenditures of between 22.3 and 25.6 percent of GDP.

In terms of content, the 'constrained scenario' would add labour-intensive public works (e.g. in roads), roofing, water harvesting, health education, and agricultural services, while the 'unconstrained scenario' would add further major investments in infrastructure for agriculture and tertiary education.

Both the constrained and unconstrained scenarios imply a need for steep increases in aid and concessional lending to Rwanda, although the 'constrained scenario' includes the kinds of activity that are already financed by foreign donors particularly through NGOs, which are not captured in the budget.

In 2002 DFID financed an *ex-ante* social impact assessment of the PRSP and associated loans by the IMF and the World Bank. The study, conducted from April to June, focused particularly on the policy debates and decisions relating to the desirable level of budget deficit, which has been the major bone of contention between the government and the IFIs. It was hoped that the recommendations of the study would help to resolve these differences.

It is not clear that the donors' behaviour shows long-term commitment to the PRS and MTEF processes. Some bilateral donor systems do not permit the provision of programme or budgetary support. They continue with a project approach, with project cycles detached from the planning and budget cycles. Accounting, banking and reporting arrangements are separate from government systems. While government systems remain weak, this is an understandable response to ensure short-term impacts. But the spirit of the PRS is a medium- to long-term strategy. In continuing project support, donors and IFIs will come under increasing pressure to demonstrate how such an approach supports the government's objectives of comprehensiveness, transparency, predictability and accountability.

The importance of this issue was well expressed in the NPRP progress report of May 2001, which described external finance as 'ad hoc and project oriented' and said that line Ministries therefore put most of their effort into 'managing different donor-driven projects rather than looking at the needs and policy requirements of their area of responsibility as a whole'. It argued for all externally funded projects to be brought within the national planning and budgeting framework, and linked both with the PRSP and with sectoral plans and policies.

7.7 Conclusions

With few exceptions, the people we met in Rwanda exuded optimism about the PRS process as well as respect for its important role in doing just the things that PRSPs are supposed to do: being the focus for efforts to develop and learn about nationally-inspired, consultative, participatory, and co-ordinated anti-poverty strategies and plans, and for improving international and intra-national inter-agency collaboration. In the words of a World Bank representative in Rwanda, 'donors are optimistic about the PRSP process in Rwanda. Some regard the process as potential best practice'.

Not surprisingly, several people also expressed doubts about many of the challenges of putting the PRSP ideology into practice. Donor coordination, cross-ministry collaboration, institutionalising 'deep' and 'broad' nationwide participatory planning, budget forecasting, and assessing outcomes, will all certainly remain difficult challenges for many years to come. Several people in agencies that would expect to play key roles, such as the media, NGOs, Ministries, and the *Fédération Rwandaise du Secteur Privé*, appeared not yet to see themselves as co-responsible or even potentially involved in the process in a significant way. But there can be no doubt that the general message is that the PRS process will bring benefits to Rwanda and that it will bring about and/or be closely interlinked with important forces of administrative, social, political, and economic change.

This chapter therefore endorses the original research hypothesis that the new process-oriented emphasis in the conditionality used by external financing agencies may be expected to lead to poverty-reduction policies, strategies, and plans which are: more strongly 'owned' by Rwandans rather than externally imposed; better co-ordinated; based on broader consultation; more results-oriented; and with better medium-to-long-term orientation. These changes in turn may be expected to lead to greater effectiveness and sustainability in anti-poverty action.

It must be emphasised, however, that much of this optimism concerns future developments that will be critically dependent on factors that are not directly part of the PRS process. Rwanda will need to make further progress towards peace, stability, reconciliation, decentralisation, and the establishment of a constitution and democratic governance. External financing agencies will have to make radical alterations to the way they finance and interact with government agencies. And there will need to be continued improvements in budgetary control, forecasting and prioritising, particularly through close linkage of the PRS and MTEF processes.

References

Bugingo, Emmanuel (2002) 'The nature of people participation in PRSP process'. Kigali: Consultancy Report to Christian Aid Rwanda [Draft March 2002].

Human Rights Watch (2001) *Uprooting the Rural Poor in Rwanda.* Kigali and New York: Human Rights Watch (www.hrw.org/reports/2001/rwanda/).

Painter, Genevieve (2002) *Quality Participation in Poverty Reduction Strategies: Experiences from Malawi, Bolivia and Rwanda.* London: Christian Aid.

Republic of Rwanda (2001) 'Governance Strategy Paper'. www.rwanda1.com/government/president/speeches/2001/strategygov.htmwww.rwanda1.com/government/president/speeches/2001/strategygov.htm

Republic of Rwanda/MINALOC (2000) *National Decentralisation Policy.* Kigali: Imprimerie Nouvelle du Rwanda.

Storey, Andy (1999) 'Economics and Ethnic Conflict: Structural Adjustment in Rwanda', *Development Policy Review* 17 (1): 43-63.

Uvin, Peter (1998) *Aiding Violence: The Development Enterprise in Rwanda.* West Hartford, CT: Kumarian Press.

Zaman, Mishka (2002) *Are We Getting Lost in Exclusive Anti-poor, Adjustment Lending Policy Cycles? A Rapid Review of Preliminary ActionAid Engagement of Poverty Reduction Strategies in Kenya, Haiti, Uganda, Vietnam, Nepal, Rwanda and Malawi.* Washington, DC: ActionAid USA (www.esrftz.org/ppa/documents/aa_).

Chapter 8: Tanzania

by Alison Evans with Erasto Ngalewa*

Despite being a relatively modest document that commits the government to little that is new, the PRSP is quite a significant innovation in the context of Tanzania. The PRSP approach has brought poverty reduction policy into line with the fiscal framework, promoted a more participatory approach to public policy-making and helped the government to adopt a policy of eliminating primary school fees. However, this chapter argues, the difference that this makes can be overstated. Much depends on the completion of complementary reforms in the management of the public services and local government. Expectations about the PRSP process therefore need to be carefully managed, keeping firmly in mind that commitment to poverty reduction is a political and not a technocratic issue.

8.1 Introduction

Since the first Tanganyika Five-Year Plan in 1964, poverty reduction has held a central place in Tanzanian development strategy and politics. It was President Julius Nyerere who first identified the three arch-enemies of economic growth as poverty, ignorance and disease; and early development strategy focused on their elimination, largely through central government investment programmes underpinned by a basic needs approach and considerable inflows of aid. Notwithstanding early and impressive gains, particularly in the areas of basic health, education and social infrastructure, expanding government social programmes without attention to policies for economic growth and strengthening capacity and participation at local level proved ill-fated.

---

* Respectively, Research Associate, Overseas Development Institute, London, and consultant with REPOA (Research on Poverty Alleviation) an independent research institute based in Dar es Salaam. The joint work involved identifying relevant stakeholders, reviewing documents and reports from the national press and interviewing government officials at central and local levels. The authors would specifically like to thank Professor Joseph Semboja, Executive Director of REPOA for his support, Ms Alana Albee, Social Development Adviser and Ms Fiona Shera, Economic Adviser DFID Tanzania for their insights and assistance in gathering information. Useful discussions were also held with other DFID Tanzania team members during the field visits. The report has benefited from comments from a number of readers and an external peer reviewer.

By the mid-1980s, economic conditions in the country had worsened dramatically and the social gains of the earlier decades began to erode. Since the mid-1990s, however, much has changed. Tanzania has undergone a gradual process of political opening with its first multi-party elections in 1995, and has embarked on a wide agenda of reforms covering almost all aspects of public policy. Gradually the state is rebuilding its core capability, and the government has resumed its focus on poverty reduction after a decade of preoccupation with macroeconomic stabilisation. The donor climate has also improved following a low point in the early 1990s. However, the challenge of political participation remains, against a background of disengagement and disenchantment among the largely rural population and continued dominance of the political machinery by the ruling party (CCM).

Within that context this chapter considers the prospects for the institutionalisation of poverty reduction and related monitoring systems through the PRSP approach in Tanzania. *Institutionalisation* refers to the process of embedding reform efforts, beyond narrow vested interests, into national debate and decision-making. It also implies a process of increasing state capability and effectiveness in the formulation and delivery of public policy.[1]

To assess the prospects for institutionalisation in Tanzania, the study attempted to examine the following:

- the extent to which formal institutional and policy changes, for example the passing of essential legislation, progress with sectoral and budget reforms and changes in the formal arrangements surrounding participation and donor engagement, are helping to embed the goals and principles of the PRSP in government systems and processes;
- the extent to which changes in the 'informal' institutional environment are helping to further the principles of the PRSP – such as increased depth of understanding about poverty and the PRSP amongst government officers at central and local levels, evidence of commitment on the part of key stakeholders, such as Parliament, to the core principles underlying the PRSP, and changes in donor/IFI attitudes and behaviour.

---

1. 'Institutionalisation' is described by Chabal and Daloz (1999) as the process whereby the realm of politics is gradually separated from society and constituted into increasingly autonomous political institutions. A key stage is the establishment of an independent bureaucracy. According to Chabal, 'the emergence of the fully institutionalised state is ... marked by the end of patrimonialism'.

8.2 Poverty reduction and the policy context

The reform context

The first round of multi-party elections in 1995 heralded a new phase in the economic and political development of Tanzania. While the preceding period was characterised largely by socialist one-party rule with extensive public sector control of the means of production, the present regime is committed to market-based reforms and increasing political pluralism. As part of this new phase, Tanzania has been pursuing a wide agenda of reforms in almost every aspect of policy, covering macroeconomic reform, public sector reform, anti-corruption, local government reform, regulatory reform, privatisation and public service delivery (Box 8.1). To date, the process of structural transformation has been slow but peaceful.

Box 8.1 Key National Reform Programmes and Poverty Plans

Macro-Economic Reforms

1981–2   National Economic Survival Programme

1982–5   SAP *(attempts to maintain improvements in income distribution and provision of basic services)*

1986–9   Economic Recovery Programme I
(The first involving external assistance focused on stabilisation/ growth objectives)

1989–92   Economic Recovery Programme II *(restored the focus on public service delivery especially the social sectors)*

1993 –   Rolling Plan and Forward Budget
(explicit focus on poverty reduction through economic policy and institutional reforms that are continued today)

Governance/Public Administration Reforms

1997 –   Local Government Reform Programme

1999 –   Public Service Reform Programme

Poverty Plans

1995   Vision 2025 (adopted 1997)

1995   National Poverty Eradication Strategy
(adopted 1997/8)

2000   PRSP

Aid Relationships

1995 & 8 –   Helleiner Process on Aid Relationships

1999 –   Tanzania Assistance Strategy Process

Since 1990, Tanzania has been the recipient of two IMF/ESAF arrangements, a three-year Poverty Reduction and Growth Facility (PRGF) (negotiated in March 2000) and a series of IDA adjustment credits. The last Policy Framework Paper was prepared in 1997 covering the period FY1998-2000 and the most recent World Bank Country Assistance Strategy (CAS) was issued in May 2000 (shortly after endorsement of the iPRSP) for the financial years 2001-3. A Poverty Reduction Support Credit (PRSC) was due to go to the Board in March 2003. Tanzania has also benefited from five Paris Club reschedulings of bilateral debt, the latest signed in January 1997. In 1998 a Multilateral Debt Fund (MDF) supported by bilateral donors was established to assist in servicing debt to multilateral creditors. Now overtaken by the HIPC Initiative, the relief, tied to the budget, was conditional on the government's commitment to sustain budgetary allocations to priority sectors. It now forms the foundation of the PRSP, MTEF and the multi-donor Poverty Reduction Budget Support (PRBS) facility.

A consultative Public Expenditure Review (PER)/Medium-Term Expenditure Framework (MTEF) process was initiated in 1997,[2] and has since become the centrepiece of the government's budget review and management process. Sector Development Programmes (SDPs) have been established in health and education, and are being proposed for agriculture and roads. Numerous thematic and sector-wide working groups are operating in an effort to integrate government and donor efforts better.

During the late 1990s, consultative processes involving regional and local government, NGOs and the donor community culminated in the preparation of three major strategy pieces: i) Development Vision 2025 (1997) – a national vision statement of economic and social objectives to be attained by 2025; ii) a National Poverty Eradication Strategy (1998) – a national strategy and objectives for poverty reduction efforts to the end of 2010; and iii) the Tanzania Assistance Strategy – a medium-term strategy setting out key principles for engaging with development partners. As will be discussed later, these strategy documents became the foundation of the Tanzanian PRSP.[3]

Tanzania's changing political economy

Reforms in the mid-1980s focused on the urgent need for macroeconomic stabilisation. The result was a squeeze on public spending, particularly in key areas of social service provision. As the urban middle classes found themselves increasingly reliant on the informal economy, so a whole new set of associations emerged to meet demands for goods and services no longer

---

2. A PER process has been in place since 1989 but was 'reformed ' in 1997 to address longer-term planning needs as well as short-term budget execution.
3. The TAS process was started in 1999, then overtaken by events surrounding the PRSP. The TAS was finally reworked in the light of the PRSP in 2002.

fulfilled by the state, including in rural areas.[4]

For many Tanzanians this was a period of retreat from the formal economy and to some extent from formal politics. This process of 'de-participation' was accompanied by weakening legitimacy for both party (CCM) and state institutions (and a certain amount of donor dissatisfaction) that proved important in the eventual push for political reforms in the 1990s.

Perhaps because of its slow trajectory, the introduction of multi-partyism in 1995 did not radically change the complexion of political relations in Tanzania.[5] Many of the same actors continue to dominate the political stage and CCM remains firmly in control of the government machinery. The withdrawal of the state from large parts of the economy and the *de facto* privatisation of some areas of social service provision did help to create a small but vocal entrepreneurial business class, based largely in Dar es Salaam. The result has been a growing alliance between the private sector and the ruling CCM. The poor and largely rural population, on the other hand, became increasingly disengaged,[6] opening the way, some argue, to a more overtly patrimonial style of politics.

While NGOs flourished in the delivery of basic services in the rural areas, few developed capacity in policy analysis and advocacy until relatively recently. The result has been a fairly small group of domestic organisations capable of engaging in public policy issues in a way that applies any real pressure on the government.

Economic performance and poverty trends

Despite the slow trajectory of political reforms, Tanzania's macroeconomic performance has continued to improve. Economic reforms dating back to 1986 have gradually stabilised the economy. Annual average GDP growth was 4 percent for the 1990s and inflation fell to single digits. The most recent data show growth increasing to 5.6 percent in 2001/2 and inflation falling to 4.6 percent. This strong performance occurred against a backdrop of slow global growth, falling commodity prices and the negative fall-out of 11 September – a possible sign of the growing robustness of the Tanzanian economy.

While macroeconomic stability and improvements in economic governance have done a great deal to restore confidence in the economy, poverty numbers suggest that the benefits are still not widely shared. Initial efforts to construct

---

4. For example, the District Development Trusts, providing basic social services outside the framework of local government and based in the 'home area' of political leaders or prominent business figures (Landau, 1998; Kelsall, 2000).
5. Others argue that it was due to the CCM's financial privilege and extensive control over the government machinery.
6. Although this was not universally true, as illustrated by the tax revolt in Arumeru District in 1998 (Kelsall, 2000).

a poverty line for the PRSP put the number of Tanzanians living in extreme poverty at between 36 and 40 percent, with over 60 percent of the rural population living below the poverty line. More recent data generated by the 2000/1 Household Budget Survey[7] suggest a small but significant decline in the proportion of people living below the poverty line (from 21.6 percent to 17.7 percent below the food poverty line and from 38.6 percent to 35.4 percent below the basic needs poverty line). Population growth means, however, that the absolute number of poor households in Tanzania increased during the 1990s, reaching nearly 11.4 million. Social indicators remain poor and preliminary results of the 2000/1 HBS indicated that income inequality is rising.

International financial institutions (IFIs) and donors generally remain optimistic about Tanzania's growth and poverty reduction prospects, arguing that it takes a considerable time to achieve the critical mass of reforms necessary for higher growth, and many important reforms have only just been completed or are still in the process of being carried out, particularly in the agricultural sector. A key question is whether the PRSP can provide added vigour and focus to this reform effort and, in so doing, help to speed up the delivery of poverty reduction targets.

8.3   The PRSP process in Tanzania

The Tanzanian PRSP process was exceptionally compressed. An Interim PRSP (iPRSP) was prepared and approved in March 2000, and endorsed by the Boards of the World Bank and IMF in April 2000. Simultaneously, Tanzania qualified for interim HIPC relief following a Decision Point meeting of the two Boards. In August 2000 the Cabinet approved a full PRSP, which was endorsed by the Boards in late November and early December 2000.

Preparation of the iPRSP was hurried and non-consultative. The document itself, which was very brief by current standards, was written with the help of Bank staff and based largely on the policy framework set out in the existing Policy Framework Paper (PFP). The rush to complete it was a reflection of the government's obvious desire to get swiftly to the HIPC Decision Point and interim debt relief. Donors were also keen to ensure Tanzania's speedy access to debt relief as an acknowledgement of progress already made in key areas of macro and fiscal policy. The lack of any real discussion around the interim document meant, however, that few national stakeholders were prepared when the full PRSP process got under way.

From initiation to cabinet approval, the full PRSP process took just six months. The preparatory process was managed by the PRSP Technical Committee, chaired by the Deputy Permanent Secretary Finance, and assisted

---

7. Completion of which was a condition for the first annual review of the PRSP and HIPC completion.

by the Vice-President's Office (VPO). Data collection, analysis, consultation and drafting were managed by a series of technical working groups. Two Dar-based research institutes – REPOA and ESRF – were responsible for co-ordinating the drafting of several chapters. Representatives from both the World Bank and the IMF participated in working group meetings. The Dar-based lead adviser for the World Bank played a pivotal role in moving the draft through its various stages.[8]

The consultative phase was particularly short-lived, focusing on seven simultaneous zonal workshops on two consecutive days in May 2000 and a national workshop to discuss an early draft in June. Participants were invited from central and local government, private sector groups, selected NGOs[9] and community-based youth/women's organisations.

The government attempted to involve civil society groups in the planning of the consultations. The Tanzania Coalition of Debt and Development (TCDD), an umbrella network of NGOs and religious groups advocating debt relief, was invited by the VPO to design and manage the participatory phase. But the rushed timetable (which put a strain on TCDD's organisational capacity) and differences between TCDD and the government over who should participate in the zonal workshops,[10] resulted in TCDD backing out at the last minute.

Official responses

Government interviewees were aware of the limitations of the process but felt that, given the relatively recent consultative exercises around the Vision 2025 and the NPES, the workshops were sufficient to support a first-round PRSP. Civil society representatives often disagreed. Few believed that the process was adequately representative or thorough, given the strategic importance (and potential influence) of the PRSP.

According to local observers, the pace of the Tanzania process was only made possible because of certain preconditions: in particular, an existing Tanzania Assistance Strategy (TAS) process which already had a consultative framework, a 'champion' in the Ministry of Finance and a framework for donor financing; ongoing work carried out as part of the PER/MTEF process, together with work on sector programmes that had created a critical mass of

---

8. Government and donor respondents were universal in their praise for the role of the local Bank adviser in the process. Many were more critical of the role played by the Washington-based country team.
9. Some say only government-friendly NGOs.
10. The VPO wanted to maintain fairly strict control over the composition of participants by sending out formal invitations to particular individuals and groups to attend. The eventual composition of the zonal workshops was criticised both by the PRSP document (as recommended by the Bank) and by the Joint Staff Assessment (JSA) for being insufficiently broad-based.

relevant information; and the beginnings of a consensus view within the government on the key priorities for reform. Finally, 2000 was an election year and President Mkapa was very keen to be seen to be doing something about poverty and the debt burden. The PRSP/HIPC initiative provided him with a crucial opportunity and he made it a theme of his re-election campaign.

Interviews during October 2000 suggested that most high-level government officials were sanguine about the value-added of the PRSP. This was described in terms of a better link between strategy and the budget (many in line Ministries were hopeful about the link between the PRSP and 'new' HIPC resources); an opportunity to turn their existing broad strategy documents (Vision 2025 and the NPES) into practicable, monitorable plans; and the opportunity to move beyond a sectoral focus to address cross-cutting challenges such as improving human capability, reducing vulnerability and increasing security.

While senior officials were generally well informed, the impression at this early stage was that this understanding did not extend very far down into the line Ministries or beyond the central government. This view was confirmed in later interviews in April 2001, which included some enquiries at district level. Few officials outside the senior staff of the Ministry of Finance appeared to have a clear understanding of the PRSP or the other conditions required for reaching HIPC completion.

Even among the senior officials, there were concerns. Some were critical of the rushed timetable; some felt that the policy framework had largely been borrowed from existing IFI documents, with little opportunity for officials to consider what needed to be done differently in order to support pro-poor growth. A few officials in the Ministry of Finance harboured some residual resentment about the change in the rules for reaching the HIPC Completion Point. Initially, Tanzania was expecting to reach this point by June 2001. However, an interim decision by the Bank-Fund Boards to extend the Completion Point until after the first annual review of the PRSP meant that this would no longer be the case. While the decision was in the past, the concern was that the rules of the game could shift again, possibly undermining the Government of Tanzania's commitment to the process.

Civil society

Civil society respondents had mixed views about the PRSP process, but were on balance more critical. Representatives of the academic/research community were among the more positive respondents, probably because many of them had been closely involved in the TAS process and in working groups drafting sections of the PRSP. Two research institutes – REPOA and ESRF – were given chapter coordinating and writing responsibilities by the Technical Committee, while individuals at the University of Dar es Salaam provided technical assistance to the working groups. As one donor representative noted, the active involvement of these institutions and individuals meant that, while the PRSP might not have been written entirely by the government, it was written largely by Tanzanians.

Representatives of advocacy civil society organisations based in Dar es Salaam were much more openly critical of the way in which the process had been managed. Plans for a participatory process had not been widely discussed with them at the iPRSP/PRSP outline stage. When they did learn of the process, the consultations were severely delimited. CSOs were critical of their lack of access to key documents and the lack of clear mechanisms for forwarding comments to drafting groups. When the PRSP draft was circulated they felt that they were being asked to endorse it rather than engage with it. The government was seen as a reluctant partner in the process.

Nonetheless, several respondents also acknowledged weaknesses among CSOs themselves. Limited organisational capacity and poor familiarity with national policy issues, reflective of a history of one-party dominance of the policy agenda, meant that few were in a position to engage directly in national debate around the PRSP. One positive outcome of the process was the experience of organising and sharing perspectives in national fora. Since then, and with the help of donor financing, the number of groups and coalitions working on policy issues has multiplied dramatically.

Follow-up in April 2001 and again in early 2002 confirmed the importance of these second-order effects. Active engagement by the Tanzania Gender Networking Project (TNGP) on the gender content of the PRSP highlighted key weaknesses that both the government and the IFIs acknowledge were important. Work by 'Hakikazi Catalyst', a local NGO, helped to transform the PRSP document into a plain language version, *Tanzania without Poverty*. Published in June 2001 with the endorsement of the VPO, the document was distributed to central and district government officials and to CSOs in an effort to 'popularise' the strategy and policy content of the PRSP. The text was also reproduced as a supplement in the English daily paper, *Daily News*, and the Kiswahili daily, *Majira*.

Donor responses

By April 2001, many donors were seeing the PRSP as the main policy framework for engaging with the Government of Tanzania, and with each other, and a core group had formed a Poverty Reduction Budget Support (PRBS) facility as a way of channelling financial support directly behind the government's implementation of the PRSP. Not all donors were in a position to make such a move but many, including those perceived to be most reluctant or unable to change their mode of aid delivery, were willing to talk about ways of coordinating more effectively behind PRSP priorities.

The extent of donor and government progress can be measured in part by the focus of the Consultative Group meeting in Dar es Salaam in September 2001. For the first time there was a common platform for discussion in the PRSP and the PRSP Progress Report, which brought together government,

IFIs, donors and CSOs. While the CSOs were critical of the way in which their participation was handled and the lack of really open debate about some key areas of the PRSP policy framework (not least the macro/growth sections), the CG meeting was a crucial first step towards building a more coherent and coordinated framework for discussion between the government and its domestic and international partners. A Policy Forum created by local NGOs as a result of the meeting is now seeking a more strategic role in discussions with the government about future policy decisions.

First year implementation and HIPC completion

After the main fieldwork for this study, Tanzania completed its first PRSP Progress Report and reached HIPC completion in November 2001. The Progress Report is impressive in its scope and particularly in its efforts to come up with a set of costings for priority areas set out in the PRSP. Despite government commitment to make the Report consultative, very little consultation actually took place, although the report did benefit from comments by MPs and other invited stakeholders during a national workshop held in July 2001. The comments and views of stakeholders reaffirmed the importance of effective implementation and monitoring of interventions, especially in rural and other pro-poor sectors.

The Report tracks a wide range of measures undertaken during the first year of PRSP implementation covering public financial management, agriculture, education, governance and implementation of the Household Budget Survey and Labour Force Survey. Notable developments included final agreement on a Primary Education Development Programme designed to assist government implement its PRSP commitment to increasing primary enrolment by removing primary school fees; completion of the Poverty Monitoring Master Plan; and creation of an institutional framework for poverty/PRSP monitoring. The first major output of the poverty monitoring system, an analytical report on 'Poverty and Human Development' was published on schedule in late 2002.

A joint donor statement on the Progress Report prepared for the Consultative Group meeting in September 2002 acknowledged the scope of the report and the considerable progress made by government (and international development partners) in prioritising the Poverty Reduction Strategy. But it pointed, *inter alia*, to continuing weaknesses in local government reform, inadequate understanding of the links between economic growth and poverty reduction and poor progress on domestic revenue collection. A joint statement prepared by CSOs (based on the Policy Forum) pointed to the lack of transparency around public spending linked to HIPC savings, weak accountability in reporting back on actual disbursements made to decentralised levels, inadequate safety nets to cushion the impact on the poor of continuing structural reforms, and the absence of institutionalised mechanisms for consulting the public before acquiring new debt.

A positive account of progress to date was felt to reflect a genuine commitment by government to reform and a galvanising of the donor community around the PRSP. But a number of outstanding issues also remain – in particular, slow progress on local government reform, high transaction costs (generated mainly by donors) arising from the participative approach taken to PRSP development and implementation, and inadequate delivery of promised debt relief by some creditors.[11] DAC donors are now pointing to the importance of a single coherent PRSP reporting and review process to embed PRSP principles further. The aim is eventually to align Tanzanian budgeting processes and the annual PER and PRSP reviews.

8.4   What difference has the PRSP made?

The earlier discussion of the reform context and the evolving political landscape in Tanzania provides an important context in which to view the prospects for the institutionalisation of poverty reduction policies, and the PRSP process. Their adoption follows an intensive period of reform and national development planning that spans almost a decade. Although the PRSP does represent a departure from past approaches to poverty reduction with its focus on growth, prioritised public actions linked to the budget and coordination across government and within the aid community, it is also part of a gradual process of economic and political change. To an important extent, poverty was already a feature of public debate in Tanzania. A key question is whether the PRSP can take this further into the systems and processes of government, and in a way that will ensure that public commitment to poverty reduction gets translated into results for the poor.

In this section, we assess the prospects for institutionalisation, in three steps. First, we examine the depth of understanding about the PRSP process within central and local government. Then we review formal changes in the policy-making and the fiscal and budgetary framework. Finally, we assess trends in the participatory/governance context related to the PRSP process.

---

11. A further stumbling block, which came to a head around the discussion of the Progress Report, was the government's decision to go ahead with a contract for a military air traffic control system to be built by a UK company under an export credit guarantee awarded by the British Government. Differences within the British Government, and between the Secretary of State for International Development and the Tanzanian Government, on the merits of this contract eventually resulted in a suspension of DFID budget support early in 2002. The matter has subsequently been resolved but illustrates well the heightened concern of some donors about the consistency of government messages about poverty reduction and the PRSP, and the extent of political influence that is possible when donors are providing budget support.

Depth of understanding

A study commissioned by DFID in March 2001 to examine the depth of understanding about the PRSP amongst government personnel confirmed many of the preliminary observations made by this study in September/ October 2000. Senior government staff, who were the most likely to have directly participated in the PRSP preparatory process, were generally well informed about the PRSP, and positive in their evaluation of the process. Central government officers located in planning departments were most likely to have engaged with, or have knowledge about, the PRSP process. Below this level there was virtually no engagement with, and very little understanding about, the PRSP. Officers in administrative departments were not aware of the process. Many respondents were not sure or able to determine how the PRSP was related to their respective sector policy frameworks or strategic planning requirements.[12]

Interviews with local government staff at district level during April 2001 revealed an almost complete lack of knowledge about the PRSP, its goals or its targets. In meetings with staff in three district councils, one city council and one municipal council, none was able to describe the PRSP process or recall any direct engagement in its preparation. Staff had been engaged in various 'poverty planning' exercises in recent years; however, none was able to link any of these to the more recent consultative exercise for the PRSP. Several staff were able to recall the consultation process surrounding preparation of the NPES and the Vision 2025, and were at pains to understand why the government now needed another national poverty reduction strategy, particularly when they had been recently asked by the President's Office to prepare plans for achieving the Vision targets for 2000-4. Officers were completely in the dark about how these strategy documents related to one another or how the PRSP was likely to affect their planning processes in the short to medium term.[13]

Although district staff were not informed about the PRSP,[14] on hearing about it most were enthusiastic, seeing both debt relief and the link between poverty reduction targets and resource allocation as critical. Nevertheless, staff were hesitant about the likelihood that districts would see any *additional* resources given their experience with the slow roll-out of the Local Government Reform Programme (LGRP) and continuing difficulties with the flow of funds (and materials) from central spending departments (see

---

12. One of the main contexts for taking forward the PRSP framework is that of sector strategies. This had happened to some extent in roads and to a lesser extent in health.
13. The PRSP targets were taken from and adjusted to a 5-10 year framework from the Vision 2025, the NPES and in some cases the relevant sectoral strategy papers.
14. A few thought they had seen something in the national newspapers about the PRSP and the link with debt relief.

Box 8.3 further on).[15]

On balance, while there has been a gradual broadening of awareness about the PRSP across central government, the *depth* of understanding about the PRSP and its targets continued for some time to be modest. The weak 'trickle-down' of information about the PRSP is probably not surprising in the relatively short time between our field visits but it is nevertheless symptomatic of important weaknesses in key areas of government, in particular in relations between the VPO and other parts of central and local government.[16] It also stems from the legacy of a highly centralised system of government in which information was not readily shared and the responsibility for taking and delivering on decisions severely disjointed.[17] Addressing such weaknesses, in particular the capacity of local authorities to take charge of planning and budgeting, is now a key challenge for the LGRP.

Impact on policy-making

Key elements of the policy framework have stayed the same, supported as they are by the World Bank's CAS and the IMF's PRGF, but there are some shifts worth noting. First, the PRSP has increased pressure for a more participatory approach to policy-making. Donors and international and local NGOs have, as a result of the process, raised their expectations about the government's willingness to engage in open debate about most areas of policy. Civil society engagement nationally in policy debates and discussions has

---

15. A tracking study of pro-poor expenditure by REPOA in 2001 found significant weaknesses in the flow of funds and the flow of materials and supplies between central and local government. Some of the key findings are reviewed in the next section on the fiscal framework.

16. The VP's Office is the institutional home of the NPES. It is also has the mandate to distribute and disseminate the PRSP. Responsibility for Vision 2025 resides with the President's Office. Supported by funds and technical assistance from UNDP the VPO has recently recruited more staff in an attempt to bolster its capacity to manage and implement its poverty eradication mandate. Its relationship with the MoF has also improved as a result of the technical support it has provided to the PRSP Technical Committee.

17. A good example of disjointedness is the fact that while the VP's Office is responsible for disseminating knowledge about poverty reduction and supporting capacity to address poverty concerns within central and regional government, it is the body responsible for Regional Administration and Local Government that is responsible for much of the planning and some of the spending that takes place at local government level. Major spending Ministries such as health and education also engage local government in planning exercises while transferring some of their resources directly and some through the Regional Administration authority.

grown significantly.[18] In 2000/1 the number of participants engaged in the PER/MTEF process increased to its largest number ever.

Second, the PRSP has become an important instrument for coordination within government. The Inter-Ministerial Technical Committee provides strategic oversight through quarterly reviews of progress on various reform efforts. Building on the strengths of the PER/MTEF process, the PRSP has also helped to forge better communication between the Ministry of Finance and key spending Ministries, although, as the section on the fiscal framework suggests, there is still some way to go before this translates into a fully comprehensive MTEF process.

Third, the PRSP created the opportunity for at least one important strategic shift in policy. The decision to eliminate primary school fees (Box 8.2) came as a surprise move in the later stages of PRSP preparation. In effect, the PRSP provided an opportunity for the government (and the President and the CCM in particular) to undertake a politically popular policy change in the run-up to the October 2000 elections that had until then been resisted by the Ministry of Education. The move not only resulted in a massive increase in school enrolment in 2001/2;[19] it also opened the way for final agreement between the government, the World Bank and bilateral donors on a Primary Education Development Programme to finance long awaited reforms in the primary education sector.

Fourth, the creation of a comprehensive poverty monitoring system promises not only improved information about performance but also a chance to improve the quality of policy. The system is still in its early stages and, as the subsequent discussion on monitoring suggests, there are still several important gaps and weaknesses in its design, including links with the budget process and back into policy/planning. As a nationally defined system, it nevertheless brings together many key elements of poverty monitoring within a framework which, if it works, has the potential to increase the level of evidence-based policy-making (at least at the centre).

The potential impact of the PRSP on policy-making appears to be quite positive so far. But past patterns inevitably persist, including an endemic gap between policy and the practice of budgeting and planning at central and local government levels. Poverty monitoring is also heavily focused on the needs of the central government, and there are as yet few signs, other than through the current participatory poverty assessment, of a more bottom-up approach to monitoring. Progress with local government reform, and linking up local government monitoring and evaluation with central planning and budgeting processes in particular, will be critical to future progress in this area.

---

18. A review commissioned by DFID of its own civil society grants programme in 2002 suggests a five-fold increase in civil society engagement in national policy debates. The number of coalitions and federations formed to engage in policy issues had tripled.

19. It exceeded the capacity of primary schools to cope.

Box 8.2 Elimination of user fees for primary education: combining the PRSP and sector reform

Faced with rapidly declining resources for education, in 1995 the government formally introduced a primary school enrolment fee. Although the fee never amounted to more than Tsh 2,000 it was strongly resented by parents, especially when they saw hard-pressed district administrations using the fees as general taxation to cover general expenditures rather than ploughing the resources back into schools. The enrolment fee failed to encourage a sense of ownership among parents of their children's schools. Poor households found it particularly onerous. At the same time university education remained free of charge. Although the impact on school enrolment was clear, as late as 2000 government maintained that user fees were essential to the operation of the education sector, and an essential component of primary education expansion (Draft *Education Sector Development Programme*).

Although lobbying for the elimination of user fees for primary education preceded the PRSP (Aga Khan, Oxfam and others worked hard on this issue), the PRSP process played an important part in the eventual policy decision to eliminate primary school fees. First, the PRSP raised the profile of 'pro-poor policies'. Second, it placed significant focus on the level and efficiency of spending in the social sectors. Third, the participatory process pointed to the priority of education as well as the financial burden that user fees imposed on poor households. It was not until late in the process of PRSP preparation that the government finally took the decision to eliminate primary school fees when it became clear that a significant part of the donor community, including the World Bank country director and other leading bilaterals, supported the elimination of user fees and would provide the necessary funds (through an education sector reform programme) for the implementation of the policy change.

A cabinet decision was eventually made and, in the context of the 2000 elections, President Mpaka announced that if he was re-elected he would eliminate user fees for primary education. The measure was only financially feasible with donor support. Once the government had found ready allies in the donor community it worked with the World Bank, donors and the NGO community toward the preparation of a Primary Education Development Programme supported by a World Bank project loan. The PEDP also included the commitment by a number of bilaterals to integrate their projects into the PEDP.

Following the elimination of user fees, school enrolment in primary education in 2001/2 doubled, reflecting great expectations by parents about the availability and quality of education to be provided. In addition the government has established a system of pooled funding to raise additional funds from donors. A number of donors have signed up to the fund.

Source: Joint Donor Workshop on the PRSP held in Dar es Salaam June 2002.

Fiscal framework and budgetary processes

The PER/MTEF process has evolved significantly since a new approach was forged in 1998. Prior to 1998 the PER process was largely external to the government and most stakeholders. Local ownership was weak and the government had little role in the review of how public money was being spent. Since 1998 a new PER approach has enabled the government to take a clear leadership position in carrying out the review.

The Ministry of Finance chairs the PER working group which is composed of members from central and local government, bilateral and multilateral donors, research/academic institutions and NGOs. Membership has been increasing gradually over the years. Independent external evaluations (by donors led by the World Bank) provide assessments of progress and problems in different areas of budget management, including the conduct of the process itself. Significantly, the PER process for 2000/1 (parallel to preparation of the PRSP) heralded a sharper focus on poverty reduction and the principle of prioritisation in the allocation of spending.

The link to the budget and, in particular, the Medium-Term Expenditure Framework (MTEF), is crucial for making progress towards PRSP targets. The MTEF process to date has been instrumental in facilitating a reallocation of resources between priority and non-priority sectors (which predates the PRSP). For example, the combined share of expenditure on education, health and water rose from 34 percent in 1999/2000 to 40 percent in 2000/1. Commitment to poverty reducing expenditures is further underlined by government plans to increase the allocations for Other Charges (OC) and development expenditures in priority sectors.[20]

Yet, to make an impact on PRSP targets, budget allocations have to be translated into disbursements. Here the record is less impressive. Budget out-turns for 1999/2000 were only 54 percent overall (that is, out-turn as a percentage of requirement) and as low as 37 percent in education (Budget Estimates, 2000).[21] It is impossible to say what this figure is at local level, but, as the study cited in Box 8.3 suggests, it is likely that budget out-turns at sub-national levels are significantly worse than this.

A background paper for the 200/1 Country Financial Accountability

---

20. This is significant, but in practice the MTEF programmes allocations of only a small part of discretionary expenditures. Personal Emoluments and external financing of the Development Budget are not allocated amongst sectors. This means that managers cannot prioritise between expenditure categories; development expenditures are determined on an individual needs basis rather than on a strategic basis taking into account the overall balance of priority expenditures (Fozzard and Naschold, 2001).
21. Budget out-turns for basic education, basic health, rural roads, etc. are the responsibility of local authorities and are currently not aggregated to national level.

Box 8.3 Budget execution

A draft report prepared for government by REPOA assessed the efficacy of budget
  execution in a number of priority areas, in particular primary education and
  health. The main observations are:
*   The cash budget system has relegated Other Charges (OC) to a residual position.
    Lack of predictability on the disbursement of OC has resulted in leakages,
    especially at sub-national level.
*   The existing system of disbursing funds is appropriate, but it does assume
    adequate transparency in information sharing and transmission. However, in
    situations of scarce resources, ownership of information is critical and resource
    distribution has consequently been skewed in favour of those having access to
    information. IFMS has helped somewhat but because it is not yet present at
    local authority level problems persist.
*   Sectoral heads have tended to re-allocate OC in favour of activities that benefit
    council staff and not service units
*   Financial reporting requirements allow for too much aggregation.
*   Materials and supplies originate from sector ministries; lack of predictability is
    a major problem especially in the supply of school materials.

Source: REPOA (2001).

Assessment (CFAA) notes the importance of accurate resource envelope
forecasts to the effectiveness of the budget process. At present, forecasts tend
to be over-optimistic, as regards both revenues and external financing. This
raises a number of concerns about accountability, since adjustments to lower
than anticipated revenue yields are made administratively by cash rationing
rather than through formal budget revisions. Since the criteria for cash
rationing are not published or approved by Parliament the resulting budget
outturns can have a very different impact from the allocations approved as
part of the budget.

To improve predictability, the government has since January 2001
introduced quarterly indicative cash allocations for non-wage expenditures
while continuing with monthly cash releases. This is intended to enable priority
sectors to plan their expenditures more effectively. There is some scattered
evidence that this is beginning to have an impact.

Recommendations on how to improve the links between the PRSP and
the budget, and to further institutionalise operational instruments such as
the MTEF, include: i) ensuring consistency between the monitoring targets
included in the budget submissions and the PRSP targets and intermediate
indicators; ii) improving the costing of strategies and assessment of the
feasibility of the 2010 targets, and if necessary revising these targets
downwards; iii) tracking expenditures and the effectiveness of service delivery;

and iv) focusing on the MTEF as a government tool, and reducing the amount of external intervention in its preparation.

Improving the budget process and embedding the government's poverty reduction targets in the fiscal framework is now a key part of the MoF's Medium Term Strategic Plan 2000-4. The CFAA found the Plan to be a coherent and effective way to build on the successful reforms of the 1990s, but noted that the introduction of planning mechanisms such as the MTEF had presupposed existing capacity in strategic planning techniques that had not been entirely forthcoming. This explains the limited benefits of MTEF planning so far in some of the weaker spending Ministries (such as agriculture).

Risks to further institutionalisation of the PER/MTEF process include a lack of synchronisation with the wider public sector reform process being managed by the Civil Service Department, and continuing shortfalls in the reporting of external assistance. The latter would undermine the government's efforts to improve resource prioritisation and develop a performance-oriented budgeting system. At present, attempts to improve the transparency of donor finances are progressing slowly. Donors are increasing the level of resources provided in the form of financial aid. Programme aid accounted for just over half of total grant assistance to Tanzania in 2001/2. But there are concerns about both the likely macroeconomic impact of continued increases in programme aid, and the slow pace of improvements in reporting (including inside the PRBS).

The governance framework

Although Tanzania now enjoys competitive multi-party elections, transformation of the political governance framework has been slow – mainly because of the CCM's control of the political institutions inherited from the era of one-party rule. The recent agreement between the CCM and the mainly Zanzibar-based CUF to investigate the events of January 2001, when CUF supporters clashed with officials following the disputed results of the election in Zanzibar, has restored a certain amount of faith in the government's commitment to political pluralism. However, problems in this regard are likely to persist.

On the PRSP itself, many of the actions and targets identified require inter-ministerial cooperation to be achieved (for example, between Agriculture and Lands, between Health and the Ministry of Women, Culture and Community Development). This requires internalisation by line Ministries not just of their own sectoral targets but of the overall road-map set out by the PRSP. While there are signs of growing coherence between central Ministries, the approach is largely untested at lower levels of government. Expected improvements in service delivery are known to depend significantly on the reform programme for local government (LGRP), started in early 2000. However, the programme has been running behind schedule, with the second phase delayed until 2003. The willingness of line Ministries to go it alone with separate donor financing is another area of continuing concern.

At the time of the PRSP consultations, the government and the international financial institutions were widely criticised by international and Tanzanian NGOs for presiding over a rushed and essentially exclusive process. Views on the superficiality of the consultative process have not really changed, but there is acknowledgement that the process served the purpose of bringing some of the more organised advocacy groups into a national debate about poverty reduction. Concerns remain that the new 'climate' of openness is one in which both government and donors are more concerned about the professionalisation of NGOs than about the institutionalisation of participation in public policy debate.[22]

Ownership of the PRSP is multifaceted. A critical test is where the locus of a strategy or programme idea resides; was it initiated by the country or not? In the case of the PRSP, this clearly is not the case. The idea was conceived in Washington. But other tests of ownership include the extent to which there is a consensus among government officials and other decision-makers on the course of action, and whether there is broad public support for the initiative. On these counts the initial findings from Tanzania are promising although, as already mentioned, commitment to implement the PRSP is still largely untested at local levels of government.

There is also potentially a large difference between willingness to comply with the process and commitment to it. While high-level political commitment pushed the preparation of the document through, the extent of commitment in Parliament and across the spectrum of government institutions to its implementation is still not clear. Progress leading up to HIPC completion was largely built around actions already undertaken or in the process of being taken. Corruption is now perceived to be a major obstacle. Tangible commitment by the government to its anti-corruption strategy is a critical part of PRSP implementation and associated donor instruments (PRBS and PRSC). The next phase, years two and three of PRSP implementation, were rightly expected to be much more of a challenge.

8.5   Monitoring the PRSP: a second chance?

In the PRSP document only cursory attention was paid to the issue of poverty monitoring, although background work had already started on some of the components of an integrated monitoring system and set of Poverty and Welfare Monitoring Indicators supported, initially, by UNDP. After PRSP approval,

---

22. This is illustrated by some by the lack of debate around various core issues at the heart of the PRSP – namely, the macroeconomic framework and future debt sustainability. Some NGOs have been taken on as 'equal partners' in some sectors such as education, but remain excluded from these core areas of debate (beyond participation in the PER process).

a core group of government staff, donor representatives and researchers/academics worked to flesh out a more comprehensive plan for poverty monitoring – the Poverty Monitoring Master Plan – which was published and endorsed by the government in November 2001 (in time for HIPC Completion).

The PMMP comprises three interrelated tiers. The poverty monitoring system focuses on the measurement of impact, outcomes and proxy indicators. Sector programmes such as those for education and health focus on tracking of output indicators with adequate monitoring mechanisms in place. The PER/MTEF processes focus on inputs with the emphasis on budget allocation and budget execution. Analytical work to be carried out as part of the poverty monitoring process is expected to establish the linkages between monitoring of impact, outcomes, outputs and inputs.

The PMMP identifies, as a minimum, the importance of regular national and sub-national data on progress against PRSP poverty targets by gender, location, administrative area and age group. Drawing from the Poverty and Welfare Monitoring Indicators and the PRSP, the PMMP identifies a 'core set' of 40 quantitative indicators focusing mainly on poverty and social outcomes. The Tanzania Socio-Economic Database (TSED), an electronic database pulling together a range of socio-economic data with a special focus on poverty-related indicators, serves as a repository for data generated by the poverty monitoring system.

At a workshop in October 2000, agreement was reached between key stakeholders (government, donors and NGOs) on the appropriate institutional design which included a National Poverty Monitoring Steering Committee representative of relevant parts of government, civil society, academia and the private sector, a Technical Committee (which would be the same as the PRSP Technical Committee) and a number of smaller technical working groups which would oversee the specific information and data needs of the system. In 2001 poverty monitoring was included in the Budget Guidelines, creating a clear institutional commitment to resourcing the PMMP, although a significant percentage of the resources still need to be found externally. Donors have supported elements of the PMMP but a small group of donors are keen to contribute to a poverty-monitoring fund to provide government with fungible resources for the PMMP.

PMMP: strengths and weaknesses

The PMMP is an impressive document. It represents the culmination of almost nine months of close co-operation between the members of the different working groups. The PMMP has many of the qualities of a country-led and country-owned process, supported by some strategic donor money and technical assistance. Although some of the more outspoken NGOs in Dar es Salaam felt marginalised from the drafting of the PMMP, in particular from the process of defining data priorities and data collection needs, the process appears to have been both comprehensive and inclusive.

The institutional framework is the result of decisions taken locally and reflects the desire for a broad-based 'stakeholder approach' that not only draws on many individual actors but also apportions responsibility for poverty monitoring across a wide group of government and non-governmental institutions. The institutional arrangements underpinning the framework for poverty monitoring build on arrangements that have been tested, in part, during preparation of the TAS, the PRSP and the PMMP itself.

During the first year of PRS implementation, there were some important achievements, not least the completion of the Household Budget Survey and of an Integrated Labour Force Survey (the first in Africa to include a child labour component). For the first time in recent years, policy makers have a clear sense of the extent of poverty in Tanzania. Progress was also made in preparing inputs for the analytical report on Poverty and Human Development that formed an important input into the second annual progress report on the PRSP.

The Poverty Monitoring Plan is nevertheless ambitious and its full implementation is going to depend heavily on sustained donor contributions.[23] It is also a complex system requiring a lot of support from the Vice President's Office (which has very limited capacity). In a number of areas, donors are currently substituting for weak government capacity (for example, on the Research and Analysis Working Group) but the sustainability of this support has to be questioned. The Poverty Monitoring Steering Committee has an estimated 30 members.

The decision not to identify a single institutional home or lead agency for the monitoring system provides an important alternative to the Uganda model, where main responsibility is housed within the Ministry of Finance. The principal concern, however, is that the current Plan is not clear on who will take final responsibility for ensuring that the relevant monitoring data are collected, analysed, reported to the persons/teams concerned and used to chart progress and take corrective action. The PRSP Technical Committee holds the key on a number of issues, including overseeing the main analytical report, but is also tasked with producing the PRSP Progress Reports, which, if the first report is anything to go by, is a major undertaking in itself.

As with many PRSPs, the minimum set of indicators for poverty monitoring focuses heavily on poverty and social outcomes that require medium to long-term monitoring, and tends to ignore those intermediate indicators that can generate information on trends and correlates in the short to medium term, and on progress with institutional change. The Plan does not really correct this, with a major emphasis on tracking poverty trends rather than other intermediate variables. It also places heavy reliance on survey and

---

23. The government budget currently allows for strengthening and production of core statistics critical to planning and policy analysis, such as semi-annual GDP, national accounts, employment and pricing data.

administrative data-gathering instruments that, amongst other things, are notoriously slow in generating data.

Considerable faith is also being placed in the synchronisation of these instruments to produce short-term data on the 2003 PRS targets. With the system of routine data collection functioning very unevenly (if at all) at present, and the capacity to reconcile data and information across administrative departments scarce at best, it is hard to imagine this happening in the time frame envisaged. The decision not to draw on 'lighter' tools for short- and medium-term monitoring is noteworthy in this context. The PPA is to be used primarily as a research tool, not a monitoring tool, and rapid survey instruments such as a Core Welfare Indicators Questionnaire (CWIQ) are only mentioned as a contingency if the multi-year survey programme falls short.

How well attuned the new system is to the demands of PRS monitoring, as opposed to more traditional poverty monitoring, is less clear. As Booth and Lucas (2002) argue, PRS monitoring is as much strategic as it is technical. Monitoring of poverty trends using large-scale surveys is critical but the demands of PRSP monitoring are somewhat different, residing more in the intermediate output and outcome indicators that relate to sector policy and programme implementation. And the links between monitoring information and planning and budgeting are vital.

Other monitoring processes

Outside of the national monitoring framework, monitoring of PRSP implementation continues through regular PRGF reviews, the PER process, the performance assessment framework linked to the PRBS, sector development programme reviews and an Independent Monitoring Group formed to monitor implementation of the Tanzania Assistance Strategy (TAS). In line with the proposed integration of World Bank PRSC support with the PRBS, it is also envisaged to agree on a joint monitoring and evaluation mechanism that would cover both PRSC and PRBS.

These processes, while technically dovetailed around the PRSP, continue to run parallel to one another and to place new and sometimes conflicting demands on government. Many are externally driven reviews that potentially conflict with the role of the national poverty monitoring system. Over time, the aim must be to streamline these review processes in such a way that the national system for monitoring is the overarching framework for PRSP monitoring and review.

8.6   Towards a new aid relationship

The history of aid delivery in Tanzania is punctuated by highs and lows. Following a low point in the mid-1990s, under the aegis of a commission on aid relations chaired by Gerry Helleiner, the climate for aid improved significantly, with donors and government committing themselves to bring about a more constructive aid relationship. The PRSP presents an opportunity to take this agenda even further.

Interviews with representatives of the donor community in 2000 mirrored the spectrum of views expressed by government officials and NGOs. There were concerns about the extent to which the Bank was taking the lead and about the weaknesses of the consultative process. But there was also praise for the government in guiding the process through so efficiently and for producing a document that was more focused and actionable than anything that preceded it. While the content was considered to be mainly a reworking of existing strategy documents and material already available in the PER/ MTEF process, most donors regarded the strategy and the process as adding value over and above the former Policy Framework Paper.

Several donors were concerned about PRSP content, pointing to the lack of a clear gender focus and to a number of governance and, particularly, anti-corruption issues. There were also concerns about the TAS process and the potential disruption to continuing efforts at aid coordination, with some donors worried that the PRSP would be allowed to expand into an overarching framework for government-donor activity, in effect replacing the role of TAS.[24] There were also fears that the PRSP was simply 'conditionality with a human face' and that it would provide the Bank and Fund with more rather than less influence over government decisions.

On balance, donors saw the PRSP as an important contribution to government efforts on poverty reduction. A few were unreserved in their opinion that the PRSP should now provide the focus of their country assistance programme. Others, particularly those without a clear country focus to their programming, expressed reservations about whether they would, or could, align fully with the PRSP in the short term. The community appeared divided between those donors ready to build on the PRSP as an opportunity to do business differently, and those that were planning to wait and see.

In April 2001, donor responses to the PRSP process were more settled than six months previously. There was clear evidence that a critical mass were now seeing the PRSP as the relevant policy framework for engaging with the Tanzanian Government, and with each other. While not all were prepared to radically change the way they were delivering assistance,[25] most were talking about the PRSP as the main starting point for their assistance programmes.

---

24. The TAS represented something of a 'turf' war between the UN system (and a few key bilaterals), which had played a crucial role in getting the TAS process off the ground, and the IFIs, which were seen as taking the lead on the PRSP and in so doing devaluing the importance of the TAS process.

25. Many bilateral donors continued to be hamstrung by restrictive legislation placed on them by their national Parliaments.

A core set of donors had, however, changed the way they were doing business. Following the modest successes of the MDF, a group of nine donors (eight bilaterals plus the European Union) decided to contribute to the PRSP by setting up the Poverty Reduction Budget Support (PRBS) facility. The PRBS channels funds directly to the government budget, based on a performance assessment framework reflecting key issues constraining the implementation of the PRSP. Two further donors are expected to join in 2002/3. It is expected that the PRBS will ultimately complement a World Bank PRSC which was pre-appraised in May 2002 and was due to go to the Bank Board in March 2003. The aim is to develop a joint policy matrix with the World Bank, which would cover both budget support and the PRSC.

The development of the PRBS is significant in a number of ways, not least because it represents a show of solidarity behind the government's PRSP by an important and influential group of donors. It also reflects a willingness on the part of donors to 'make the first move' in a context where worries remain about the quality of the government's fiduciary framework,[26] progress with civil service reform, especially pay reform, and the political situation with Zanzibar. The introduction of new public finance and procurement legislation in 2002 led to some improvements in the fiduciary context. Most PRBS donors have also now moved to multi-year frameworks for budget support.

Beyond financial aid, donors have used the PRSP as an opportunity for improving coordination, including joint donor statements at the decision point, on Bank/Fund Joint Staff Assessments and on PRSP progress at the September Consultative Group. While donors have generally worked closely with the Bank and Fund representatives in Dar es Salaam, there has been residual feeling amongst some that missions from Washington continue to arrive at short notice, without agreed terms of reference and with little lead-time for donors to prepare. Donors themselves have also faced challenges in coordinating their actions because of unclear or inconsistent messages from national headquarters. Different levels of delegated authority assigned to donor offices at country level make it possible for some to move ahead quickly and flexibly in response to the PRSP process, while others remain reluctant or fearful because of the lack of clear direction from headquarters.

8.7 Conclusions

Poverty reduction remains the biggest of challenges. Tanzania's social indicators are some of the worst in the region, and income poverty levels are higher than would be predicted based on the country's resource endowment.

---

26. The Country Financial Accountability Assessment (CFAA) carried out in early 2001 points to some areas of high fiduciary risk, although the report is also complimentary about the steps the government has taken so far to improve the quality of the budget process.

The reasons for this are inevitably complex, but lie in part in the endemic weakness of the agricultural sector (and of agricultural sector policy) and the true extent of erosion in basic service delivery following the economic collapse of the 1980s. The question is whether the PRSP can make any difference.

This chapter has argued that the PRSP represents something quite important in the Tanzanian context. It has demonstrated the importance of bringing poverty reduction strategy in line with the fiscal framework. It has translated broad strategy intentions into specific actions and targets, with some initial sense of how much it will cost. It has also promoted a more participatory approach to public policy-making and helped the government to make a strategic shift in policy with the elimination of primary school fees. Yet the PRSP is a relatively modest document. It commits the government to very little that is new.

A broad policy agenda for reform already exists, including the Local Government Reform Programme and the Public Service Reform Programme. Legislation has also been passed that seeks to strengthen accountability and audit rules within government. The question is whether these formal institutional changes are sufficient to embed the goals and principles of the PRSP, and ultimately to make progress on poverty reduction goals. The answer is not simple. On the one hand, yes. Delivering on the PRSP depends on progress in local government reform, on improvement in the quality of public sector performance and on improved budgetary accountability. On the other hand, it is too early to say whether these reforms can deliver the qualitative institutional changes that are required to get long-lasting results on poverty reduction or deliver the kind of political change that will strengthen the link between government and people (by effectively reducing the scope for patrimonial politics).

The specificity of country circumstances makes it hard, if not dangerous, to come up with general policy messages. Nevertheless, there are a few that may be of use to countries only now entering into the PRSP phase.

First, it is important to manage expectations about the PRSP process. It is not a panacea, and is likely to have the greatest prospect of working if it builds on ongoing strategy and policy processes (however imperfect), if it identifies feasible (streamlined) goals and targets, and if it acknowledges potential difficulties and uncertainties in reaching them. It is now up to the IFIs, donors and the government to be clear about these inter-dependencies in order to bolster the credibility of the process during implementation.

Second, the PRSP is not the only show in town, and the extent of institutional capacity being taken up by other major reform processes (and government priorities) needs to be brought more forcefully into the field of vision. The international donor community needs to be aware of the potential conflicts between its own non-PRSP reform and review processes and the demands of the activities surrounding the PRSP. That is why alignment of processes is so critical.

Third, politics matter, and while political and governance issues may come onto the PRSP agenda, the response (at least from the IFIs) is generally technocratic. This may be an area where bilateral donors have a comparative advantage, particularly in supporting longer-term reforms in support of the embedding of the PRSP document and process in national debate.[27]

Finally, it is not possible to judge ownership in simple terms. In the Tanzanian case, it is possible to identify pockets of clear ownership within the wider system. These pockets are the result of a coming together of people (personalities), specific relationships with donors, and key events – the PER, TAS and PRSP processes within the Ministry of Finance, for example – backed up by a broad technocratic commitment to reform (in this case macroeconomic reform). Political commitment at the top of government and the party is also evident, but this becomes noticeably diluted as one moves down the layers of government – hence the concern of some observers that measures critical to PRSP effectiveness, and a source of donor confidence (anti-corruption, for example), will not be taken. It is possible that the coming together of key reform processes around the PRSP – the LGRP, the PSRP and the key sector strategies and programmes already under way – will help to lock in the necessary political commitment to reform. Whether this happens will depend less on the detail of the PRSP document and more on its significance as an opportunity – politically and technically – for doing things differently.

---

27. The Netherlands Institute for Multi-Party Democracy (IMD) is in the process of supporting cross-party debates between the national chairpersons of Tanzania's political parties, designed to encourage the development of 'policy platforms' and capacity for policy formulation. The first debate took place in September 2002 on the issue of poverty reduction – the role of government, donors, NGOs and the private sector.

References

Booth, David, and Lucas, Henry (2002) *Good Practice in the Development of PRSP Indicators and Monitoring Systems*. London: Overseas Development Institute, ODI Working Paper 172, July.

Chabal, Patrick and Daloz, Jean-Pascal (1999) *Africa Works: Disorder as Political Instrument*. Oxford: James Currey and Bloomington, IN: Indiana University Press.

Fozzard, Adrian and Naschold, Felix (2001) 'Tanzania Country Financial Accountability Assessment – Planning, Budgeting and Budget Execution'. Draft Report, 23 February. London: Overseas Development Institute (mimeo).

Government of Tanzania (2001a) 'Poverty Monitoring Master Plan'. Second draft for review by the Technical Working Groups, the PRS Technical Committee and the Poverty Monitoring Steering Committee.

Government of Tanzania (2001b) 'Monitoring and Evaluation of Poverty Reduction Strategies in Tanzania'. Paper presented at the 'Building Evaluation Capacity for Poverty Reduction Strategies' Workshop organised by the World Bank's Operations Evaluation Department and the Inspectie Ontwikkelingssamenwerking en Beleidsevaluatie (IOB), Ministry of Foreign Affiars, The Netherlands, The Hague, March.

Government of Tanzania (2001c) 'Country Financial and Accountability Assessment'. Draft.

Kelsall, Tim (2000) 'Governance, Local Politics and Districtization in Tanzania: The 1998 Arumeru Tax Revolt', *African Affairs* 99 (397): 533-51.

Landau, Loren (1998) 'National Politics in Post-Nyerere Tanzania. Potential Implications of the 1995 Multi-Party Elections', *Ufahamu* XXVI (Winter): 4-33.

REPOA (2001) 'Pro-Poor Expenditure Tracking'. Draft. Dar es Salaam: REPOA.

World Bank (2001) *Tanzania at the Turn of the Century: From Reforms to Sustained Growth and Poverty Reduction*. Washington, DC: World Bank, April.

Index

countries
participation 3, 28, 34-5, 41, 51 *see also under individual countries*
parties, political 8, 10, 30, 34, 49, 60, 61, 80, 95, 104, 120, 190-1, 197, 232
opposition 5, 9-10, 30, 49, 61, 79, 80, 104, 120, 122, 136, 156, 170, 171, 190-1, 197
partnership 7, 14, 34, 43, 44, 86, 107, 115, 142
Patel, Nandini 120
patrimonialism 9-10, 13, 156, 171, 251, 271
patron-client relations 11, 13-14, 42
patronage 8, 13, 23, 30, 51, 75, 94, 101-8 *passim,*112, 114, 121
planning 12, 15, 22, 37, 69, 98, 107, 132, 138, *see also under individual countries*
pluralism, institutional/legal 59, 60
political 249, 264
Policy Framework Papers 2, 69, 123, 125-6, 162, 173, 181, 194, 220, 222, 250, 252
politics 8-15, 23, 25-6, 29-30, 34, 45-50 *passim; see also under individual countries*
population 67, 220; growth 58, 93, 154, 220, 252; movements 218
Poverty Action Fund 113, 231
poverty reduction 3, 6, 7, 14-21, 25, 37 *see also PRSP under individual countries*
mainstreaming 16-21, 47, 48, 100, 102-5 *passim,* 109, 113, 159
pre-PRSP policies 14-15 *see also under individual countries*
PPAs 31, 38, 41, 96, 97, 99, 218, 228, 232, 237, 238, 260, 268
PRGF *see* IMF
PRSC *see* World Bank
prebendalism 9
predictability 21, 236, 244, 263
prioritisation 21, 29, 30, 66, 68, 72, 78, 104, 107, 130, 131, 179, 199-201, 203, 235, 245, 262
private sector 5, 27, 30, 36, 93, 96, 101, 112, 171, 198-9, 204, 220, 228, 229, 239, 245, 251, 253
privatisation 45, 75, 162, 168, 249, 251
Progress Reports, PRSP 255, 256, 267
projects 13-15 *passim,* 22, 41-2, 49, 59, 86, 96, 100-1, 103, 134, 164, 180, 230, 235, 241, 242, 244
public works 72, 74, 242

Putzel, James 104

radio 9, 59, 62, 79, 121, 129, 167, 190
Raffinot, Marc 153-85
Rebelo, Pamela 187-216
reform 11, 13, 16, 20-5, 32-3, 36, 47, 49, 57, 63, 78, 86-8 *see also under individual countries*
budget 21-3 *passim,* 49, 71-6, 85, 132-4, 171-3, 191, 201-2
civil service 21, 133, 171, 183, 264, 270
civil society 12, 21, 86, 88
conditionality 149-50
financial 12, 21-4, 71, 108, 200-3, 234-6 *passim*
institutional 21-5, 31
legal 32, 77
public expenditure 132-4, 147, 234
public sector 16, 21, 22, 40, 191, 201, 204, 249, 264, 271
regionalism 120-1, 174, 190
religious bodies 60, 61, 97, 198, 205, 228, 230
rent-seeking 11, 13, 42, 59, 62, 69, 101, 171
REPOA 253, 254, 263
reporting 172, 209, 234, 235, 244, 256, 257
Républiquain, Le 168
research 34, 35, 41, 253, 254
resettlement 219
results orientation 7, 12, 21, 37, 45, 71, 245
revenue 8, 11, 12, 72, 101, 122, 134, 174, 192, 201, 202, 220, 222, 225, 227, 234, 256, 263
review, PRSP 4, 28, 35, 36, 43, 49, 51, 71, 127, 145-6, 254, 256-7, 268
Reynolds, A. 120
rights
human 59, 212, 219, 242
inheritance 32
land/property 219, 220
riots 198
risk 34, 43, 52
roads 188, 200, 242, 243, 250
Russia 163
Rwanda 3, 9, 14, 16, 17, 23, 26, 30, 32, 38, 39, 47, 217-46
and accountability 233, 234, 241, 244
and aid 217, 221-2, 230-1, 242-5
budget 227, 234-6, 245; support 230, 237, 242, 244
capacity 219, 230, 236, 242